WILSONIAN DIPLOMACY

ALLIED-AMERICAN RIVALRIES
IN WAR AND PEACE

Edward B. Parsons

FORUM PRESS

Published simultaneously in Canada.

Printed in the United States of America.

Library of Congress Catalog Card Number: 77-80967

ISBN: 0-88273-006-1

Cover design by Michael Toti

CONTENTS

PREFACE

Extensive research has expanded our knowledge of the extent to which the Allies' economic and territorial war aims aroused Woodrow Wilson's 1917-1919 animosity toward them. Discussion in *Wilsonian Diplomacy* points out the novel fact that this animosity stemmed largely from the Allies' threat to the realization of Wilson's own expansionist goals for America's navy, merchant marine, export markets, and access to foreign petroleum deposits. While agreeing with the traditional view of Wilsonian historians that the President possessed high ideals, this book ascribes a much larger influence on the course of the war and the Peace Conference to Wilson's surprisingly intense anti-British hostility and his somewhat Machiavellian strategic thinking. Chiefly because of his anti-Allied antipathy, so research has revealed, the President tried to get a peace conference convened soon after he entered the war so as to achieve the compromise peace without victory for either side that he still desired. Among the additional new facts that this work brings to light are that 1) Wilson's animosity toward the Entente's economic and territorial goals contributed to the demoralization of the war efforts of Russia and Italy, and 2) at Armistice time, the President sought to keep the German emperor at his throne.

Research has also revealed the major reason for Wilson's refusal to take an influential senator or political leader to Paris as a peace negotiator — a reason quite different from those generally accepted. This work also shows that it was not only the President's ideals, but above all his economic ambitions that exacerbated his quarrels with the Allies in Paris and hardened his resolve to deprive Italy and France of Middle East protectorates while he got some for the United States. Also brought to light are the real reasons for Wilson's abandonment of his "freedom of the seas" plank in 1919 and his ironic refusal to support the British Peace Conference effort to outlaw submarine attacks on merchant ships.

I wish to acknowledge the generous assistance of members of the staffs of the Manuscript Division, Library of Congress, the National Archives, and the Office of Naval Records and Library in Washington, D.C.; of the Public Record Office, the British Museum, and especially the Beaverbrook Library in London. I am also grateful for help from the staff of the Lockwood Library of the State University of New York at Buffalo, the King Library of Miami University, and the National Maritime Museum at Greenwich, England.

Research for this manuscript was supported by a Summer University Research Fellowship in 1968 from the State University of New York at Buffalo and by a Research Grant for 1973-1974 from the Graduate School of Miami University.

I am indebted to Paul Guinn, State University of New York at Buffalo, for his comments which improved the structure and scope of this work in its initial version. I am also grateful to Clifton K. Yearly, Milton Plesur, Charles R. Planck, and Selig Adler for their helpful criticisms of the initial version of this manuscript. In addition, I acknowledge the invaluable editorial assistance of Dorothy L. Ilgen in the preparation of this book. I alone, however, am responsible for any errors of fact or interpretation that might be found in this work.

INTRODUCTION

Writing half a century ago, Ray Stannard Baker set the tone for most subsequent portrayals of Wilson's war-connected diplomacy in *Woodrow Wilson and the World Settlement*. He presented an idealistic President who was largely frustrated by the selfish Allies, the American voters, and the Senate. For example, Thomas A. Bailey argued cogently in his 1944 study of *Woodrow Wilson and the Lost Peace* that the President clung myopically to his concept of a diplomacy of nobility and ignored too many realities of international and domestic politics. Hence he failed to achieve a durable peace. In his 1966 work, *Politics is Adjourned: Woodrow Wilson and the War Congress, 1916-1918*, Seward K. Livermore concluded that the American electorate's failure to sustain the President in the 1918 elections "tragically altered the course of history."

W. B. Fowler, in *British-American Relations, 1917-1918: The Role of Sir William Wiseman* (1969), and V. H. Rothwell, in *British War Aims and Peace Diplomacy* (1971), observe that Wilson's dislike of the Allies' war aims marred his diplomatic relations with them during America's participation in the war. Rothwell points up the President's animosity toward the Entente's aims as Wilson took them to mean from the Allies' Paris Economic Conference of June 1916 onward.

William Diamond, in his 1943 analysis of *The Economic Thought of Woodrow Wilson*, wedded the President's idealism to economic ambitions for America's global expansion. Echoes of this economic ambition resounded in N. Gordon Levin, Jr.'s *Woodrow Wilson and World Politics: America's Response to War and Revolution* (1968) and in Carl P. Parrini's *Heir to Empire: United States Economic Diplomacy, 1916-1923* (1969).

William R. Braisted (in his 1971 study of *The United States Navy in the Pacific, 1909-1922*) and David F. Trask (in his 1972 work, *Captains and Cabinets: Anglo-American Naval Relations, 1917-1918*) have pointed out that the United States delayed, in April-June 1917, committing many of its destroyers to the Allies' struggle against the U-boats and altering its naval construction from an emphasis on capital ships to one on anti-submarine craft. These historians attribute this delay chiefly to Wilsonian concern that an anti-American coalition led by Germany and Japan might ensue from the war, to traditional isolationism, to a Mahanian stress on dreadnoughts afloat, and to ignorance of the extent of the U-boat danger to the Allies.

The present work is based on the premise that all the motives attributed to Wilson by these various historians did influence Wilson's conduct of the war and his role at the Peace Conference of 1919. In the belief that the world would be better off dominated by American democracy and economic might, the President resolved to prevent both the Central Powers and the Allies from imposing their expansionist peace terms on the world. To enable him to impose his own peace terms on both sides, he restricted, not only in April-June 1917, but until the end of the war America's naval and merchant marine aid to the Allies to the minimum necessary to the prevention of a German victory. He husbanded the nation's maritime, military, financial, and manpower resources in both 1917 and 1918 while the Europeans, who had started the war, were allowed to expend a large portion of theirs against each other. Then, during his Armistice and Peace Conference struggle against his ostensible partners, the Entente, he brandished America's economic and maritime resources at them. He did so to prevent the Allies from imposing their peace terms — terms which would restrict America's economic growth, deprive Americans of equal opportunities with Allied nationals in many of the world's markets, and bar Americans from access to many of the world's raw materials (including oil deposits).

Proof of this thesis comes from an examination of the mission of Admiral William S. Sims, Commander of the Naval Forces the United States, sent to European waters in 1917-1919. Until Armistice Day, the U.S. Government refused to send him more than one-fourth of its anti-submarine vessels for use in the war against the U-boats. The government also declined to act on his urgings that it divert many of the ships of its expanding merchant marine from distant, profitable routes where they were building up America's exports to carrying war supplies to the Allies through U-boat infested waters.

Wilson also encouraged General John J. Pershing to minimize his casualties by delaying his divisions' combat debut, not only owing to nationalist, domestic political considerations, but also in order to preserve the nation's manpower and gain leverage over both sides at a peace conference. The President's aversion for the war aims of both sides animated his peace without victory, without annexations, without indemnities slogans. He intended to use his Fourteen Points and the League of Nations to protect and advance America's economic and maritime interests by rendering the Allies' secret economic and territorial treaties harmless, by fettering British naval power, and by giving the world a just and durable peace.

Had President Wilson given the Allies all the maritime and military aid that he could muster before the summer of 1918, he might have enabled them to win the war sooner, but they would have claimed the right to dictate the peace terms because they had defeated the Central Powers mainly with their own forces and only with some help from American forces. The Entente would have brushed aside Wilson's freedom of the seas claims and, in his view, have inflicted permanent damage to vital American interests.

In 1916-1919, the President endeavored to mobilize domestic and world opinion behind him for potential use against the Allied and German governments. He and his Chief of Naval Operations, Admiral William S. Benson, sought to preserve German naval power at Armistice time as a balance against the Royal Navy's preponderance. His Armistice and Peace Conference position, however, was weakened by the deterioration of his public support, both at home and in Europe. Theodore Roosevelt and Admiral Sims called for a maritime partnership between America and Britain; Wilson rejected this notion because he believed that America's expansionist interests could best be served by independence from obligations to Britain and a navy and merchant marine at least equal to hers.

During their Armistice and Peace Conference struggles, Wilson and British Prime Minister David Lloyd George continued their wartime efforts to constrict each other's economic and maritime power. Each sought the support of France and Italy against the other. The President's quest for territorial mandates at the expense of the economically exclusionary French and Italians, however, lessened their willingness to support his anti-British maritime position. His opposition to Japanese and British military advances in Russia added to his tensions with Tokyo and London.

Their mutual distrust of each other's motives hardened Wilson's and Lloyd George's opposition to each other's effort to improve the peace settlement. This meant that first the Prime Minister and then the President was all the more inclined to side with French Premier Georges Clemenceau against the notion of giving the Germans fewer grounds for instigating a second world war.

1

WILSON'S REFUSAL
TO AID THE ALLIES

June 1916-April 1917

WHEN THE UNITED STATES formally entered the Great War, the Allies and Admiral William Sowden Sims (the American sent to London to coordinate with the Allied Admiralties the use of naval units which Washington might dispatch to the war zone) urged that all American anti-submarine craft (destroyers, gunboats, Coast Guard cutters, tugs, submarines, and converted yachts) be rushed to European waters, the only waters where U-boats were active. By June 1917, because of the heavy losses suffered by the British Grand Fleet in the Battle of Jutland in May-June 1916, Sims would begin pressing the Department of the Navy to send a limited number of battleships to join the Grand Fleet. He feared that the Germans, aided by U-boats, would again give battle, especially since more than half of the British fleet's anti-U-boat craft had been removed, in an attempt to protect the dwindling remainder of the Allies' merchant ships. The German surface fleet was somewhat more powerful than that of the United States; each had about half the firepower of the Royal Navy's vessels. But German inferiority in dreadnoughts compared to those in the Grand Fleet was less striking.[1]

The Department of the Navy, however, would refuse to the end of the war to send more than about one fourth of its anti-submarine vessels to the war zone; furthermore, it would long delay sending the few dreadnoughts that it *did* finally dispatch. It would also long decline to send Sims a staff, although from late April 1917 it made him commander of all its warcraft in European waters. Similarly, the War Department would decline the Allies' plea of May 1917 that half a million troops be rushed to France for rapid training and early use on the Western Front. President Wilson would also restrict America's financial, merchant marine, and moral aid to the Allies in 1917 and 1918. From the day he entered the war, Wilson sought to preserve the bulk of the United States' maritime and military resources in case one or more of the Allies joined a hostile combination of powers against America after the war and because he feared the damage the Allies would do to America's economy and ideals if they held the power to impose their peace terms on the United States as well as the Central Powers. The grudging contributions that he did make to the Allies' war effort in 1917 and 1918 were intended to prevent the Germans from imposing their peace terms on Europe, the Russian Empire, and the Middle East, and to help him impose his peace terms on both sides. The Germans escalated their war aims in mid 1916-early 1917 in response to their failure to break the British blockade at Jutland; the outcome of the Russian military offensive of June-August 1916; and the war and peace terms set by the Allies at their Paris Economic Conference of June 1916.

Although Emperor William II rejoiced at his High Seas Fleet's Jutland performance, its commander, Vice-Admiral Reinhard Scheer, urged that unrestricted U-boat warfare held brighter promise than another surface battle of breaking the wearying Entente blockade by forcing the Allies to the peace table. The Entente's armies and industries were more rapidly susceptible to strangulation by sea than were the Central Powers. By an accelerated launching of U-boats, Germany would frighten the British out of removing anti-submarine craft from their Grand Fleet to protect cargo ships, lest Scheer try for a decisive victory at a second Jutland, where he would have U-boats strew mines in the path of the Royal Navy's dreadnoughts (as he had planned to do at Jutland) and then have his dreadnoughts and U-boat torpedos sink the surviving British warships.[2]

The Germans stepped up their U-boat construction from the summer of 1916, pending their final decision on unrestricted use of them. In August 1916, they decided on a second means of nullifying the effects of the Allies' blockade. William II concluded that the war's "decision lies more than ever in the East."[3] Field Marshal Paul von Hindenburg and General Eric Ludendorff were placed in overall command of all German fronts; they were to "tackle Russia militarily so as to push her out of the coalition, which will probably drag France down in her wake, and so give us a free hand against England," Chancellor Bethmann Hollweg anticipated.[4] By January 1917, all of Rumania's oil fields lay in Central Power hands; Berlin and Vienna were then joined by rail to their allies in Constantinople and Baghdad. The Germans had seized Russian Poland and Lithuania. They anticipated that the Allies would never be able to impose the dreaded terms of their Paris Economic Conference of June 1916 upon them. Instead, Germany would establish a league of nations to uphold the peace settlement; she would dominate a Common Market-style bloc from Brussels and Stockholm to the Persian Gulf. German capital and organizational skills would develop its backward areas. German engineers would irrigate parts of the Ottoman Empire. There, cotton would flourish as well as oil wells. With strategic annexations from Russia, and retention of the richest of France's iron mines (held since 1914), the Reich would possess economic resources equal to those of the United States. No future enemy could sap Germany's industrial, agricultural, and military might through blockade.[5] These ambitions threatened America's prosperity and security.

Early in 1917, the British were depressed by the debacle in Rumania and by the deepening demoralization of Russia. A separate peace by Petrograd would make the wheat, oil, and ores of southern Russia available to the Central Powers. From Russia's March revolution until November 1917, however, the British and French, owing mainly to the U-boat decimation of their cargo space, dispatched only token quantities of war supplies to their collapsing Slavic partner.[6] They unavailingly urged the American President to rush full scale aid to Russia as well as themselves.

To President Wilson, the economic ambitions of the Allies had become as alarming as those of the Central Powers; both menaced global open-door policy opportunities for American economic expansion in the postwar world. At the Paris Economic Conference of June 1916, the Entente laid plans which poisoned American relations with them through the remainder of the war, and into the Peace Conference period. American diplomats quickly sent the "secret" terms of this conference to the President. An alarmed Senate requested and got these terms from him.[7] These terms hardened Wilson's resolve to be slow and miserly in providing ships, troops, money, and moral support to the Entente if the United States declared war against Germany.

At their Paris Economic Conference, the Allies planned to keep the Central Powers, especially Germany, economically crippled for the indefinite period of "reconstruction." They would thwart the publicly avowed American hopes of investing capital in the war-ravaged consumer-producing sections of their economies. They would prevent the realization of anticipated profits and high worker employment rates from the export of American commodities and consumer goods to the denuded warehouses of Hamburg, Prague, Budapest, and Constantinople. They would constrict the volume of exports to the Allies' empires, which covered over half of the world. They would impede America's access to shipping space and to the raw materials of the world.[8]

Wilson administration spokesmen tried to reassure American businessmen and farmers. They averred that the war was forcing both sides to exhaust their capital and labor forces. All American raw material exports had long been cut off from the Central Powers, who were eager for their resumption. Both sides had converted their surviving factories to military production; a vast European demand had been created for investments out of the enormous accumulation of capital which the war was bestowing on the United States. Both sides would have to buy American goods.[9] These government officials, however, left it to the President to formulate and to bring about the "peace without victory" conditions which the avoidance of a postwar depression seemed to require.

President Woodrow Wilson. Underwood & Underwood photo.

Between June 1916 and America's break with Germany, administration spokesmen also evaded coming to grips with other menacing terms of the Paris Economic Conference. For the duration of the postwar "reconstruction period," the Allies pledged to each other that the raw materials of their home and overseas territories would be available exclusively to themselves, as long as they "needed" them. After Allied commercial requirements had been met, requests from outsiders such as Americans could be considered. The Allies assigned similar priorities to the use of their merchant marines and the world's cable networks; most of the transoceanic message network was in Allied, especially British, hands. The Entente would seize the German and Austrian merchant marines; they would give first priority in their use to their own cargoes and a low one to those of Americans.[10]

If America entered the war, how could the President force the Allies to give up their peace terms and accept *his* terms — except by setting limits on the maritime, military, and financial aid he gave them so that he would possess stronger resources than they when he confronted them at a peace conference?

By 1917, the war aims of both sides threatened to damage vital American interests, to trample the rights of weak nations, and to sow the seeds of a great war of revenge. Hence in August 1917, Wilson implicitly warned the Allies (in his reply to a papal peace proposal) against clinging to terms that would "cripple some nations [the Central Powers] and embarrass [damage] others [the United States]." That he felt very strongly about the Allies' aims even after he became their ostensible partner, that he felt sufficiently hostile toward them to delay and limit help to them against the Central Powers in 1917 and 1918 is suggested by the fact that in August 1918 he ordered that Australia's Prime Minister, William M. Hughes, be refused entrance to the United States for his impending scheduled visit because he had recently praised the terms of the Paris Economic Conference. Although he eventually let Hughes in, he did so only after he warned Britain's Prime Minister, Lloyd George, who had also recently lauded the Paris Economic Conference, that he would denounce both men by name in public if Hughes mentioned the Paris Conference while in America. In his speech of September 27, 1918 (after the Central Powers' collapse had begun), Wilson implicitly warned the Entente that he would tolerate "no selfish economic combinations" or "any form of economic exclusion . . . from the markets of the world" in the peace settlement. Only the League of Nations was to decide if anyone was to get exclusionary economic treatment, he declared.[11]

By 1917, it was obvious that the Allies' Paris Economic Conference's provisions to prevent the Germans' "dumping" of postwar goods into their empires could readily be applied against the Americans; the Germans had no goods to dump. The Reich would require some time after the war to retool, to recruit and retrain a labor force, and to fill the chasm of its own domestic demands. Moreover, the Allies' terms would suppress German exports by imposing enormous indemnities, and by confiscating the German merchant marine. How could America buy from and sell to a penniless Germany? It was the Americans who would have the most goods to "dump" in competition with the Allies after the war.

Allied assurances in Washington of the innocuousness of their terms were unconvincing. Secretary of the Navy Josephus Daniels noted the February 1917 statement of a French official to him that the Allies would apply their Paris Economic Conference aims against postwar Germany, but not against the United States. Daniels added, however, that American leaders "said the Entente powers intended to control the trade of the world." Secretary of State Robert Lansing urged Wilson to act against both the immediate wartime threat of the Allies' economic policy and to their threat to America's postwar commerce. He also warned that Germany would not accept the President's "peace without victory" because she feared the Allies' Paris plans.[12]

These Allied designs helped force America into the war; in its unrestricted U-boat warfare announcement of January 1917, the German government stated that the Paris Economic Conference required the measure in self-defense.[13] The Allies' terms hardened Wilson's resolve to arrange the timing and quantities of America's contributions to the "common" cause against the Central Powers in 1917-1918 so as to give him the power to impose his own peace terms.

Washington was angered by more immediate aspects of the Paris Economic Conference. The Allies' new "blacklist" practice tightened their control of American exports. The Royal Navy detained and sometimes confiscated offending cargoes. Allied control over export clearances through their agents in American ports was humiliating. Americans suspected that the British were using information thus gleaned to inform their own traders of American commercial secrets.[14] The penalty for refusal to comply with these Allied regulations was a prohibition of all trade by the offender with the dominions and territories of all of the Allies.[15]

Wilson nourished strong economic expansionist goals for the United States. The Allies were rivals of America; their 1915 Treaty of London and their Paris Economic Conference goals meant that they must not be allowed to win the war with sufficient power intact to dictate their peace terms. To advance his ambitions for the United States, Wilson would have to impose his peace terms on *both* sides if he entered the war, even if he had to allow both sides to exhaust each other while he husbanded the bulk of the nation's maritime and military resources safe from combat risk in order to come out of the war with strength sufficiently superior to that of the Allies and the Germans to bend them to his will.

Wilson's idealistic principles nurtured his vision of America's global economic expansion. In a 1914 address, he declared that

> there is no man who is more interested than I am in carrying the enterprise of American businesmen to every quarter of the globe. . . . I have been preaching it year after year as the great thing that lay in the future of the United States, to show her enterprise and influence in every country in the World.[16]

As N. Gordon Levin has put it, Wilson sought a "type of liberal world order of commercial freedom in which the genius of American capitalism would win its rightful place in the markets of the world." As Wilson himself emphasized in his election campaign of 1912, the nation's industries had outgrown the capacity of the domestic market "until we now have a surplus of manufactured goods of which we must get rid or do an unprofitable business." A little later he declared that "we must have an outlet in foreign fields, or else there will be a congestion which will operate calamitously upon the economic conditions of this country."[17] In 1915, Wilson rejoiced that the war was making the country a creditor nation for the first time in its history. He exhorted America's businessmen:

> Lift up your eyes to the horizons of business . . . let your thoughts . . . run abroad throughout the whole world, and with the inspiration . . . that you are Americans and are meant to carry liberty and justice . . . wherever you go, go out and sell goods that will make the world more comfortable and happy, and convert them to the principles of America.[18]

The World War brought European threats to this Wilsonian mission. The British historian V. H. Rothwell contends that

> Wilson suspected the British of harbouring the most sinister economic war aims. Like many Americans, he misunderstood the resolutions of the Paris Economic Conference of 1916 which he regarded as a blueprint for Entente, chiefly British, world economic domination, though his self-righteous policy had not prevented him, during the early months of the war, from initiating a policy by which his administration would aid American businessmen in replacing German and British trade in the western hemisphere.[19]

But, as will be demonstrated, during 1917-1919, the British would seek to regain the commercial leadership of the world which the war was transferring to the United States and the British would (especially during the Peace Conference) use means that closely resembled those of the Allies' 1916 blueprint to do so. France, Italy, and Japan would seek territories in Asia from which they planned to exclude American goods and capital. Moreover, France and Italy sought exclusionary control of the Balkans; Britain, France, and Italy intended to control most of the Middle East's oil resources which the American government and people believed vital to their nation's future.

Rothwell more correctly describes Wilson's Latin American policy. The President tried from 1913 onward to oust German and British capital. This hardened both the German and British authorities against allowing Wilson to dominate a peace conference. The President's first military intervention in Mexico (in April 1914) "served well the American oil interests who found that Huerta favored British capital as against American." The President had explained to a British official that America's endeavor to "champion the open door" lay behind his impending use of force there; he intended to "secure Mexico a better government under which all contracts and business and concessions will be safer than they have been."[20]

In December 1914, the President urged Congress to fund the construction of American merchant ships in order to seize and keep markets that the war was forcing European belligerents to abandon. "The Government must open these gates of [Latin American] trade, and open them wide, open them before it is altogether profitable to open them . . . . "[21] In July 1916, he angrily told Colonel Edward M. House that the British wanted to use certain provisions of the Paris Economic Conference "to prevent our merchants from getting a foothold in markets which Great Britain has hitherto all but dominated. Polk and I are compounding a very sharp note. I really feel obliged to make it as sharp and final as the one to Germany on the submarines."

In September, he told the nation's voters that the Federal Reserve Act he had sponsored had helped bring the nation to the brink of world financial and commercial supremacy. He enjoined them: "not only when the war is over, but now, America . . . must take her place in the world of finance and commerce upon a scale that she has never dreamed of before."[22]

Although Wilson's first term attacks on monopolistic trusts aroused suspicions in the American business world, he sought opportunities for businessmen to get ahead, both at home and abroad. In order to help them abroad, he was willing to give advantages to larger corporations. In December 1916, he stated privately that it was necessary to circumvent the anti-trust acts to help Americans against rival Britons and Germans: "Congress will be expected to aid . . . trade expansion. American firms must be given definite authorization to cooperate for foreign selling operations, in plain words, to organize for foreign trade just as the 'rings' of England and the cartels of Germany are organized."[23]   This led to the Webb-Pomerene Act of 1918 (which exempted such American cartels from anti-trust prosecution) and to the Edge Act of 1919, which "applied a similar exemption to banking." [24] These acts were designed to help thwart British and German efforts to regain lost markets, or to gain new ones, as the war ended. A similar purpose was served by Washington's wartime censorship of mail to Latin America. Wilson sanctioned this when Lansing urged him to do so in May 1917, in part to frustrate "an effort on the part of the Germans to build up their trade after the war."[25]

Rugged individualism among nations was the precept Wilson followed in international relations. His version of the League of Nations would suppress Europe's military and economic alliances. It would leave the United States free to use her superior natural resources and skilled manpower to achieve her global destiny. For example, en route to the Paris Peace Conference, he declared his plan to thwart the Entente by seeing to it that each of Germany's colonies was made "the common property of the League of Nations." Then "the resources of each colony should be available to all the members of the League." [26] The United States, he intended, would be its leading member.

Even before the outbreak of the war, the President had urged the nation to build a great merchant marine. Only in 1915, however, did he become convinced of the need for a similar expansion of the Navy. In both cases, he saw Britain's maritime and commercial supremacy as the most compelling incentive in his struggle for America's maritime independence and ascendency.

As a presidential candidate in 1912, Wilson had called for a great revival of the American merchant marine. For decades, the nation had been dependent on foreign ships for trade; the American merchant marine was far too small to carry more than a fraction of it. And, Wilson had pointed out, foreign carriers discriminated against their American rivals in carrying their goods. The German and Austrian withdrawal of their merchant fleets from the seas in August 1914, accompanied by the partial withdrawal of Allied ships from the

American trade in order to concentrate on war material, left some American goods stranded. The President and Secretary of the Treasury, William G. McAdoo, seized this opportunity to begin their two-year crusade to persuade Congress to sanction federal funds for merchant ship building.

Ships were needed to carry the stranded cargoes; they were essential to seizing markets and keeping them from the Germans and the British after the war. McAdoo put it succinctly to Wilson: "Without ships we can do nothing. With them we can quickly establish business and political relations . . . in Latin America of inestimable value . . . perhaps for all time." These appeals won only minor 1914 concessions from a Congress that feared that the President's proposals were socialistic. The pressure for new American ships eased as the Allies bought up and carried away stranded cotton cargoes. A boom of exports to the Allies was established. But in December 1915, the President warned Congress that the Latin American and Asian markets Americans were gaining were in danger of being wrested back after the war by Europeans who had the merchant ships to do so. America's exports were still too largely dependent on rivals' (particularly British) ships. "We are not likely to be permitted to . . . use the ships of other nations in rivalry with their own trade," Wilson declared. More markets could be acquired while the war lasted, if only Congress would act: many more ships must be launched to "move constantly back and forth between the Americas . . . taking immediate advantage of the great opportunity that awaits us," the President importuned.[27]

Congress was converted in the summer of 1916. The booming economy gave the government a tax base to support a merchant marine; the expansion of markets in Latin America and Asia led to rising expectations of more. Illustratively, Wilsonian prodding helped to drive American exports to Brazil up from $48,000,000 in 1915 to $79,000,000 in 1916. The United States had advanced from its 1911-1913 position behind Britain and Germany into a strong first place in Brazil's import markets.[28] The news from the Paris Economic Conference gave Congress a final push toward approval of both a great merchant marine, and a navy to protect it. The terms of that Conference were cited by supporters of the great navy bill, which passed first. Thoughtful Americans "believed that they could glimpse what was to come from the results of the . . . economic conference [at] Paris . . . . If the war was at bottom a struggle for commercial supremacy, only adequate seapower would guarantee the entrance of our goods into all ports . . . . " A few days later, the great merchant marine act passed. Obviously, "entrance of our goods into all ports" required both merchant ships and warships. Federal funds enabled the government to buy, build, own, and operate merchant ships until private capital had enough ships to supply the nation's needs. A government shipping board now operated the government's ships; it also set the routes and rates for all privately owned ships flying the American flag.[29] Wilson chose anti-British board members who were anxious to expand exports, especially Edward N. Hurley (chairman in

1917-1919) and Admiral William S. Benson (chairman upon his retirement from active naval duty in September 1919).

By the end of 1916, about the time the incentives of the 1916 merchant marine act began to become effective, private capital had expanded the ocean going merchant marine to about 2,200,000 tons, or double its 1914 tonnage; but it raised the percentage of American sea-borne trade carried in American ships from 10 percent only to 17 percent. In 1916, the Allies still carried about 65 percent (consisting largely of war supplies); other neutrals carried 18 percent. When America entered the war, the government's Shipping Board sought to keep its expanding cargo space safe; it refused an Allied request that it divert ships "engaged in other [more profitable] channels into the [U-boat infested] North Atlantic trade."[30]

From April 1917 to November 1918, Allied-American cooperation against the common foe was to be hampered by the naval, merchant marine, and trade rivalry between the United States and Britain. London, Paris, and Rome would assert that as their merchant marines shrank and America's grew, the United States was using its new ships primarily to expand its export trade instead of helping with their worsening shortage of ships by carrying war supplies through the torpedo-riddled waters of the U-boat zone.

> While the nation's leaders were interested in expanding commerce with Latin America, their perspective was world wide, embracing such areas as China, India .... Precisely because the opportunity which the European war seemed to offer the United States to expand her commerce at the expense of England and Germany, business and administration officials were almost from the beginning of the struggle greatly concerned about what would happen after the war was over and Europe attempted to regain her former markets. In 1915, Roland G. Usher of Washington University predicted a clash between the victor of the struggle and the United States over Latin America ....[31]

American officials, as will be discussed, shared Usher's concern. Because of it, they would seek to keep the nation's maritime resources safe in 1917-1918.

From the outset of Wilson's campaign for a great merchant marine, the Allies increasingly resented his maritime ambitions, while he, in turn, resented their plans to thwart him. This enhanced the prospect that neither side would cooperate fully with the other to wage the war or to forge a just and lasting peace. After America entered the war, both Washington and London would lay "plans to ensure that the other used its shipping in terms of immediate military necessities."[32] This, however, left the advantage with the United States. Wilson could risk, even welcome, a peace without victory while the Allies desperately sought to avoid one. British losses and America's gains of mercantile profits meant that Washington would have a relatively stronger financial base for a postwar race in both merchant marine and naval building. Anglo-American, not German-American or Japanese-American rivalry, was the chief impetus to America's shipbuilding.

In October 1914, the President sided with the pacifist Daniels against Assistant Secretary of the Navy Franklin D. Roosevelt and a majority of the senior officers who sat on the Navy's General Board: Congress would be asked to fund only two (not four) dreadnoughts in 1915. The board cited only a latent German threat to the Monroe Doctrine and Japanese resentment at America's exclusion of Asiatic immigrants as the chief reasons for the larger program.[33] The Allies had not yet agreed to their 1915 Treaty of London; the Germans had not yet sunk the *Lusitania*. It was not yet clear that the war would last long enough to provide the United States with the opportunity to garner large new markets that the Germans and British had to abandon owing to the Allied blockade or to British war needs, and that the war would bring America the money to build a large merchant marine and a navy to support it.

By July 1915, however, it was clear that the war would probably last for some time. Moreover, in April 1915, the Allies concluded the Treaty of London. This threatened America's opportunities for access to trade markets and raw materials in what was believed to be the world's largest store of both proven and unproven oil deposits — the Middle East, by dividing all of the Turkish Empire outside of Anatolia among Britain, France, and Russia. Britain had earlier established a sphere of influence in oil-rich Persia and was competing with the United States for Mexico's oil; she now would get the proven oil deposits of Mesopotamia (Iraq) and an expanded sphere of influence in the petroleum rich Arabian peninsula. France would get Syria, which was believed to have oil deposits. In the Balkans (and Anatolia), Italy would gain a strong foothold from which she could impose her exclusionary practices against American goods. (See Chapter 4 for details of this treaty.) In May 1917, Colonel House would tell British Foreign Secretary Arthur James Balfour that these terms were "bad, all bad." Wilson's animosity to these terms would help constrict his 1917-1918 aid to the Entente.

In July 1915, the President instructed Daniels and Secretary of War Lindley M. Garrison to encourage their senior officers to provide justification for Congressional approval of greater military prepared-ness. Daniels and the General Board correctly understood that this was primarily a call for a naval race against Great Britain, Germany, and Japan. Garrison, however, obtusely pressed for a parallel, large expansion of the Army for possible large-scale fighting against Germany. The Navy Department's arguments led to Congressional passage of the largest construction program in American history with the emphasis on capital ships instead of anti-U-boat craft. The new dreadnoughts would be neither available nor needed for the ongoing war against Germany; if America entered the war, she already had enough afloat to give the British a more comfortable margin of safety against a second Jutland. The President helped bring about this capital ship emphasis. On February 3, 1916, he enjoined the nation to build "incomparably the greatest navy in the world," not a large array of anti-submarine craft. On February 10, Garrison resigned after telling Congress that the Wilsonian policy for expanding the Army was "quite inadequate."[34] Neither the public nor the President was anxious to muster a great army; it would enhance pressure to use it in the event of another *Lusitania*, and Wilson intended to conserve the nation's manpower instead of expending it as the belligerents were doing — even if he eventually had to do some limited fighting over the U-boat issue. The President gave first priority to naval expansion to prepare for a possible confrontation with Britain, rather than for a more imminent one with Germany or Japan.

The President recognized that a war against Germany was likely when he made his effort in the spring of 1916 to pressure Britain into accepting his peace mediation effort. He told House to tell London that it was "probable that this country must break with Germany on the submarine," and that if the United States entered the war, it "would undoubtedly be prolonged."[35] Presumably he intended this prolongation spectre to warn Britain that her financial and maritime resources would be further depleted by a refusal to cooperate with his peace conference endeavor, and that if he did enter the war he would not rush much military or maritime aid to her. At any rate, in February-July 1917, he did not hasten to alter the great 1916 naval building program which stressed dreadnoughts rather than anti-U-boat craft for a war against Germany.

That Japan was not the primary incentive behind Wilson's naval construction policy is demonstrated by his rejection of the construction expansionists in October 1914, despite the Mikado's nearly completed seizure of the Marianas, the Carolines, the Marshalls, and Shantung. Although Tokyo's Twenty-One Demands on China in February 1915 were unacceptable to Washington, American pressure had been a factor in Japan's decision to give up the most offensive of them by May 1915 — without a presidential call for accelerated construction. Then, the President, from July 1915 until July 1917 adhered almost unfalteringly to a stress on dreadnought building. His naval building policy, embodied in the August 1916 act, encouraged the Berlin authorities to risk war with the United States. America's "comparatively great strength in battleships was rendered unnecessary [for an Allied-American struggle against Germany] by the overwhelming power of the British and other Allied navies . . . [in capital ships]. It was largely on this deficiency of American and Allied destroyers that Germany counted for the success of her submarines, and hence final victory."[36]

Although the Reich had a modest superiority over America in dreadnoughts in July 1917, she lacked bases in North American waters necessary for a successful fight there against the American Atlantic Fleet. In 1916, as well as 1917, the American navy needed to build proportionally more anti-submarine craft than dreadnoughts for a more "balanced" fleet and a better chance of success in a battle against either the German or the Japanese fleet.

Yet, even after America declared war, those officers who sought to wage it to the utmost were to be hampered by the anti-British bias of their superiors. In June 1917, Assistant Chief of Operations Captain William V. Pratt would argue to Chief of Operations William S. Benson that the surest way to eliminate the German Fleet as a future danger to America was to help the Allies defeat William II with anti-submarine vessels. To do this, the first four construction priorities should be "(1) submarine chasers (2) destroyers (3) scout cruisers (4) submarines . . . . " He pointed out that the American navy was "already stronger" than Japan's; for a possible war against Britain at the end of the existing war, "no amount of feverish building of dreadnoughts or battlecruisers could hope to put us in a position to cope with her Fleet." For "such a contingency our efforts should now be directed towards augmenting our submarine Fleet, both offensive and defensive."[37]   Thus, submarines would be effective against German submarines soon, and as a threat to British dreadnoughts and merchant ships later.

On August 29, 1917, the General Board threw its weight behind the move to change Admiral Benson's naval building policy from dreadnoughts to anti-U-boats to help save the Allies from defeat. It pointed to other benefits that would accrue. The Navy was "top-heavy" in capital ships; for success in battle against the Japanese fleet or the German fleet if it were "no longer contained" by the Grand Fleet, highest priorities should be given to "building (1) scouts and cruisers (2) destroyers. . . ."[38] Benson's testimony to a 1920 Senate committee suggested that he had, in 1915-1917, been more anxious to prepare for a challenge to Britain than to build anti-U-boat craft to help save the Allies' merchant marines. When a senator pointed out that the Battle of Jutland had demonstrated the need for more American smaller craft for a possible battle against the German surface fleet, and that they had obviously been needed to fight the U-boats, the Chief of Naval Operations replied evasively: he was familiar with Jutland only "in a very general way"; it was Congress that had enacted the August 1916 three-year program.[39]

Just before Congress had acted on the Department of the Navy's 1916 construction recommendations, the Allies' "blacklist" practice that had issued from their Paris Economic Conference had angered Benson and the President. If the Entente judged that an American firm's shipment to another neutral country were ultimately destined for a Central Power, no ship carrying this firm's goods could get coal from the British bunkering stations that held a virtual monopoly across wide seas. Similar punishment was meted out to any firm that held stock in a company that was tied in any manner to Central Power interests. Ship owners shunned cargoes of the blacklisted. Wilson induced Congress to grant him retaliatory powers to "prohibit loans and restrict exportations to the Allies" when he might find it advantageous to do so. In September 1916, the President proclaimed that "American energies are now directed towards the markets of the world." He alluded to the foreign markets which the war had from the outset forced the Germans, and then gradually the British to abandon to Americans; his administration had plans for "the re-creation of an American merchant marine and the revival of the American carrying trade indispensable to our emancipation from the control which foreigners [mainly British] have so long exercised over the opportunities, the routes, and the methods of our commerce with other countries." He proclaimed his "very great enthusiasm for the triumphant development of American enterprise throughout the world." [40] In a September 1916 discussion, House warned him that the British were coming to see the Americans in the same baleful light they had seen the Germans in 1914. The United States had "undertaken to build a great navy . . . [and] our commerce was expanding beyond all belief . . . . The President replied [House noted] 'let us build a navy bigger than hers and do what we please.' I reminded him that Germany had undertaken to do that and Great Britain had checked her before she could accomplish her purpose, and in the spring of 1914 I had predicted that she would. I thought it unlikely the British would be willing to permit us to build a navy equal to theirs if they could prevent it." House later noted that at the Paris Peace Conference, many British "authorities thought the 1916 bill would make us not equal but superior to any navy in the world." [41]

In December 1916, the President called upon both sides to agree to a peace conference; he observed sardonically that "the objects which the statesmen of . . . both sides have in mind are virtually the same, as stated . . . to their people and to the world." An American professor protested (through Secretary of War Newton D. Baker) that the President should not have placed Britain's war aims on the same moral level as Germany's. The President rejoined that if the protestor "had lived with the English statesmen for the past two years and seen the real inside of their minds I think he would feel differently." [42] In April 1918, during the formidable German land offensives against the British in France, an American admiral would plead that American dreadnoughts should be sent to bolster the Grand Fleet in case Scheer tried to support the Hindenburg-Ludendorff drives with a sea offensive. Wilson would refuse, saying that he anticipated he would "come out of [the] war hating [the] English." That he preferred the survival of the German Fleet in German hands to a world dominated by the Royal Navy would be illustrated during the Allied-American rows at Armistice time. The President would cable Pershing to try to keep the Entente from determining the fate of the Reich's U-boats. He would summon acting Chief of Naval Operations Pratt and instruct him to cable Benson (in Paris) to insist that the Kaiser's dreadnoughts must be merely "interned" until the Peace Conference returned them to German control. "I lean backwards" (so Pratt recalled him saying) to avoid having "a weakened Germany." This suggests that Wilson had long shared the view that Benson and his handpicked staff would express on November 4, 1918, about "Great Britain and her fugitive allies" as a menace to the growth of America's economic prosperity: "The German Navy should remain . . . sufficiently strong to exercise a distinctly conservative influence on . . . British Sea Power." The staff elucidated: "If the German Fleet were destroyed, Great Britain would be at liberty to do with our new merchant marine as she thought fit, since her naval power would so far outbalance our own . . . ." Her power would ruin "the idea of a League of Nations." In December

1918, the President was to state that had not the U-boats forced his hand against Germany, he "would have been ready to have it out then and there with Great Britain . . . ."[43]

Britain's commanding position would also frustrate the Wilsonian ambition to sell goods to her enemies in a future war. In March 1917, Lansing rejected a Mexican protest that America had prolonged the bloodshed by her exclusive exporting of supplies to the Allies; he paraphrased his reply to a similar 1915 protest from Austria: the United States' "inability to ship munitions of war to the Central Powers was not of its own desire or making, but wholly due to the naval superiority of the Allies." In that same month (August 1915), the General Board had added Britain as a potential enemy to its October 1914 expansionist arguments against Japan and Germany (which Wilson and Daniels had overridden).[44]

Other auguries had persuaded the President to abandon his October 1914 stance. No peace conference had seemed likely to halt the rising export boom to the Allies in the near future or release British maritime power for a struggle to reverse the trend of America's success in her rivalry with Britain for markets elsewhere in the world. The rising tax base would make the cost of new construction more palatable to the American taxpayer. The public harbored a residual anger at the *Lusitania* sinking — anger which interventionists such as Theodore Roosevelt fanned. Admiral Austin K. Knight (of the Naval War College) "held that the current war was fundamentally a struggle for industrial and commercial supremacy between Great Britain and Germany. The victor . . . would inevitably face a challenge from the United States." Britain was not only the largest naval power, she had an alliance with Japan. The navy should therefore be prepared "for the ultimate threat of war against the two." Alternatively, it should be prepared for the possibility of a war against Germany and Japan; "Japan was cultivating Germany." The General Board had essentially agreed with Knight in July 1915. It voted seven to one for building a navy as powerful as Britain's (the dissenter wanted one even more mighty). "The United States must defend its expanding economic interests in a world dominated by selfish national policies"; America was increasingly "a competitor of Germany, Britain, and Japan." The Board warned against Japan's growing claims on Britain for postwar support in the Pacific that the war was enhancing.[45] Obviously, America's entry into the war as Britain's ally would establish claims on Britain that could be stronger than Japan's. Tokyo was giving only token assistance to the Allies struggle in European waters. On the other hand, the danger from the Anglo-Japanese partnership was weakened by the 1915-1918 distrust between London and Tokyo. In January 1916, Ambassador Walter Hines Page wrote from London that the British government was "disgusted and distrustful of Japan" while "the more sensational Tokyo press was declaiming on the uselessness of the Anglo-Japanese alliance to Japan."[46]

Yet the President held some fear of the "Yellow Peril." After the diplomatic break with Berlin, he even toyed with the notion of passively enduring German U-boat depredations out of concern for the fate of "white civilization" if the United States entered the war. This may have been rationalization for limiting America's commitment of military and naval units to the "common cause" against the Germans. The Board also warned that "the current war . . . would be followed by others of comparable magnitude" and that "the defeated belligerents with the connivance of the victors might try 'to recoup their losses and expand at the expense of the new world.' "[47]

News of the Paris Economic Conference prodded Congress into action that exceeded the administration's hopes. The ten "super" dreadnoughts the administration was asking to have funded in five years were to be funded in three. Informed Americans, it will be recalled, saw that "only adequate seapower would guarantee the entrance of our goods into all ports." But less informed, as well as ardently pro-Allied sections of the public, were persuaded to support expansion on less logical reasons. The administration did little to combat such reasons. The Germans might overrun France and Britain, destroy Britain's fleet, and send an armada against the United States. The German fleet "could quickly and easily destroy our existing Navy. . . . German armies, millions strong, would brush aside our puny army, and advance at will, destroying our cities, committing unmentionable atrocities, and generally laying waste our fair countryside."[48] The greater navy would save the nation from such a fate. When the United States declared war, many Americans wanted the navy kept at home to guard them against such a fate. The President declined to tell them that the Allies needed the bulk of America's anti-U-boat vessels in European waters (see Chapter 2).

Quickly following Berlin's January 31 submarine announcement, Secretary of the Navy Daniels wrote the President of Benson's revulsion at the notion of entering the war "on either side". The Secretary then allowed a German press correspondent to use the navy's cables to inform the Berlin authorities that "the highest sources" in the American government had requested that he let them know that they were striving to avoid giving any provocation for a German declaration of war. The German government reciprocated a month after Washington's formal declaration of hositilities. On May 8, the Reich's Admiralty ordered that no American merchant ship bound for the United States outside of the blockade zone off Europe was to be sunk, but that it was to be regarded as still neutral. If American warships were encountered, they were not to be fired upon unless they fired first. The failure, or deliberate oversight, of the American government to comply with the legal requirement of notifying Berlin through Switzerland (the power representing America in Berlin since the diplomatic rupture) that a state of war existed was cited as justification for this restraint. Although Lansing drew Wilson's attention to this legal "oversight" on May 12, the President declined to rectify it.[49] The Germans wanted to encourage anti-war sentiment in the United States. They did not want to send their few long-range submarines to the western Atlantic because they would lose time getting to the relatively fewer targets there and back that could be spent sinking ships in the denser traffic off Europe. Wilson wanted to limit America's participation in the war (see Chapter 2).

For some time after Berlin's January 31 U-boat announcement, it looked as if the President and the Kaiser would succeed in avoiding serious fighting against each other. Wilson did ask Daniels not to send any more soothing messages to Berlin because the Imperial authorities might take them as an encouragement to sink American cargoes without fear of retaliation. Secretary of War Newton D. Baker, however, successfully urged that no special meeting of the National Defense Council be held; it could provoke Berlin. Both Baker and Daniels vigorously protested a Cabinet colleague's suggestion that conscription might become necessary; it was un-American.[50] The two secretaries had, for some time, clandestinely yielded to the professionals' insistence that contingency plans for war against certain nations be made. When, in 1915, Wilson discovered that the military officers had been doing this, he called for their punishment. He was dissuaded, but his writ against all war plans still ran. Thus, in February 1917, the navy had only a *sub rosa* plan for a war against Germany. This bore little relation to the realities of the ongoing U-boat warfare; it merely envisaged a surface battle between the United States' Atlantic Fleet and the German High Seas Fleet in the mid-Atlantic, in the approaches to Cuban waters, or in the Caribbean Sea. Despite reports to Washington in the autumn of 1916 about accelerated preparations for unrestricted U-boat campaign, even to the end of the war, the Navy Department drew up no relevant plan.[51] The President hoped to mediate the war. Such a plan might have encouraged bellicosity among his admirals before April 2, 1917, and the sending of full scale naval help to the Allies in April 1917-November 1918.

Following the diplomatic rupture with Berlin, Daniels and Benson contentedly took their cues for the lack of serious naval preparations from Wilson. Despite Germany's unrestricted U-boat warfare announcement of two weeks earlier, on February 15, 1917, the President instructed against "any great preparedness — he anticipated that Europe would be man and money poor by the end of the war." Presumably he was not going to incur a similar loss in American manpower and financial strength. He also declared in February 1917 that he still believed in a "peace without victory" and that he wished to see "neither side win."[52] Neither the army nor the navy hastened to undertake any "great preparedness."

The nine weeks of transition to a formal state of war (following Berlin's January 31 note) saw naval preparations guided by an "ahead slow speed" policy. The army, too, dawdled. At the National Council of Defense's routinely scheduled meeting of February 16, the Chief of Staff fell asleep. "Mars and Morpheus in one" and "nothing got done" complained the hawkish Secretary of the Interior, Franklin K. Lane. Early in 1918 the British Cabinet would read a letter from Theodore Roosevelt which blamed much of the meagerness of America's contribution to the fighting in Europe to date on Wilson's decisions to keep "an amiable professional pacifist" as his Secretary of War and "two old fuddy duddies" in succession as the Army's Chiefs of Staff. [53] Perhaps he felt that these gentlemen had too passively acquiesced in Wilson's overall war policy.

However, "an amiable professional pacifist" seems an apt appellation for the rotund Secretary of the Navy. Daniels' numerous critics asserted that he was the personification of rusticity, Billy Sundayism, and ineptitude. Yet he was a shrewd populist; he was an evangelical friend of William Jennings Bryan. After Bryan's 1915 resignation as Secretary of State, Wilson may have felt that the importance of the populist-progressives demanded that he retain Daniels. Even Colonel House received an icy rebuff when, in 1915, he urged the President to remove him for incompetence. [54]

When Cabinet members suggested the feasibility of providing naval "escorts" or "convoys" for terrified merchant ships sheltering in New York harbor, Daniels rejoined that his admirals damned them. They would present a double target; they would endanger naval craft and their use might prove provocative in Berlin. The President declined to order naval escorts for American merchant ships. [55] Ignoring the General Board's February 4 urging of several trial measures, including an attempt to escort single merchant ships, and a mobilization of ships, men, and material, the Secretary informed the President on March 27 that his admirals held that no measure would meet the U-boat menace. [56]

Although the Chief of the Bureau of Navigation (the misnomer for the Bureau of Personnel), Rear-Admiral L. C. Palmer, and his able assistant, Captain Harris Laning, wanted to muster the reserves, they had no legal authority to defy the Secretary by doing so. In February, 1917, the navy was short by 27,000 of the 86,000 officers and men authorized by Congress in 1916 (in manning tables which ignored the swollen requirements of anti-submarine warfare). In the face of Daniels' prohibition, Palmer and Laning risked their careers by smuggling in a few officers at a time. Occasionally Daniels found out. He upbraided them; sometimes they had to send these badly needed officers back to civilian life. [57] Perhaps he feared that they would criticize him and the Department's war effort and he could not silence them with threats to their normal careers. Yet, until early 1918, Sims' anti-U-boat forces would have no adequate staff to direct their operations; his vessels were destined to remain short of officers until virtually the end of the war. The pacific Secretary did not want the responsibility of directing a fighting navy during a major war. He waited until March 27, 1917, to appeal for civilian volunteers to bring the navy up to its authorized peacetime strength. His appeal elicited a feeble response. Daniels would wait until the draft, enacted in May, gradually drove enough infantry dodgers onto his decks to man them adequately. [58]

After the war, Benson would testify that the navy's preparations during this transitional period were inadequate to those necessary to seek a redress of grievances from either side. He thought that it was in the national interest to keep the Allies or Germany from dictating the peace; he sought to safeguard and expand American naval power while doing so in preparation for a postwar confrontation with either side that might win. Until the President had signed the war declaration on April 6, however, Benson had deferred to the President's policy and to his own opinion that the American people were generally against serious preparations for entering the fray.[59]

Soon after the United States declared war, the American Winston Churchill, (who had graduated from Annapolis and then given up a naval career to win fame as a novelist), undertook research (at Franklin D. Roosevelt's secret prodding) in the Navy Department to write a series of articles. This research would supposedly popularize the navy's role in the war, but FDR intended it to expose Daniels' and Benson's shortcomings in waging it. In July 1917, Churchill resolved to let the President know what candid discussions with officers of the several bureaus had disclosed. He felt that "Admiral Benson . . . has many good qualities; and though not a war college man himself, he chooses these men as his assistants. Most of . . . these are able. But the general opinion of Admiral Benson is that he is not quite up to the place. He is not constructive enough, assertive enough, and has not had the training." As for Daniels, "the chief, the universal comment concerning him from all who have had dealings with him, has been of his dilatoriness, of his unwillingness to act on matters great and small, the result of which has been to delay and at times almost to paralyze the activities of the Naval Service."[60]

Although access to his papers is restricted to Benson's biographer, Dr. Mary Klachko, she has given this writer some information about him. Other sources for the following points of interest about the admiral are Daniels' diary, and Benson's testimony at the 1920 Senate Committee Hearings.

William Shepherd Benson was born in Macon, Georgia, in 1855, of British stock. He was graduated from the U.S. Naval Academy in 1877, where he was the captain or leading player of several sports teams. Soon thereafter, he married a Roman Catholic and converted to her faith. His Anglophobia may have been fueled by Irish-American clerics. During the Spanish-American war, Benson served as Commandant of Midshipmen at Annapolis. Later, his assignments increased in importance until he commanded the battleship *Utah*; in 1913, he was assigned as Commander of the Philadelphia Navy Yard, where Daniels discovered him.

Benson sustained the President's and Secretary Daniels' disinclination, in February and March 1917, to do much to prepare to fight Germany. Participation in the war did increase the latitude of Benson's decision-making powers.[61] Wilson and Daniels needed *someone* to implement the details of expanded wartime activity; they trusted him to carry out their anti-British policy in doing so.

The nine weeks between the German U-boat declaration and the President's war request message (January 31-April 2) saw no serious public indignation swell up against the Navy's 'ahead slow speed' policy. The clamorous pro-war minority wanted troops called up; the army was even more inadequately manned for war than was the navy. This sector also called for naval protection of American merchant ships, preferably accompanied by a declaration of hostilities. Wilson balked. In early March he brushed aside such promptings, partly because they supposedly would enrich the Republicans' munitions-making friends. Above all, they would lead straight to war. He did finally arm the nation's merchant ships — by removing guns from the navy's fighting ships. Nevertheless, the mid-March torpedoing of American merchant ships persuaded the President to summon Congress to formal action.[62]

These weeks of transition to a state of war witnessed mammoth peace rallies. Bryan threatened to demand a people's referendum if Wilson took preparatory measures. Benson was suspicious of the British capacity for winning a possible second Jutland. He also rather expected the Allies' defeat to be brought about on land. So did much of the American press.[63] As leader of his party, the President had to consider future elections. To the traditional isolationist sentiment were added the strong feelings against the Allies among Irish and German voters (and smaller ethnic groups such as the Hungarians). Many among these groups were also susceptible to anti-Allied Vatican influences. By November 1916, the Irish proportions of the vote which usually went Democratic had fallen so low that Wilson had barely squeaked through for reelection. From party workers and from his ambassador at Rome, the President had been informed that this decline had been due in some measure to the Pope's request that his American bishops use their pastoral functions to work against Wilson's reelection. The President's Latin American policies had been partly responsible for this Vatican instruction; his seeming coolness to the Irish cause had encouraged obedience to it.[64] In January-March, 1917, Pope Benedict XV endeavored to prevent the United States from joining the coalition against the Central Powers; he urged that Wilson cite his difficulties with the Japanese and Mexicans as requiring the husbanding of America's resources at home. Alternatively, the Pontiff urged that Wilson insist on America's neutral right to ship munitions and other war supplies to the Central Powers, that he uphold his own assertions about freedom-of-the-seas.[65] Wilson's secretary Joseph Tumulty (an Irish-American) red-penciled for him some of the press's widespread insistence that, if the United States had to be dragged into this war by the U-boat, its naval and military efforts must be completely separate and free from those of the Allies. America must also remain at liberty to leave the war the moment Berlin might relent its submarine policy — the only grounds on which an American declaration of war might be justified. These journalists gave public demand to the President's private intention. No naval or military effort could be allowed to commit America to the Entente's "lust for territorial conquest and domination." If defeat overtook the Allies, the United States must in no way be obligated to join them in a peace of humiliation or surrender; neither could America be obligated to fight on to rescue them from such a fate.[66]

When Wilson summoned Congress to meet on April 2, a tearful

Daniels supposed that there was no other way to legalize the use of his own and Britain's navy to protect the American merchant marine. "From such evidence as is available, however, one might hazard the guess that even as late as April 1, 1917, the majority of the people were still firmly for peace."[67]

Quickly following Wilson's March 20 decision to ask Congress for a war declaration, the principal preparatory measure was taken with regard to the Atlantic Fleet, which usually contained all fifteen of the navy's dreadnoughts. It steamed from Cuban waters into Chesapeake Bay. Its commander, Rear-Admiral Henry T. Mayo, was a dynamic, capable officer. Since January 31, he had been straining to keep his complaints to Benson within respectful bounds. Although Benson would soon be excusing his refusals of Sims's pleas for warcraft and men in the war zone on the grounds that the Germans might defeat the Grand Fleet and Mayo's Fleet would have to fight, the Department did little to prepare Mayo's forces for that possibility. In the months ahead, Mayo found himself with a deteriorating fleet. Part of this decline was caused by Daniels' procrastination about getting sufficient manpower to repair and man Mayo's vessels. In January, only twelve of Mayo's dreadnoughts were fit to take part in his winter training exercises off Cuba. He reported in February and March that even these twelve needed repairs if they were expected to fight or even to operate outside of coastal waters. He asked that his cruisers and smaller craft that were still policing Latin American waters be returned to him.[68] Despite his May 5 protest that the Atlantic Fleet was not fit to engage the German Fleet or even to do much "cruising outside of inclosed waters," the department moved sluggishly to repair Mayo's ships. Only in November did he feel that his vessels were fit to resume "work as a fleet." [69]

Despite the department's dilatory approach to getting immersed in the ongoing war, Wilson made no move to replace Daniels with an energetic advocate of a quick and full use of the navy in the war zone, such as Assistant Secretary Roosevelt. This suggests that the President felt that Daniels' procrastinations had their advantages.

As for the calamity that loomed in the waters of the shipping funnel southwest of Ireland, sister craft of Mayo's Fleet were doing little to combat it. Indeed, in April 1917, no American vessel arrived in the war zone, where nearly 900,000 tons of merchant ships and their vital war cargoes went to the bottom.

Wilson found Daniels useful in husbanding the nation's maritime resources. The President pursued a similar policy of restricting military and financial aid to the Allies in 1917-1918, not only to ensure that the nation did not become "man and money poor by the end of the war," but also to ensure that his principles were backed by powerful resources at a peace conference. He first applied America's financial power in late 1916 to help get a peace without victory for either side.

By November 1916, Great Britain, the financial mainstay of the Allies, was running low on gold and American securities with which the pound sterling needed to be propped up in order to continue making purchases and receiving loans in America. The President, through the Federal

Reserve Board's president, W.P.G. Harding, and McAdoo, threatened to stop their loans and credit unless they sold "our own and foreign securities" that they held to Americans. He made this threat just before his call for a peace conference; he probably intended it to enhance his bargaining power over peace terms. The Wilson-Harding statements added that if the Allies decided to fight on without American financial support, the United States did not fear a depression; they asserted that her trade could be "stimulated in other directions." This was a bluff. Other nations were unlikely to make purchases on the scale that the Allies were doing. They added that if the Allies made a compromise peace with the Central Powers, American capital and exports would profit from Europe's need "to be rehabilitated after the war." The uncertain prospects on both sides of final victory led Wilson to hope that his summons for a peace conference would be accepted, and a general return to the *status quo ante bellum* reached. Otherwise, America "must inevitably drift into the war over the submarine issue," he told House.[70]

Allied counter-pressure lay behind Wilson's relaxation of his coercion over war exports in December 1916. The British and French said that their naval power would no longer give support to the Monroe Doctrine after the war if they were forced to make an unsatisfactory peace and a new coalition of great powers challenged the United States' position in the world. (See Chapter 3)

Although both sides rejected the President's peace without victory, he continued to use financial pressure, in an attentuated form, to bring about a compromise peace favorable to American interests. Washington's feeble response to the Allies' April-May 1917 appeals for help to reduce the U-boats' toll and for troops to stem the weakening of their military position signified the continuation of his policy. Had Washington rushed most of its anti-submarine craft and the 500,000 troops for training and early use in combat in France that the Balfour mission would ask for in April-May 1917, or, even had Washington agreed that these troops could form cadres of an early, large, independent American army, the scales might possibly have been tipped against the Central Powers. (These requests and Washington's response will be discussed and documented in Chapters 2 and 3.)

But, in these circumstances, the Entente would too strongly dominate a peace conference, owing to their larger military and naval success in forcing the Central Powers to the peace table. The Allies would impose the terms of their Paris Economic Conference and their territorial pacts. Hence, as Wilson would confide to House in July 1917, he would wait until the Allies were delivered "among other things, financially in to [sic] our hands." Only then "can we force them to our way of thinking," force them to accept "our real peace terms, those upon which we shall undoubtedly insist even though they are not now acceptable to either France or Italy (leaving Great Britain for the moment out of consideration)."[71]

In addition to financial, naval, and military leverages, the President intended to use moral power against the Allied governments. He would seek support from the Allied peoples against them. He would try to encourage the German and Austrian moderates so that they might acquire sufficient power over the militarists to accept his peace terms. He would remain distrustful of the "imperialists" who led the London Cabinet: David Lloyd George; Alfred, Viscount Milner; and George, then 1st Earl Curzon of Kedleston. These men seemed determined to fight on for complete victory and their own peace terms.

As the war progressed, Wilson would try to repair the rents in his moral armor. He defined the crux of his problem when he told Lansing on March 20, 1917, the day he decided on war, that he could not truthfully say that it would be a war for democracy. [72] Aspersions on his motives were cast widely in Allied as well as in Central Power countries. For example, the *Sydney Sunday Times* had editorialized that "the American vampire" was "busy making money" out of "the world's agony" while "John Bull fights for civilisation." Illustrative too was the attack leveled against him in the Jesuit paper of Florence in March 1917 following his refusal of the Pope's request that he halt war supplies to the Allies. In "a classical example of selfishness, the United States . . . have used their vaunted neutrality to gain millions and billions to the rhythmic beat of preparing ammunition which were [*sic*] used to scatter broadcast death and destruction throughout Europe." America should "stop the war immediately by preventing the exportation of munitions." Wilson knew of this indictment; yet he probably did not know that Vatican opinion held that he would now enter the war because he realized that in the eyes of both sides he was *non grata;* that by participation in the war he would achieve participation in a peace conference; that otherwise even the Japanese would advance their anti-American interests in his absence. [73]

The man — William Snowden Sims — the Navy Department selected late in March 1917 to go to London to arrange a limited naval cooperation (no more than that required to protect American merchant ships) held that Wilson's and Benson's basic premises were morally wrong. Sims would protest that their wartime naval policy was animated by a narrow nationalism. As were Wilson, Daniels, and Benson, Sims was of entirely British descent. His mother, as was Wilson's, was born in northern England. Her father, Major William Snowden, brought her as a girl to Port Hope, Ontario, where she met and married an American engineer from a comfortably well-off Philadelphia family, Alfred Sims. In Ontario, on October 15, 1858, William Snowden was born. Ten years later, the family moved to Pennsylvania, where the father acquired lucrative mining and iron-smelting interests. [74]

William entered the Naval Academy in 1876, and was graduated twenty-eighth in his class of fifty-six. In November 1917, Captain Pratt, who had served as Sims's second in command of the Atlantic Destroyer Flotilla and had become Benson's chief assistant (and would, in 1930, become Chief of Operations) advised Daniels about his former commander. Sims possessed a high order of intelligence. He excelled in choosing the right man for the right job, and in winning the fierce

Admiral William S. Sims, London, December 1918. Photo courtesy of William S. Sims II.

loyalty and best efforts of those who served under him.[75] A jovial raconteur of after-dinner stories and an exponent of officers' physical fitness through sports and exercises, Sims's striking countenance and muscular physique gave him the aura of the ideal naval officer.

After varied duties at sea, Sims was assigned in 1897 as Naval Attaché to Paris, Madrid, and St. Petersburg simultaneously. On this duty, he first met his bride-to-be, Anne, daughter of the St. Louis businessman chosen by President McKinley as envoy to Russia, Ethan Allen Hitchcock, future Secretary of the Interior under McKinley and Theodore Roosevelt. Later, on the China Station, he became fast friends with Captain (later Admiral Sir Percy) Scott. Through this association, Sims learned of the new gunnery techniques with which Scott had brought the British Far Eastern force to the most efficient standard in the world. Sims's gratitude to the older officer for confiding his secret, still guarded from the main units of the Royal Navy, gave a powerful impetus to the American's conversion to a devoted and unwavering admiration for the British navy, Empire, and people. Sims's biographer and sometime son-in-law, Elting Morison, wrote that although "America was his country, and therefore more to him than England," he believed that "the two together were the English-speaking race and the sum was greater than the parts. The race stood for free men, free minds, and free spirits; it stood for the highest form of culture on earth; it stood especially for the dignity of men."

Improving on Scott's technique, Sims won President Theodore Roosevelt's support against his complacent naval superiors. When tests showed an average of 13 percent of hits on targets in contrast to British scores of an average of 81 percent, a ruffled Rough Rider commanded that Sims be given charge of the navy's gunnery training program. On target strikes rose by 500 percent. Sims married Miss Hitchcock in Roosevelt's presence at St. John's Episcopal Church near the White House. A stint as a White House aide confirmed Sims's devotion to Theodore Roosevelt. So did Roosevelt's leadership of the pro-British, pro-war wing of the Republican Party during its 1916 campaign to prevent the reelection of the President who had "kept us out of war."

In 1910, Sims received his first letter of reprimand from the Secretary of the Navy, George von L. Meyer, and President Taft. The sentiments which earned him this admonition were fairly widespread among American naval officers. Their envy vied with their admiration for the world's greatest navy and empire. At a London banquet, Sims declared that "if the time should ever come when the British Empire is menaced by a European coalition, Great Britain can rely on the last ship, the last man, and the last drop of blood from her kindred across the sea." [76]

When Benson, Daniels, and the General Board independently selected Sims to carry out their policies in England, they wanted Britain to do something for them. They needed an admiral towards whom the British authorities felt well disposed. And if anti-U-boat craft had to be dispatched to Europe to prevent a German victory, Sims was an excellent commander of war craft, especially destroyers. On March 20, when the Cabinet had agreed with the President that a formal war declaration had become necessary, a sorrowful Daniels had concurred. A *sauve-qui-peut* policy of stingy naval support in the war zone would serve two alternatives. If the Allies became so weakened and desperate from the U-boat losses that Wilson had to increase his contributions, they would become beholden to their eleventh-hour savior. On the other hand, if the Allies went down with their ships, few American naval craft would be caught by Scheer in their catastrophe. Tearfully, Daniels agreed at this Cabinet session, that a formal declaration of war was required as "our present attempt by Armed [*sic*] guard would not be wholly effective, and if it succeeded, we must cooperate with English and let them convoy [somehow escort or protect in the war zone] our ships while we patrolled this coast. Having tried patience, there was no other course open to protect our rights at sea." Wilson here denounced both "G[erman] militarism on land and E[ngland]'s militarism on sea." In carrying out a wartime policy, Daniels doubtless would also not forget the statement the President made to his Cabinet of two days after the German U-boat announcements: he did "not wish to see either side win." [77]

On March 25, the Sims mission was authorized when Wilson told the Secretary to send an officer to England sanctioned "to study and cooperate to protect our merchant ships . . . [instead of] asking them to send officers here." The President concluded in a letter to Daniels on March 24, that "the main thing is no doubt to get into communication with the Admiralty [Sims's task to be] and work out a scheme of cooperation. As yet sufficient attention has not been given . . . by the authorities on the other side . . . to the routes to be followed or to plans by which the safest approach may be made to British ports." He made no allusion to convoying. [78]

On March 27, the day Mayo's Fleet began arriving in Chesapeake Bay, Sims reached Washington from the War College at Newport, Rhode Island, to be briefed on his mission to England. Benson couched his instructions in phrases meant to ensure that Sims carried out the Wilson-Daniels-Benson policy, rather than his own or the General Board's, whose report of April 5 named Sims as the best choice to head a mission to Europe. Although the board, on this date, cautioned that the navy must be prepared to stand alone against possible postwar enemies, it repeated its recommendation of February 4 and 17: "As most important, arrange, as soon as possible, plans of cooperation with the naval forces of the Allies for the joint protection of Trans-Atlantic commerce and for joint offensive operations against the common enemy." To accomplish these ends, Sims and the fourteen officers the Board urged should accompany and assist him were to "immediately obtain from the Allied powers their views as to how we can best conform our preparations and acts to their present needs." [79] But Benson and Daniels gave Sims no staff; they did not contemplate any "joint offensive operations against the common enemy"; neither did they intend to make the United States Navy ready to meet the Allies' "present needs." Instead, Benson admonished Sims not to "let the

British pull the wool over your eyes. It is none of our business pulling their chestnuts out of the fire. We would as soon fight the British as the Germans." When Sims later reported these instructions to the 1920 Senate Committee, Benson testified that his words were intended to warn Sims against "letting his feelings towards the British" guide his actions. Besides, Benson added, "I had very serious doubts as to the Allies whipping Germany." [80] Presumably he did not wish the American navy to be seriously committed to a losing struggle.

At these same Senate Committee Hearings, Daniels averred that even after the American declaration of war, he had intended that Sims avoid agreeing to any joint effort that might imply a junior American partnership of "subserviency" to the Royal Navy. [81] He did not explain how the American navy could act jointly with the much larger British navy without playing the junior role.

Sims was not much discouraged. With his aide, Lt. Commander J. V. Babcock, he sailed for England at the end of March. Babcock soon suffered a mental breakdown because Sims tried to use him as his entire operational staff in a mission that Sims determined would be broader even than that envisaged by the General Board.

Notes on Chapter 1

[1] George T. Davis, *A Navy Second to None* (New York, 1940), 171-72; Harold and Margaret Sprout, *The Rise of American Naval Power 1776-1918* (Princeton, 1939), 323, 344-45; Arthur J. Marder, *From the Dreadnought to Scapa Flow* (London, New York and Toronto, 1961-70), III, 37-38.

[2] Marder, *Dreadnought to Scapa Flow*, III, Chs. 2-4, *passim; ibid.*, 202-07; summary of British intelligence sources on pronouncements of German leaders through May 1916 on need to break the blockade in study for British War Cabinet's Reconstruction Committee, "German Post-War Economic Policy," Jan. 1917, CAB/17/73, Public Record Office (hereafter P.R.O.).

[3] Fritz Fischer, *Griff nach der Weltmacht* (3rd ed., improved; Düsseldorf, 1964), 306-09.

[4] *Ibid.*, 306.

[5] *Ibid.*, Ch. 8; William H. Maehl, "Germany's War Aims in the East, 1914-1917: Status of the Question," *The Historian*, XXXIV (May 1972), 381-406.

[6] CAB/24/9, Jan. 1917; CAB/21/73, Jan. 1917, and 88, Jan. 16, 1917; CAB/24/10, Mar. 1917, and 17, Apr. 1917, P.R.O.

[7] William G. Sharp, ambassador at Paris, to Lansing (Secretary of State), June 22, 1916, Papers of Josephus Daniels, Library of Congress (hereafter Daniels Papers); Ray Stannard Baker, *Woodrow Wilson: Life and Letters* (Garden City, 1927-39), VI, 313n.

[8] Baker, *Wilson*, VI, 229-30; see also documents cited in note 6, above.

[9] Robert S. Lovett in *New York Times*, Oct. 9, 1916; Secretary of Agriculture David F. Houston's proposed campaign speech in fall, 1916, n.d., Papers of President Woodrow Wilson, Library of Congress (hereafter Wilson Papers), Sers. 2, Box 155 (hereafter the series and box number of this collection will not be cited unless a missing date or some other deficiency precludes ready location in the chronological order in which these documents are arranged or the document is not in Sers. 2); speech of Senate majority leader John Sharp Williams, Dec. 11, 1916, and speech of Secretary of Commerce William C. Redfield, Dec. 13, 1916, *ibid.*, speech of President, Oct. 26, 1916, *The Public Papers of Woodrow Wilson*, Ray Stannard Baker and William E. Dodd, eds. (New York and London, 1925-27), hereafter *PPWW*), V, 377-79.

[10] "Economic Conference of the Allies," CAB/24/10, June 21, 1916, P.R.O.

[11] British liaison representative to House Sir William Wiseman to Br. ambassador to U.S. Lord Reading, Aug. 20, 27, 28, and 30; Sept. 5, 12, and 15, 1918, FO/800/225, P.R.O., on Wilson's anger at the two prime ministers and related grievances; PPWW V, 93-96, 253-61.

[12] Entry for Feb. 27, 1917, in E. David Cronon, ed., *The Cabinet Diaries of Josephus Daniels, 1913-1921* (Lincoln, 1963) (pagination follows chronology of entries); Baker, *Wilson*, VI. 229-30.

[13] Many American newspapers which reported the text of this German note, including the *New York American*, can be seen in the Library of Congress.

[14] Baker, *Wilson*, VI, 107-08, 327-32; W. H. Page to Wilson, Sept. 15, 1916, Wilson Papers.

[15] "Econ. Conf. of the Allies," CAB/24/10, June 21, 1916, P.R.O.

[16] *PPWW*, IV, 143.

[17] N. Gordon Levin, Jr., *Woodrow Wilson and World Politics* (New York, 1968), 18; *PPWW*, II, 357-58, 408.

[18] *PPWW*, IV, 229, 233.

[19] V. H. Rothwell, *British War Aims and Peace Diplomacy, 1914-1918* (Oxford, 1971), 279.

[20] William Diamond, *The Economic Thought of Woodrow Wilson* (Baltimore, 1943), 152; Baker, *Wilson*, 4, 292.

[21] *PPWW*, III, 220, 216.

[22] Baker, *Wilson*, VI, 312; *PPWW*, IV, 314.

[23] Cited in Diamond, *Economic Thought*, 136.

[24] David A. Shannon, *Between the Wars: America, 1919-1941* (Boston, 1965), 21.

[25] Lansing to Wilson, May 5, 1917, Wilson Papers.

[26] Cited in Arthur Walworth, *Woodrow Wilson* (New York, London and Toronto, 1958), II, 217.

[27] Baker, *Wilson*, V, 108, 110, 111-12; *PPWW*, III, 415-16, 418.

[28] W. H. Koebel, *South America: An Industrial and Commercial Field* (London, 1918), 208-209.

[29] Davis, *Navy Second to None*, 223; Baker, *Wilson*, VI, 309.

[30] Jules Nahoum, *The Key to National Prosperity* (New York, 1923), 257-58; Postmaster General A. S. Burleson to Wilson, Mar. 30, 1917, Papers of Newton D. Baker, Library of Congress (hereafter N.D. Baker Papers), Box 4.

[31] Burton J. Kaufman, "United States Trade and Latin America; The Wilson Years," *The Journal of American History* LVIII (Sept. 1971), 361-62.

[32] Baker, *Wilson*, 5, 110; David F. Trask, *Captains and Cabinets: Anglo-American Naval Relations, 1917-1918* (Columbia, Mo., 1972), 170.

[33] William Reynolds Braisted, *The United States Navy in the Pacific, 1909-1922* (Austin and London, 1971), 174-75, 178.

[34] Baker, *Wilson*, VI, 29, 162-64; Braisted *Navy in Pacific*, 141, 194, 202.

[35] Charles Seymour, ed., *The Intimate Papers of Colonel House* (Boston and New York, 1926-28), II, 231.

[36] Dudley W. Knox, *A History of the United States Navy* (New York, 1936, 381-85; Diary by Josephus Daniels (not in his hand), Apr. 24 and June 30, 1917. Records of the Department of the Navy, Naval Records Collection of the Office of Naval Records and Library (Record Group 45), 1911-1927, National Archives, Washington, D.C. (hereafter USNSF), U file.

[37] Pratt to Benson, June 7, 1917, USNSF, UB file: Miscellaneous Correspondence of Admiral Benson.

[38] Board report GB 420 (no SSN), Aug. 29, 1917, Office of Naval Records and Library, Washington Navy Yard, D.C. (hereafter ONRL)

[39] U. S. Congress, Senate, *Hearings Before the Subcommittee of the Committee on Naval Affairs*, 66th Cong., 2d Sess., 1920 (hereafter *Hearings, 1920*), II, 1834-41, 1881.

[40] Baker, *Wilson*, VI, 312, 317; *PPWW*, IV, 278, 310.

[41] Seymour, ed., *House Papers*, II, 316-17, 316n.

[42] *PPWW*, IV, 404; Wilson to Baker, Dec. 26, 1916, N. D. Baker Papers, Box 1.

[43] Cronon, ed., *Daniels Diaries*, Apr. 15, 1918; Baker, *Wilson*, VIII, 521; unpublished autobiography of William V. Pratt (© 1939), Naval Historical Foundation Collection, Library of Congress, (hereafter NHFC) chap. XIV, p. 28; Memo., No. 65, USNSF, TX file: Planning Section; Arthur Walworth, *Woodrow Wilson* (New York, London, and Toronto, 1958), II, 217.

[44] Lansing to Ramon Di Negri (in charge of Mexican affairs in the United States), Mar. 16, 1917, USNSF, VP-2 file: Belligerent Governments . . . ; Braisted, *Navy in Pacific*, 188-89.

[45] Braisted, *Navy in Pacific*, 187-90.

[46] *Ibid.*, 194.

[47] Anne Wintermute Lane and Louise Herrick Wall, eds., *The Letters of Franklin K. Lane: Personal and Political* (Boston, 1922), 237; Braisted, *Navy in Pacific*, 189.

[48] Sprout, *Rise of American Naval Power*, 338-40, 320.

[49] Daniels to Wilson, Feb. 2 and 7, 1917; Wilson to Daniels, Feb. 8 and 13, 1917, Daniels Papers. Mr. Herman Duncan, of Washington D.C., was kind enough to provide me with a photocopy of a German Admiralty order of May 8, 1917, which he had found in Record Group 45 (Naval), National Archives. It is headed "Supplement No. 63, Chief of the Admiralty Staff, B.0/1. Berlin, . . . " The text begins with: "It has been *officially* ascertained that the U.S.A. notified neither us nor . . . Switzerland of . . . a state of war . . . therefore we are not at war with the U.S.A. In order that no excuse may be offered . . . for accusing us of the first act of war . . . ships proceeding to America outside the barred area are to be treated . . . as if the United States were a neutral country."; Lansing to Wilson, May 18, 1917, Wilson Papers; Sims to Secretary of Navy (Ops.), Apr. 14, 18, and 19, 1917, Sims Papers.

[50] Wilson to Daniels, Feb. 8 and 13, 1917, Daniels Papers; Baker to Wilson. Feb. 18, 1917, Wilson Papers; Cronon, ed., *Daniels Diaries*, Mar. 24, 1917.

[51] Frederick Palmer, *Newton D. Baker* (New York, 1931), I, 40-41; Daniels at *Hearings, 1920*, II, 3077-79, 2884-93, 2911-22; Benson, *ibid.*, 1886.

[52] Lane and Wall, eds., *Lane Letters*, 236; Baker, *Wilson*, VI, 455-56.

[53] Lane and Wall, eds., *Lane Letters*, 237; T. R. to Rudyard Kipling, Jan. 6, 1918, printed for King and War Cabinet, Feb. 19, 1918, CAB/21/41, P.R.O.

[54] Joseph L. Morrison, *Josephus Daniels, the Small - - d Democrat* (Durham, 1966), provides a sympathetic, well-done biography; Cronon, ed., *Daniels Diaries*, 206n.

[55] Lane and Wall, eds., *Lane Letters*, 234, 236, 239; Benson at Hearings, 1920, II. 1839-40.

[56] Daniels to Wilson, Mar. 27, 1917, Wilson Papers.

[57] *Hearings, 1920*, I, 452, 454-56.

[58] Cronon, ed., *Daniels Diaries*, Mar. 27 and July 8, 1917; *Baltimore Sun*, Apr. 5, 1917; *Hearings, 1920*, I, 400, 452, 454-56.

[59] Trask, *Captains and Cabinets*, 47-48; Benson at *Hearings, 1920*, II, 1820-23.

[60] Frank Freidel, *Franklin D. Roosevelt* (Boston, 1952), I, 308-09; Churchill to Wilson, n.d., marked by archivist "ca. July, 1917," Wilson Papers, Ser. 2, Box 161.

[61] *Hearings, 1920*, II, 1887-88.

[62] Cronon, ed., *Daniels Diaries*, Mar. 8, 1917; Baker, *Wilson*, VI, 472-73.

[63] Frederick Dixon (ed., *Christian Science Monitor*), on conversation with Bryan, to Wilson, Feb. 15, 1917, Wilson Papers; Benson at *Hearings, 1920*, II, 1905-08; R. R. M. Emmett to Sims, mentioning Benson's views, May 19-June 25, *passim*, Papers of William S. Sims, NHFC (hereafter, Sims Papers).

[64] Hugo Muensterberg to Wilson, Oct. 24, 1916, Portland, Oregon Customs Inspector Thomas C. Burke to Wilson, Oct. 14, 1916, Wilson Papers; T. N. Page to Lansing, Jan. 22, 1917, *Foreign Relations: The Lansing Papers* (Washington, 1939), I, 751.

[65] T. N. Page to Lansing, Dec. 29, 1916, Feb. 17 and Mar. 20, 1917, *Lansing Papers*, I, 744-45, 755-57, 760-61.

[66] Rabbi Stephen S. Wise to Wilson, Apr. 11, 1917, F. Dixon to Wilson, Feb. 23, 1917, Wilson Papers; H. C. Peterson, *Propaganda for War: The Campaign Against American Neutrality, 1914-1917* (Norman, Okla., 1939), 241-42; *New York American and San Francisco Examiner*, Feb. 1, 2, and 4, 1917; Tumulty to Wilson, Mar. 24, 1917, with clippings from several newspapers: the *New York Evening Post* on Mar. 22 and *New York Times* on Mar. 24 called for no commitments to Allied aims if America entered the war.

[67] Seward K. Livermore, *Politics is Adjourned: Woodrow Wilson and the War Congress, 1916-1918* (Middletown, Conn., 1966), 8-13; Cronon, ed., *Daniels Diaries*, Mar. 20, 1917; Arthur S. Link, *Woodrow Wilson and the Progressive Era, 1910-1917* (New York, Evanston and London, 1954), 275.

⁶⁸Mayo, Admiral C. P. Plunkett (wartime commander of U. S. Submarines), Admiral A. W. Grant (wartime commander of Mayo's battleship Force I), and Benson at *Hearings, 1920*, I, 579-85, 521, 550, II, 1850, respectively.

⁶⁹*Hearings, 1920*, I, 551-52; 579-84.

⁷⁰Baker, *Wilson*, VI, 269-78; Seymour, ed., *House Papers*, II, 390-95.

⁷¹Baker, *Wilson*, VII, 180-81.

⁷²Daniel M. Smith, *American Intervention, 1917: Sentiment, Self-Interest, or Ideals?* (Boston, 1966), 187.

⁷³U. S. Consul-General at Sydney to Lansing, Oct. 12, 1915, National Archives mf. 581 (roll 1) *Records of the Department of State Relating to the Political Relations Between the United States and Great Britain, 1910-1929* (hereafter USDSM 581); T. N. Page to Lansing, Mar. 20, 1917, *Lansing Papers*, I, 760-61.

⁷⁴Unless otherwise noted, this summary of Sims's early life derives from Morison's *Sims*, interviews with Sims's son, William S. Sims of Washington, D.C., and Sims's biographical sketch issued by the Navy Office of Information, Jan. 15, 1959.

⁷⁵Pratt to Daniels to Wilson, Nov. 12, 1917, Daniels Papers.

⁷⁶Davis, *Navy Second to None*, 112-13.

⁷⁷Cronon, ed., *Daniels Diaries*, Mar. 20, 1917; Lane to George W. Lane, Feb. 9, 1917, Lane and Wall, eds., *Lane Letters*, 234.

⁷⁸Cronon, ed., *Daniels Diaries*, Mar. 24 and 25, 1917; Wilson to Daniels, Mar. 24, 1917, Daniels Papers.

⁷⁹Board to Daniels, Feb. 4 and Apr. 5, 1917, 425 SN 666 and 699, ONRL.

⁸⁰*Hearings, 1920*, I, 1; II, 1880-82.

⁸¹*Ibid.*, II. 1994, 2005.

2

WILSON AND BENSON'S "AHEAD ONE-THIRD SPEED" ON NAVAL WAR

April-July 1917

SPEAKING BEFORE CONGRESS on April 2, 1917, Wilson declared that
the war was going to make the world "safe for democracy" (despite
his recent statements to Lansing). He warned the Germans that
America would ultimately wield a powerful sword to deny them victory
— unless they meanwhile accepted his olive branch. On the other hand,
the American people were going to "conduct . . . [their] operations
without passion." They were entering the war only because they had
been "forced into it" by the U-boat campaign. They desired "nothing
so much as the early restoration of intimate relations of mutual
advantage between . . . [the two peoples] ."[1]

Although the German government's U-boat warfare announcement
had stated that the German people demanded that their submarines
sink munitions destined to kill their soldiers and break the blockade
that threatened to starve their children, the President was appealing to
the German people to pressure their government into abandoning the
submarine campaign and negotiate peace on his terms. The phrasing of
his message to Congress intimated to the directors of America's armed
forces that their preparations for fighting "without passion" against
Germany were to be restrained. Sims soon discovered that this was so.
On July 11 he appealed to the President to intervene with Daniels and
Benson to send him warships, the men to man them, and the officers to
direct the operations of those he had. Otherwise, America could not tip
the balance against Germany. Sims pleaded that even if the war were
lost, history should demonstrate that the United States had done what
it could against the U-boats by sending him all of her "destroyers,
submarines, armed tugs, yachts, light cruisers, revenue cutters, mine
layers, mine sweepers, gunboats . . . and similar craft."[2] However,

Wilson did not order the bulk of America's anti-U-boat craft sent to Europe. He still sought to conserve America's resources.

In October 1916, Wilson had pointed out that "from 40 to 60 percent of the skilled mechanics of Europe have been called into the field . . . . The debts of these nations are piling up . . . . " These nations had ceased to produce dyestuffs "and other things that they . . . sent to the American markets . . . the whole . . . energy of these nations will require a generation, say, to recover . . . . " The United States should be prepared to ship goods and capital to them; after "this war, they will need us" to revive their economies. "It will be America's opportunity . . . . [not merely to make profitable advantage of Europe's plight], but to do something very much greater than that." The American people must abandon their fears that Europe would have postwar goods to dump on the American market. Then they must join a league of nations and use their "physical force" if necessary to "see to it that . . . no group of nations tries to take advantage of another nation . . . . " He feared a worse postwar contest than the war itself, a "contest based on radical economic rivalry [sparked by the quest for exclusionary access to the world's raw materials as envisioned by the Paris Economic Conference and the German-sponsored common market-style combination, he doubtless foresaw] which would breed deeper antagonisms than the antagonisms of actual force." He assailed "exclusive combinations" at home and abroad. His League of Nations would suppress them and protect "competitors of merit alone."[3] After Berlin's U-boat announcement, he rejected "any great preparedness" for imminent combat in February 1917 as he anticipated that "Europe will be man and money poor at the end of the war."[4]

Minimizing America's combat role in the war would help achieve the "early restoration of intimate relations of mutual advantage" with the German people that Wilson wanted. Restraint in the use of his armed forces would help prevent a boycott of American goods by angry Germans after the war. He had told the nation in November 1916 that "the real foundation of good business" was to avoid alienating potential customers: "America cannot reap the harvest . . . unless the soils of the world . . . yield to her . . . they will not yield to hatred . . . or enmity . . . . " House would remind him in September 1918 that his avoidance of declaration of war against Germany's ally Bulgaria "will mean after war reconstructing and financing" of that country by Americans. In February 1917 (as noted), Wilson told his cabinet that he did "not wish to see either side win" the war. As he polled the cabinet about a war declaration on March 20, 1917, he denounced both "G[erman] militarism on land and E[ngland]'s militarism on sea."[5] Enroute to the Peace Conference, as noted, the President would exclaim that had not Germany's unrestricted U-boat campaign forced him into the war in 1917, he "would have been ready to have it out then and there with Great Britain . . . . " One remembers Benson's admonition to Sims as he dispatched him to London in March 1917: "we would as soon fight the British as the Germans."

On the other hand, both Benson and the President wanted

America's role in the war to be a creditable one that would bring prestige to the navy and to its commander-in-chief. Hence they relied on Sims's competence in commanding what vessels were risked in the war zone. On April 12, Daniels noted that recruiting results were poor. In May, the Department of the Navy protested British press reports that six American destroyers had arrived in the war zone to help against the U-boats' depredations. Daniels and Benson held that these reports "intimately concern the welfare of the U.S." and must not be repeated. Not only did this news tend to undermine the German-American posture Wilson desired to maintain, it made the pacific Daniels uneasy over the safety of the vessels (despite assurance from Sims that few Allied destroyers had been sunk as "subs are afraid of them").[6]

In April, the President told the people that the nation was entering the war over the U-boat; but in May the navy seemed to be doing little to combat it. The people found little in the President's war message to stir them — he had not even called for victory over Germany. Although he was never to do so, beginning with his answer to the Pope's August 1917 terms for a peace conference, he did make the people aware that they had a greater stake in the war than the principle of freedom of the seas. If the Allies faltered, Americans would have to do some serious fighting. Wilson would have to unite them behind his war leadership for this purpose. This had been pointed out to House by British Foreign Secretary Sir Edward Grey in July 1915: "nothing short of being actually involved in the war will stir your people sufficiently to . . . enable the President to exercise on the terms of the peace conference all the influence that is possible." In April 1916, House had advised Wilson that if America entered the war, "it will strengthen your position at home and with the Allies," and that his "influence at the peace conference would be enormously enhanced instead of lessened." Moreover, "we could still be the force to stop the war."[7]

But the task of strengthening his peace conference position was plagued, in April-October 1917, by the dichotomy of his purposes as understood by his people from his speeches. Tumulty advised the President of "a spirit of indifference" in the "attitude of the people toward the war." On June 20, Lord Northcliffe (coordinator of British war missions in America) reported that Secretary of the Interior Franklin K. Lane had told him that Irish-Americans needed to be conciliated over Ireland; they exercised a "power in the Press," and their workers had "much to do with the various metal trades." Appeasement of them "would mean a 10 percent increase in war activity." The administration worried over criticism of its war purposes. In May, it began to act "against the threat of . . . pacifists, socialists and others to make trouble over the conscription." Yet Ambassador Sir Cecil Spring-Rice reported on July 27, 1917, that the Hearst Press was urging that the destruction of British naval supremacy was "the first and foremost interest of the U.S." Sir Cecil also reported that certain Irish-American organizations were asserting that "an Irish republic under German protection will be the most powerful engine to destroy British naval supremacy . . . . "[8]

In October, however, a change in public opinion began to occur. The Russians were in retreat. The administration's suppression of war critics also helped to arouse the majority behind the President. Walter Lippmann wrote Wilson to protest that the Attorney General's censorship of the mails was alienating a liberal minority, as well as to tell him that his rejection of the papal peace conference terms (as too pro-German) had won him support from "the masses." On October 24 the Italians began their paralyzing retreat from Caporetto. British naval intelligence reported that the current American Liberty Bond campaign had "brought home to the people . . . the issues of the war and enthusiasm had grown." On November 7, the Bolsheviks seized power and Lenin quickly announced that Russia was suing for armistice terms. On October 12, the President exhorted the nation to gird its loins against the growing German territorial economic empire "from Hamburg to Bagdad" and the Reich's unfair methods of economic competition. He warned that Russia might otherwise remain doomed to domination by Germany. Wilson castigated both Russians and Americans who would end the war under such conditions. He won the support of the majority of union workers by his public enforcement of AFL goals. By late November, most Americans had become aroused behind "an energetic conduct of the war." By May 1918, Irish-America had temporarily demoted its anger over British rule in Ireland to give priority to "the general enthusiasm for the war."[9]

While Sims was still en route to England, the first British and French naval missions to visit Washington, following the U.S. declaration, arrived. Benson's visitors, Vice-Admirals Sir Montague E. Browning and R. A. Grasset, commanded their nations' cruisers in North American waters; these guarded shipping against virtually non-existent Atlantic surface raiders and enforced the blockade rules. [10]

By this time official Washington had received ample information about the U-boat-wrought plight of the Entente. In February and March, American diplomats had written from Paris and Rome about the growing dearth of essentials which was created by the U-boat menace. House advised Wilson that the French badly needed "steel . . . coal, and other raw materials." From Rome, Ambassador Thomas Nelson Page warned that increasing privations and demoralization meant that a successful Austrian offensive in the north could bring a Marxist revolution to Italy. House warned the President that the cumulative sinkings meant that "the strain upon the English to furnish materials for Russia, France and Italy has been so great that they are now unable to recruit for the army any further."[11] The British redoubled their efforts to supply the Allied armies whose consumption of ammunition and other war materials steadily increased, while many more such cargoes were sunk. In April, the United States seized the 720,000 tons of German shipping which had been stranded in its ports since 1914. The Allies hoped — largely in vain — that this would soon be used to carry war supplies and food to them.[12]

Theoretically, the Allies should not have felt such a desperate need for American anti-submarine craft. But, when, in January 1917, Lloyd

George had addressed an inter-Allied naval conference in London, he had appealed in vain to the Italians and French for release from the old agreement by which the British kept destroyers and battleships in the Mediterranean. The first type was needed to combat U-boats in British and northern French waters; the older battleships needed to be retired to release their crews to man newly launched anti-submarine craft. Nevertheless, the Italians had adamantly refused. They had insisted that the Austrian surface fleet might any day sail forth to give battle, or that it might choose to raid Italy's eastern cities. Moreover, lack of coal was fast paralyzing Italy's warships. Their delegates had declared that either the British and French would continue to sustain Italy with their naval presence and rush coal to her factories and navy or their government would no longer feel obligated to remain in the war. The French had been almost as unyielding about the Royal Navy's units in the Mediterranean; both were obsessed with the notion of preserving their own warcraft for the power they might exert over a peace conference.[13] Minor Latin concessions had been made; but the French and Italian naval vessels continued to make only rather ineffective efforts to save merchant ships in the Mediterranean — through which one-fourth of the world's shipping passed.[14]

As Browning and Grasset arrived in Washington, the British and French stood in desperate need of both financial and naval help. The Italians had recently told the British that their factory owners were refusing to sign any more war contracts until they had a glimpse of the money with which they would be paid. The British had curtailed their own purchases in the United States. By now much of America's and the remaining neutrals' shipping had forsaken the U-boat-infested waters off Europe to concentrate on the profitable and safe waters of Asia and Latin America, as 150 British merchant ships were being recalled from such distant trades. Most of the doomed ships belonged to the British; most of the remainder belonged to other Entente owners or to neutral owners in Norway and the Netherlands who had been coerced, owing to their vulnerable location, by the Allies into plying the war zone.[15]

Another cause of Washington's reluctance to join the fray against the U-boats was Wilson's antagonism towards Lloyd George's "fight-to-the-finish" Cabinet. In the fall of 1916 (while still the War Secretary) Lloyd George had publicly rebuked the President for attempting to set a peace conference in motion. Soon after forming his own Cabinet, however, he had grasped the fact (so Wilson was informed) that the United States could, through financial pressure, "force the Allies to their knees."[16] Moreover, by April, he realized that American naval help was needed. He had begun tacking to the Wilsonian wind. In February, he had sent word to the President that he looked forward to America's participation in the war "especially because it meant he would receive the President's cool and patient and humane counsel . . . at the peace conference." Ambassador Walter Hines Page let Wilson know what else Lloyd George wanted — and at once, a week before the Allied naval mission's arrival. His administration could "save itself from becoming a black blot on American history only in . . . putting our navy to work — vigorous work . . . with the British Navy whereby we can best help." Rush American troops to France for rapid training for early combat use and grant a large loan, Page also enjoined.[17]

Lloyd George's protestations of a rapid conversion to Wilsonian principles were not, however, sufficiently convincing. The program worked out at the Navy Department on April 10 and 11 remained guided by the "ahead slow speed" policy of recent weeks. At the outset, Benson informed Browning and Grasset that the United States Navy would only help them patrol American waters from Maine to Texas. The next day, in Daniels' office, the foreigners were told that the basic war policy of the United States would be to preserve its navy "intact" in American waters. Thus, only six of its sixty-six destroyers would be sent to the war zone "to cooperate with the Allied anti-submarine forces in that area."[18]

On the day before this Washington conference with Browning and Grasset began, Sims had taken to a lifeboat; his liner had limped to a mooring in Liverpool with a hole blown in its side by a U-boat-laid mine. In London on April 10, the First Sea Lord Admiral Sir John Jellicoe informed Sims that in February the Allies and neutrals had lost 536,000 tons of shipping; in March another 603,000 had gone down. The April rate indicated that during this month at least another 850,000 tons would go down.[19] During the first 30 months of the war, the Allies had lost 4,500,000 tons of merchant ships. They lost "approximately that amount in the first seven months of the new submarine warfare." In 1917, 6,100,000 tons with vital cargoes went down; only 2,700,000 tons were launched. American merchant ships, however, remained shy about entering the blockade zone. Benson saw the strategic need to deflect sufficient commerce to the transatlantic trade to insure full support of the Entente powers in February 1917,[20] but he did not seek to do so with American ships before or after April 6, 1917.

Responding to Sims's postwar public assertion that the Navy Department had withheld the bulk of its anti-submarine craft from the war zone owing to the paucity of American ships in U-boat-stalked waters and its indifference to the sinking of Allied merchant ships, Benson would reply merely that the number of American merchant ships sailing to Europe had not been "very large." In July 1917, about 3,000 British ships entered or departed a British port, but only 160 (5 percent of the British number) American ships did so. In November, Daniels noted that "of 354 ships that go daily into French and English ports only twenty-six (or 7 percent of the total) are American." In February-March 1917, 59 percent of the world's tonnage sunk were British. In April-May 1917, 62 percent of the ships sunk were British. In the summer of 1917, British officials tried (but unavailingly) to persuade Wilson to send many more ships (especially German ships America had seized) to succor the Allies. The British fruitlessly assured him that the war had forced their merchant marine virtually to abandon Latin American and Asian shipping routes so as to concentrate their dwindling cargo space on the carriage of vital military supplies for the Allies. They assured the President that Britain could not regain the distant markets she had been forced to give up — at least not while the war lasted. The United Kingdom was devoting 75 percent of its building capacity to anti-U-boat craft, and only 25 percent to merchant ships, they added.[21]

Jellicoe told Sims that the British were " 'building destroyers, trawlers . . . as fast as we can . . . . but we shall need all of the assistance [from America] that we get' " to avert a U-boat-forced end to the war.[22]

Sims began his struggle, which would be frustrated to the war's end, to induce Washington to send all operational anti-submarine craft to European waters. His cables of mid-April pointed up the starkness of the war at sea. These were shown to the President. "Supplies and communications [which includes transporting troops] of forces on all fronts, including the Russians, are threatened and control of the sea is actually imperiled . . . . regardless of any diversions such as raids on our coast [two long-range U-boats would come over in May 1918, and inflict moderate damage] . . . the critical area in which the war's decision will be made is in the eastern Atlantic at the focus of all lines of communication." Sims pointed out that it would be a waste of German sea weapons to send long-range U-boats, of which there were few, to American waters. The time lost on the round-trip voyage, and the meager rewards to be found in the widely dispersed traffic scattered from Boston to Brownsville, could be much more profitably spent on shorter forays to prey upon the concentrated swarms of inbound ships in the lanes approaching the coasts of southern Britain and northern France. It was here that the British and French were so short of anti-submarine vessels. The Allied navies were "dangerously strained".[23]

Sims's April 19 cable (shown to Wilson) informed the Navy Department of the news that he was working to overcome the Admiralty's objections to convoying. Meanwhile, patrols against submarines were the only remedy agreed to. Even for these, all seaworthy American destroyers and all other anti-submarine craft must be rushed to him. Merchant ships, too, should be hastened to the rescue.

In April 1917, Jellicoe was more amenable to the notion of convoys in the eastern Atlantic than Lloyd George subsequently made him out to have been. Jellicoe believed, however, that he needed many American anti-U-boat craft to make a convoy system effective and the risk of removing more destroyers from the Grand Fleet for it to be acceptable. He and Admiral Sir David Beatty, commander of the Grand Fleet, were frightened at the risk they had already taken in transferring destroyers from guarding the Grand Fleet against U-boats to convoy ore ships from Scandinavia through the North Sea and escort hospital ships elsewhere. On April 25 the First Sea Lord wrote a friend that he feared "the convoy on the East Coast will fail" for want of enough anti-submarine vessels. Jellicoe added that he had "no destroyers at all to carry it out in the western approaches" to the United Kingdom. On April 27 he demanded that the Cabinet give up the Greek expedition "at once" to release naval craft "to assist in providing protection for convoys of ships bringing into this country essentials . . . but, even with this we shall be very hard put to it unless the United States think to help us to the utmost of their ability." On May 7, Beatty fanned his fright: "We are so very short" of destroyers with the Grand Fleet that "what would happen if the enemy [Fleet] came out . . . to engage in mortal combat I can't think as he would certainly have 100 subs and we have today 37 destroyers *here*. 14 at Rosyth!!!"[24]

Late in April, Jellicoe agreed to adopt the convoy system in the western approaches without an assurance that significant American help in naval craft would be forthcoming to make it effective. On May 1, Sims cabled Washington a detailed plan which required American participation in the new system. The Navy Department would have to supervise the assembling of the cargo before sailing for Europe; it was too dangerous to let them mill around to assemble and await escorts in the war zone, and there were hardly enough anti-submarine craft to guard a whole convoy, certainly not to "convoy" individual ships. American cruisers must escort them part way toward Europe to guard against the remote possibility of a surface raider and to insure that they had got used to keeping together. Above all, the new system demanded that the Navy Department dispatch to him at once convoy escorts for the U-boat zone: destroyers, gunboats, armed yachts, tugs, and any other fast craft (such as Coast Guard cutters) which would drop the new British device, the depth charge, on the slow-moving submerged vessels whose torpedo wakes made their position rather clear. Guns on their merchant ships' decks, however, only made certain that U-boat commanders would not give warning to man lifeboats before they drove their torpedoes into the merchant ships' sides.[25]

Even if Washington gave full-scale cooperation, there would not be enough British and American warcraft to escort ships outbound from Europe through the danger zone. Yet Sims's cables of April 19 and May 1 elicited no cooperation; the Navy Department refused for many weeks even to acknowledge receipt of his convoy appeals. At the end of April, all he had heard was that the six destroyers promised to Browning and Grasset had sailed on April 24; they would arrive at Queenstown about May 4. What he wanted was hundreds of anti-U-boat craft, including submarines, for convoy and patrol duty in the war zone. On April 24 he cabled, largely repeating his previous arguments.[26]

As Sims wrote Palmer on May 1, he realized that his own voice was suspect in the department, and that he could only rely upon the Balfour and Viviani missions, which had recently reached Washington, to persuade the American authorities that his advice on the war at sea was not "extravagant."[27] Wilson told House he supposed that there was no way short of an open breach to stop the Balfour mission from coming. House was able to get the British to agree not to send any naval figure of stature with Arthur James Balfour; the world must not be encouraged to conclude that the U.S. Navy was about to become a junior partner of the Royal Navy. House induced Balfour to announce that he had not come to seek any Anglo-American agreement about fighting the war; trade matters of mutual interest would be discussed. President Poincaré wrote President Wilson that M. René Viviani, former Premier of France, and Marshal Joseph Joffre, popular hero of the Marne, would be the luminaries of the simultaneous French mission. They were coming merely to congratulate the United States upon its entry into the struggle against Germany.[28]

The Balfour and Viviani missions actually came to press for large scale American naval contributions, including, after April 30, craft for convoying; loans and credits; and 500,000 American troops to France immediately after the conscription bill before Congress passed (which it did in May). There combat experienced Allied officers and NCO's could train them far more quickly than could be done in America. There was a possible fourth purpose; if the President wished, the mission would negotiate the political price he wanted the Entente to pay for all of this.[29]

Daniels passively noted that the visitors regarded "the German submarine warfare as very serious." Even when Franklin Roosevelt and Lansing suggested sending destroyers to England on condition that Whitehall agree to turn over new British dreadnoughts to the United States in exchange, Daniels merely noted their proposal with no comment of its merits.[30]

Largely from what it learned from these missions, the Navy General Board divested itself of much of its traditional linguistic restraint. On April 28 and May 3 it called for a radically different policy from Daniels' and Benson's. All of Sims's recommendations were vigorously urged — except for convoying. It concluded that if Sims were not rushed all possible anti-submarine craft at once, the President would never impose his peace terms upon either side. What the German and Japanese prospects for acquiring overseas investment and export markets at American expense would then be, the Board did not need to specify. Its report of April 28 urged that

> the success of the war . . . rests primarily upon Great Britain. The failure of any of the other contestants might result only in protracting the war; but the collapse of Great Britain would be followed indubitably by the collapse of the . . . Allies, and Germany would . . . demand heavy indemnities. Her enemies, except for the United States, . . . will be in no position to pay. The United States will have to pay or fight the released activities of Germany — an army of millions of veterans and a war-trained fleet superior to that of the United States, and a possible ally in the Pacific . . . . If the success of the Entente cause depends primarily upon Great Britain, and . . . [this] depends upon adequately meeting the U-boat menace; then . . . it is imperative for the United States to combat to the fullest extent of . . . [its] resources the submarine peril as it effects Great Britain now. By a powerful reinforcement of the patrol of . . . surface craft about the British Islands now, we would fight our battle a hundred times more efficiently . . . than . . . by an endeavor to combat submarines on our own coast . . . . Great Britain's condition is now extremely critical . . . the people of the United States generally have no conception of the intimate connection between our safety in the future and Great Britain's safety now . . . .[31]

On April 26 and again on April 28, perhaps partly in response to Sims's and Page's cables, Benson had ordered six destroyers "fitted out" for distant service — a process requiring one to two weeks.[32] But despite the fact that the British mission would present a detailed plan for convoying on May 5 and may have already broached the subject, the Board's April 28 report included its opinion that "no better means than surface patrol craft have yet been devised to meet the submarine menace."

By May 3 Benson had only agreed that a total of thirty-six destroyers and no other anti-submarine type craft would be sent to Sims; the General Board therefore sharpened its tone. As the naval head of the Balfour mission, Admiral de Chair, informed London, it was difficult to persuade the Navy Department's decision-makers to budge from their "inclination towards keeping their forces, particularly destroyers, within the limits of American waters". Admiral de Chair handed an unreceptive Daniels a list of 320 anti-submarine craft which, "in addition to as many [tugs] as can be procured," Britain "very urgently required" to cope with the U-boats.[33] The General Board, however, reacted differently. Its May 3 report stated that it had inventoried the navy's anti-U-boat resources; 200 craft were available or could be made so within sixty days — these must be rushed to Sims. Tugs were included; Sims wanted them for dropping depth charges on U-boats and rescuing slowly sinking ships. "With all the emphasis at its command," the Board insisted that the 200 anti-U-boat craft be dispatched to Sims within sixty days. "The emergency exists *now*, . . . time . . . is of overwhelming importance . . . action [must] be immediate." Although addressed to Daniels, Benson, as a Board member, automatically received a copy of this unwelcome document. Another six destroyers could be dispatched at once (giving Sims a total of forty-two). Fifteen armed yachts and navy gunboats, and ten revenue cutters were ready; at least fifty tugs which could be readily requisitioned, and at least eighty other vessels for patrol and depth-charge work could be requisitioned from civilian owners. Although Sims had mentioned his desire for submarines on April 19, the Board omitted them from its list. Sims's requests for these would soon become more pressing; the British were finding theirs to be effective ahead of convoys and at sinking U-boats.

Sims did not get these 200 anti-submarine craft within the Board's sixty day limit. By July 1, he had been sent thirty-four destroyers and seven armed yachts. By September 1, about 120 days beyond this limit (and five months after the official American war declaration) he had been sent forty-one of the sixty-seven destroyers in commission, twelve of the thirty-seven armed yachts; one of the thirty-five Coast Guard Cutters, and none of the other types. He then had in hand or en route a total of sixty-three of the 200 urged for July 1. By December 1, he had been sent a total of ninety-four anti-U-boat vessels, including three of the Department's forty-six submarines. By this time the Department would have mulled for some months over whether or not to send any of the many tugs it had requisitioned from civilians beginning in July. It had been settled that none of the navy's own tugs would be sent. Finally Daniels and Benson decided to let Sims have one or two occasionally.[34] On May 1, 1917, Wilson told Daniels to withhold some of the destroyers from the war zone for later use as escorts for troopships. When Benson arrived at Sims's headquarters in early November, he had dispatched only 20.9 percent of all U.S. anti-submarine craft in commission to the war zone.[35] Why, one wonders, could not all the destroyers have been sent over and those designated to escort troopships into Brest at a later time have meanwhile been used to help keep Allied merchant ships safe from U-boats?

After the war, with these considerations on his mind, Sims charged that the half-hearted policy adopted by the Navy Department for months after America entered the war had made it more likely that the enemy might win. Moreover, by weakening the Allies, it had prolonged the war at the cost of thousands of Allied and American lives, and unnecessary expenditure of great treasure. Benson, on the other hand, would only admit that any additional tonnage lost by his refusal to adopt Sims's policy had had "a demoralizing effect upon the Allies." He had been concerned about "the question of commercial competition with Great Britain." As Benson put it at the 1920 Senate Committee Hearings, his overriding motive in the war had been "in the beginning, during, and always . . . to see that our own . . . interests were safeguarded". He had seen that it was his "duty to safeguard America's interests . . . regardless of any other duty, of humanity, or anything else, and that was the underlying motive in all the actions that I took"[36] (or did not take, one might add). Asked what had taken him so long to send Sims the limited number of craft and staff members he finally let him have, Benson replied that he had felt constrained to give "due deliberation and careful consideration to all of the conditions surrounding the situation." He had decided that "the main fleet should be kept here, whether it was necessary to guard the coast or not." Benson had believed that Sims's demands for reinforcements had stemmed from an exaggerated notion of "the importance of his mission." Thus, Benson implied that he himself had placed a higher value upon a different goal than aiding the Allies in their ongoing struggle against the German navy.[37] From the fall of 1917 to August, 1918, Benson added that he had also sought to keep the bulk of his forces safe in case the Germans broke through in the west and he needed them to protect a Dunkirk-type evacuation of Pershing's army.[38]

The Balfour and Viviani missions also tried to get troops and money from the Washington administration. Wilson tried to obtain their acquiescence in his peace terms, and their agreement to attend a peace conference as soon as the Germans proved willing to do so. Both sides would be disappointed with the results of their efforts. Two weeks before the General Board pressed Daniels and Benson for 200 warcraft for Sims, the President received a naval staff officer's study, which urged that the navy rush the maximum force to Europe: "the result of the war hangs on the submarine issue." American troops were needed in France at once, as it was doubtful if Germany's divisions had reached their potential strength. If they had, so had those of Britain, "while those of France have been on·the decline for some time." It was doubtful that Russia would survive "without greatly increased assistance from without in munitioning the Russian armies". Even if the Allies could get through U-boat-infested waters to her with help, Russia lacked "cohesion and unity."[39]

In late May, Secretary of War Newton D. Baker supported this naval report's view; he, too, was probably impressed by the Balfour and Viviani missions' plea that 500,000 American toops be rushed to France for rapid preparation by experienced Allied personnel for a combat role. He was probably mindful of the disastrous effect on the French army of its ill-fated April-May offensive. He wrote Wilson that "soldiers in our own army" advocated rushing troops to France for rapid training, lest critics be able to say that America intended "to continue here a long drawn out process of training with the ultimate intention of doing fighting on a large scale at some later time." To continue to train troops mostly in the United States increased "the chance of the French or Russians breaking down . . ." In France, "our own officers" would keep the American recruits out of the "fighting until their training is perfected." But they could soon take over quiet sectors of the front while "better prepared men of the French and English armies . . . [undertook the more] trying operations." The only prospect of ending the war soon lay in using an "overwhelming aggregation of forces, including our own." Joffre pressed France's desperation on House; American soldiers should be rushed "at once" to France and sent to the front five weeks after their arrival.[40]

The President, however, was not anxious to help the Allies bring about an early defeat of the Central Powers. By July 1917, Baker was able to assure House of his conversion to a policy of delay to win Wilson more leverage over rival powers. The large, independent army of the future would put "us into the war as a great power conducting *pro tanto* a war of our own" so that, at a peace conference, "where the various nations involved will each have its own particular kind of interest to work out," the maximum pressure on behalf of that of the United States could be brought to bear through "complete diplomatic and military individuality." This policy would avoid any "identity of diplomatic interest" through military association with the Allies and leave America "in a neutral attitude as between the English and French."[41]

For more than a year after the American declaration of war, the ordeals of the Allied armies were punctuated by costly British offensives, undertaken (according to Chief of the Imperial General Staff General Sir William Robertson's *ex post facto* explanation) to distract German attention from the demoralized French army as well as that of the retreating Russians.[42] This year of American waiting to take the field would see the virtual collapse of Italy, the advent of the Communists to power in Petrograd, and Lenin's capitulation to the

Central Powers almost in time to make the Germans invincible by breaking the effects of the Allied blockade.[43] In American eyes, however, this war was of Europe's making. Europe should bear most of its sacrifices.

The Balfour and Viviani missions also got cold comfort in the area of finance. As had been noted, Wilson told House in July 1917, that he aimed to get the Allies "among other things, financially in to our hands" in order to force his peace terms on them. To his financial advisers, the ambition to overtake Britain in world trade and investments and his intention of preventing her from achieving the aims of the Paris Economic Conference called for stingy treatment of the Entente. On April 16, 1917, the chairman of Wilson's Tariff Commission, F. W. Taussig, began to press him for permission to go to Europe to question the Allies about all of the terms of "The Paris Economy Pact." The Commission intended "to be prepared . . . even before . . . [an armistice] to give constructive aid to the President and Congress" in thwarting the Allies' aims. However, Lansing implied to the President that a possible effect of such a hostile inquiry, coming on top of niggardly contributions to the fighting, would tend to propel the Allies to a peace table from which Wilson would be virtually excluded.[44] This view did not, however, prevent Benson, when he sent Mayo to England in August, from instructing him to make "certain inquiries into the matters [*sic*] of seeking for trade." The combat-eager Mayo, however, did not allude to any such inquiries, if he made any, in his written report of his visit.[45]

The Balfour and Viviani missions got no specific promise of financial help, or so Treasury Secretary McAdoo subsequently averred. A few weeks after the Balfour mission's departure, Lord Northcliffe, the new coordinator of British war purchases in America, was lamenting to Lloyd George about his humiliation at watching "this poor man [Sir Richard Crawford] practically begging for financial assistance from McAdoo." A month later (on July 17), he repeated this theme: "our attitude is that of beggars." Canada's Minister of Trade and Commerce, George E. Foster, complained to Lloyd George that Canada's proportionately larger (than America's) sacrifices for the "common cause" were being shabbily rewarded by Washington. Northcliffe and Foster unavailingly told the Americans Britain's loans were always made to her allies "without prescription that they were to spend the money in England." Now, however, the United States' economic policy, which demanded that all Washington loans be spent in America, "means . . . that our [Canada's] industries become dismantled and closed." Canada's agriculture was also suffering from Wilson's loan policy.[46]

On the one hand, McAdoo implied America's need to continue to profit from the Allies' war effort as long as the conflict lasted; on the other hand, he was premature, at least in the President's view, in urging that the British, French, Italians, and Russians be monetarily pressed into accepting American control over their military and naval conduct of the war. He and his assistant, Oscar T. Colby, were also too hasty in seeking to force the terms of the eventual peace onto the Allies before they were sufficiently at Wilson's mercy. In the first instance, as the Secretary McAdoo told the President in May, 1917, "the Allies in the next twelve months will spend from four to six billion, we from two to three billion . . . in our markets." Cargoes destined for Entente countries were now stranded in America for lack of shipping space, and thus provided leverage for gaining an American seat "on the London International Commission which determines the needs of . . . [the several Allies]." There the Americans could wrest supreme authority from the British by exploiting the "considerable dissatisfaction" of the other Allies at London's "preponderant" control. Earlier, McAdoo had induced Congress to phrase a recent act on Allied credits so as to enable "this Government to impose such terms and conditions upon the borrowing powers as would give us a potential voice in the use of such credits."[47]

In July, when Balfour reminded the President that "His Majesty's Government, have, singlehanded, borne the burden of financing the whole of the Allied powers," and Chancellor of the Exchequer Andrew Bonar Law sent word that "our resources . . . for payments in America are exhausted," McAdoo and Colby saw the more fortunate aspects of Britain's predicament. "The magnitude of our loans" meant that the United States should begin to direct the military and political conduct of the war.[48]

But, from aversion for any entanglement in their "political" aims before they were delivered into "our hands," Wilson hesitated to join any inter-Allied committee. He issued strict orders that no discussion of war aims was to involve American representatives until he found the time propitious to take personal charge of them. Hence, in July 1917, he agreed with Lansing's advice that McAdoo be instructed to delete words to the Allies that American credits in no way implied American assent to the Entente's war aims. Nevertheless, McAdoo was allowed to state that the Balfour mission had received "no positive undertaking" about war credits. Moreover, he and House demanded proof from Northcliffe and his French opposite number, André Tardieu, that credits to Russia were not to be used to refurbish her deteriorated railroad system so as to enhance her postwar economic position. The British were required to guarantee that no American loans or purchases were to be used to construct dreadnoughts.[49] In his July 17 letter cited earlier, Northcliffe accurately predicted continued "great difficulty" over war expenditures. He cited Washington's alleged betrayal of its promise to the Balfour mission of a $400,000,000 loan; he was sure that the Americans' "seizure of the [merchant] ships we are building" (through American contractors) boded ill for the future.

If McAdoo's assertion about Wilson's material power over the Allies was extravagant, Sims and the Allies felt that Wilsonian claims that Washington's war aims were purely altruistic were extravagant too. In November 1917, Sims advised the Navy Department that "the most serious naval problem" had become finding sufficient total cargo tonnage for bringing over and supplying Pershing's army "without immobilising [sic] too much tonnage necessary to supply Allied countries." This was aggravated by the aversion of the several powers at war with Germany to contribute ships; they were full of "mistrust of [the] intentions of various nations" because of "the probable condition of their oversea trade after the war." He soon elaborated to Benson: Allied mistrust of America was rooted strongly in "envy of the position which the United States is likely to occupy after the war is over. This is accentuated by our commandeering all vessels being built for belligerent and neutral countries. I have heard it said [he was writing from Paris] . . . that the real object of this measure was to try to get as many ships into our hands as possible in order to seize the trade of the world when hostilities are ended." Sims recommended that the Wilson administration announce that it would replace or return these ships after the war at their originally contracted prices.[50] No such offer was forthcoming. The British did not think that the Americans intended to even wait until after the war to use their ships to "seize the trade of the world." In October 1917, Lloyd George mulled over the U-boat-wrought ruin of "numerous industries" in his country and over the mounting evidence that Washington was not fulfilling its pledges to commit certain American ships to the transport of its own troops. Instead, as Britain's shipping controller Sir Joseph Maclay told the London Cabinet, the Americans were forcing the British to undertake this unprofitable task while they "were actually opening new lines in South America" with their ships. Maclay insisted that the evidence proved that the United States "were out for *post bellum* developments of which they always suspected us."[51]

In November 1917, the London Cabinet lamented a report that during the first ten months of 1917, Britain had lost 3,173,000 tons of merchant ships to the enemy; America had lost only 164,000 (or 5 percent of theirs) during this period. In November-December 1917, America lost 16,000 tons, Britain 433,000. During 1917, the British merchant marine shrank to 15,800,000 tons while the American ocean-going merchant marine grew from 2,200,000 to 4,000,000 (from about 12 percent to 25 percent of Britain's), owing mainly to new construction, the seizure of interned German ships, and the avoidance of U-boat-ravaged shipping lanes. The United States' exports to Latin America climbed from $390,000,000 worth in 1916 to $585,000,000 in 1917 to $705,000,000 in 1918 (and to $930,000,000 in 1919).

> The role of the American government in this increase was . . . significant . . . . the government controlled the movement of capital, *the disposition of shipping tonnage* [italics added] . . . . By 1919 the government was accustomed to committing its power and prestige to economic affairs . . . . Businessmen and government officials . . .were anxious to take advantage of Europe's weakness by continuing the expansion of the United States' economic influence which had been facilitated by the war through the retention of at least some of the wartime administration machinery for their benefit.

With Wilsonian prodding, between 1915 and 1920, the "United States' percentage of all goods imported into Latin America grew from under

16 percent to almost 42 percent."[52]

Wilson and Benson held similar views about the wartime use of America's merchant marine. They also held similar views about not sending staff officers to Europe in 1917 in order to avoid pressure from them to step up America's participation in combat. When Secretary Baker (in April) urged that a staff be sent to France to hasten coordination necessary for sending large numbers of troops for rapid combat training, the President did not cite a patriotic aversion the American people might display if their troops fought under an Allied command that has been given since the war as the main reason for the delay of Pershing's entry into large-scale combat. Domestic politics were doubtless one factor in this delay. But the President did not seek to overcome it. His reply to Baker only implied his apprehension that an army staff would accelerate combat aid to the Allies before it had been proven necessary to avert a German victory. "We are in danger of creating too much machinery," he reproached Baker. The few officers already in Europe (war observers and attachés) would suffice to arrange what cooperation was needed, although they were "out of touch with conditions [meaning policy] on this side of the water." Baker should keep all officers at home instead of sending some "parleying to England and France." Benson argued in May-June 1917 against sending Sims a staff; the officers he might send over were "in danger of becoming obsessed with all things British to the detriment of clear judgement"; Sims already was, he observed.[53]

A number of navy (and army) officers seemed deaf to the "nationalistic" argument against prompt and full support of the Allies in April-July 1917. Pratt unavailingly urged that crewmen be taken from obsolete battleships and cruisers to man warcraft for Sims. Department officers laboring to help Sims encountered the Secretary's baleful eye. Daniels found that Rear Admiral Palmer and his assistant Captain Laning were striving too hard to send crewmen to combat. He found the vigorous Assistant Secretary, Franklin D. Roosevelt, and the Paymaster General, Samuel McGowan, were "war mad lunatics." Charged with responsibility for naval contracts and for drawing up an annual budget to recommend to Congress, Roosevelt nevertheless joined with Commerce Secretary Redfield in trying to prod the sluggish Daniels and the skeptical Benson into laying what eventually gave promise of becoming an effective mine barrage from Norway to Scotland and across the Straits of Dover to block the egress of U-boats. The British had made some efforts at this; but until a suitable mine was later developed in America, these proved largely futile. Roosevelt used strident words to the Secretary; in July 1917, he wrote him that "more *destroyers*" were needed, "*the estimates should go in now.*" When construction of the mine barrage was finally sanctioned in October 1917, Roosevelt wrote that he hoped that "amiable discussion" would now give way to action. He was sure that Daniels would not mind that he had taken his case to the President.[54] Daniels did mind (as did Wilson) when after the war, but before Sims had brought his charges against the department which resulted in the Senate committee hearings, Roosevelt publicly assailed the navy's 1917 war effort. For some days, Daniels considered asking for his resignation. He would have done so, had he known that Roosevelt had also written to Sims to congratulate him for publicly indicting Daniels for deleting the names of combat officers to be submitted for congressional approval for medals and for substituting the names of many who had done nothing in particular. Congress then forced Daniels to reverse himself.[55]

Roosevelt also recommended the construction of small wooden "sub-chasers" for Sims's use. These were easily, rapidly, and cheaply constructed; they also would require few regular personnel to man them — college undergraduate volunteers would do. When, at Benson's insistence, they were tried as convoy escorts, it was found that in a rough sea they bobbed about and lost track of their merchant ships. Nevertheless, Sims would find less important uses for them in confined and calmer waters.[56]

In the summer of 1917, the American novelist Winston Churchill (who was well regarded by Wilson) charged the President to inquire of any naval officer what should be done. Wilson would find that most officers regarded Daniels as incompetent, Benson as not quite up to the job. He would find that they were all for Sims. The President should ascertain what Sims wanted done and see that it was done.[57]

Pratt also tried to help Sims. At the 1920 Senate committee hearings, Pratt would risk Daniels' wrath to testify that had it been in his power to do so, in April 1917, he would have rushed Sims every anti-U-boat craft the navy had. He would have manned those short of personnel with crews from osbolete battleships and cruisers. Nevertheless, he counseled Sims that only if he kept insisting that he be sent American submarines could he hope to get any. In October 1917, six months after Sims's first request, Benson at last agreed that five could go over. In January 1918, five more were sent.[58]

The cold reception accorded his convoy promptings was perhaps even more disappointing to Sims than the failure of the Balfour and Viviani missions to get him many more warcraft. Weeks passed with no word from the Navy Department on his May 1 request for cooperation in assembling and shepherding convoys out of American ports. His May 1 cable stated that the Admiralty was anxious to start convoys from the United States. "American cruisers [largely occupied in patrolling safe Western Hemisphere waters for nonexistent surface raiders] will [have] to be diverted to" escorting convoys on the start of the voyage from New York and Hampton Roads. The Admiralty officers "do not know that they have enough vessels in the British Navy to carry out this work." The merchant ships would make the longest stretch of their voyage, across "deep water," in formation, but unescorted. Escorts of destroyers, gunboats, Coast Guard cutters, or converted yachts loaded with depth charges would meet them at the edge of the danger zone; twelve to eighteen cargo ships would make up a convoy. Action was needed at once; shipping was being lost so fast that the British did not think that they had space to evacuate 100,000 malarial troops from Salonika.[59]

Rear Admiral Sims with the Assistant Secretary of the Navy, Franklin D. Roosevelt, 1918. Photo from Elting E. Morison, *Admiral Sims and the Modern Navy* (Boston: Houghton-Mifflin Company, 1942).

Sims kept on badgering the Navy Department. There was "great anxiety as to the final outcome of the war . . . caused by the present success of the submarine." If the department would only help with the departure of half the convoys from America, even though it would "strain British resources . . . to the limit," the Admiralty would furnish the cruisers for those to sail "every fourth day" from either New York or Hampton Roads. This elicited no response. Daniels did dutifully record in his diary that Baker had told him that "we should send them [troops] at *once*"; that the General Board had stated "that submarine situation [is] critical and action must be taken at *once* [.] Advised destroyers, trawlers, mines, tugs, etc. at once. Thought in a few months England would be starved *into submission* [.] "[60]

On May 24, William E. Buckler, First Secretary of the U.S. Embassy, in London, appealed to House and Wilson. They regarded him as much less of an Anglophile than Page; he mingled with anti-war liberals and socialists and kept House and Wilson informed on how the President's efforts at a compromise peace were being received by these groups. Now he urged that all possible anti-submarine craft be rushed to Sims; they were desperately needed, "even if they were only used with convoys [instead of with patrols]."[61] Buckler added, perhaps to improve the chances of favorable action, that much British shipping had been withdrawn from distant trades.

On June 20, just over two months after Sims's first cable urging the convoy system, Benson made his first reply on the subject: "In regard to convoy, I consider that American vessels having armed guards [with anti-U-boat guns] are safer when sailing independently [than they would be in a convoy]."[62] Sims protested Benson's anti-convoy decision, his expression of concern only for the fate of American ships, and his implied indifference to Allied ships. "All Allied shipping" must be protected, "for it is on the remainder of this shipping that our success against the enemy is entirely dependent." By hinting that he suspected the Washington administration was hoping soon to achieve a compromise peace, he tried to shame the department into action. "The comparative immunity of American shipping from submarine attack is due to German hopes that it will strengthen German peace propaganda in the United States . . . this is clearly indicated by the German press . . . ." Future history would show that, if the war were lost for want of sufficient American warcraft, Washington's policy had been the cause.[63]

The next day Sims cabled Benson that the Admiralty would attempt to escort all of the convoys without American help. In this cable, Sims went on to suggest that he sensed that the administration intended to withhold significant help from him until, if it did not meanwhile achieve a negotiated peace, it had expanded its navy to the point that it could exercise a more pronounced influence over the Allied naval policy. He had already been told something of this by Pratt; later he would receive more details from Laning. This policy of keeping men and ships at home to prepare men to man the greater American navy and merchant marine of the future contradicted Benson's later excuse for having no American plan to fight that war: British naval superiority had dictated that he would adopt whatever policy the Admiralty pursued. Nevertheless, Sims argued to Benson that American help in the "assembly of convoys, and furnishing one cruiser or reserve battleship a week for high sea escort would not interfere with personnel training, for which . . . they [the ships] are being used."[64]

But Benson remained immovable. With words that sounded generous, he told Sims that he was not going to adopt the convoy system; neither was he going to send him many more anti-U-boat craft. The department would send Sims "all anti-submarine craft *which can be spared from home waters* [italics added] when [in Benson's opinion, Sims correctly surmised] they become available."[65] On June 23, almost simultaneously with this June 24 cable from Benson, the Navy Department sent the State Department a belated announcement of its war policy for transmission to the Allied governments. This policy had been determined "after careful consideration of the present naval situation . . . and possible future situations which might arise." It was to be one of "the most hearty cooperation with the Allies to meet the present submarine situation in European or other waters compatible with an adequate defense of our own home waters . . . . " Against what menace was not explained, but a general hint was provided: "While a successful termination of the present war must always be the first *allied* [italics mine] aim, . . . the future position of the United States must in no way be jeopardized by the disintegration of our main fighting fleet." Sims observed to a confidant: "You know what this means." But he protested to Benson that he could not understand what was meant by this feared "disintegration". He pointed out that the German High Seas Fleet was bottled up by the British, even though he knew from Emmett that Benson felt that it might not stay bottled up.[66] This elicited little help. Sims knew, too, that the department was concerned about a domino effect which the collapse of one or more of the major Entente powers might have upon the others, as well as upon Japan's possible consequent change of sides. This will be discussed shortly.

There was more to the Navy Department's statement. Probably to shift the blame for the U-boats' toll onto British shoulders, as well as to prepare the ground for a dominant American control over Allied naval policy (which Wilson would soon try to achieve), the department insisted upon the necessity of attacking the Reich's home naval bases — despite their fortifications. However, Daniels and Benson carefully avoided committing any American forces to participation in such an enterprise; they certainly did not intend to launch such an assault on their own. "The Department cannot too strongly insist that . . . the offensive must always be the dominant note in any general plan of strategy prepared. But as the primary role in all offensive operations must perforce belong to the Allied powers, the Navy Department announces that *in general* [italics mine] it is willing to accept any joint plan of action of the Allies . . . when after joint consultation of all the admiralties concerned [the Navy Department being an admiralty here] the emergency is deemed [by Washington] to warrant it." The department proclaimed "its willingness to discuss more fully plans for joint operations." To combat the present U-boat campaign, it was willing "to send its minor forces . . . in any number not incompatible with home needs." This was hardly a "most hearty" response to the June loss of 675,154 tons of merchant ships.

Notes on Chapter 2

[1] R. S. Baker and W. E. Dodd, eds., *The Public Papers of Woodrow Wilson*, (New York and London, 1925-27), (hereafter *PPWW*), V, 11, 14-15.

[2] Sims to Wilson, July 11, 1917, Wilson Papers.

[3] *PPWW*, IV, 378, 380, 376, 358, 361.

[4] A. W. Lane and L. W. Wall, eds., *The Letters of Franklin K. Lane: Personal and Political* (Boston, 1922), 234

[5] *PPWW*, IV, 390, 392; House to Wilson, Sept. 18, 1918, Wilson Papers; Lane to George W. Lane, Feb. 9, 1917, *Lane Letters*; E. David Cronon, ed., *The Cabinet Diaries of Josephus Daniels, 1913-1921* (Lincoln, 1963), Mar. 20, 1917; quoted in Arthur Walworth, *Woodrow Wilson* (New York, London and Toronto, 1958), II, 217.

[6] (Senate Naval Affairs Subcommittee) *Hearings, 1920*, II, 1820-23; USNSF, U file: Diary by Josephus Daniels; Lansing to Wilson, May 12, 1917, Wilson Papers, Sers. 5A; Spring-Rice to First Lord of Admiralty (Sir Edward Carson), May 17, 1917, Balfour Papers, 49704; Cronon, ed., *Daniels Diaries*, Apr. 24, 1917.

[7] Charles Seymour, ed., *The Intimate Papers of Colonel House* (Boston and New York, 1926-28), II, 55; *ibid.*, 330.

[8] Tumulty to Wilson, May 31, 1917, The Papers of Robert Lansing, Library of Congress (hereafter Lansing MSS), Vol. 28; Lloyd George Papers, F/41/7/8; USNSF, file WY: International Situation . . . British Intelligence Reports, No. 198, May 29-31, 1917; Spring-Rice to Balfour, Balfour Papers, 49740.

[9] Lippmann to Wilson, Oct. 17, 1917, N. D. Baker Papers, Box 2; USNSF, file WY, Br. Naval Intelligence Report No. 241, Oct. 26-29, 1917; *PPWW*, V, 118-20; USNSF, file WY, Reports No. 248, Nov. 20-22, 1917, and 250, Nov. 27-29, 1917; French Finance Ministry representative in New York J. de Neuflize to Lord Duncannon, Lloyd George Papers, F/47/7/25.

[10] Thomas G. Frothingham, *The Naval History of the World War* (Cambridge, Mass., 1927), III, 41-48.

[11] A. H. Frazier, First Secretary, U. S. Embassy, Paris, to House, Feb. 16, 1917, Wilson Papers (Sers. 2); T. N. Page to Wilson, Mar. 28, 1917, *ibid.*, House to Wilson, Mar. 19, 1917, *ibid.*

[12] Minutes of Br. War Cabinet meetings, Dec. 1916-Apr. 1917, CAB/23/1, *passim.*

[13] Report of Allied Naval Conference of Jan. 23 and 24, 1917, CAB/21/9, P.R.O.

[14] Admiral Sir Charles Maddox to Jellicoe, Apr. 4 and 27, 1917, Papers of Sir John Jellicoe, British Museum, London (hereafter Jellicoe Papers), 49009; roving Br. diplomat Mark Clark from Taranto to Jellicoe, May 29, 1917, *ibid.*, 49036.

[15] See note 21, below.

[16] Lord Grey to Lloyd George, Sept. 29, 1916, Lloyd George Papers, E/2/13/5; House to Wilson, Jan. 16, 1917, Wilson Papers.

[17] W. H. Page to Wilson, Feb. 16, 1917, Burton J. Hendrick, *The Life and Letters of Walter Hines Page* (Garden City, 1922-25), III, 319-20; Page to Secretary of Agriculture David F. Houston, Apr. 1, 1917, *ibid.*, II, 226-28.

[18] Mayo, Rear Admiral Henry B. Wilson, and Benson at *Hearings, 1920*, I, 587, 897, II, 1897.

[19] Sims, in collaboration with Burton J. Hendrick, *The Victory at Sea* (Garden City, 1920), 8-9, 14.

[20] John Buchan, *A History of the Great War* (Boston, New York . . . , 1920-22), III, 554; Sims, *Victory at Sea*, appendixes VIII, IX, David F. Trask, *Captains and Cabinets: Anglo-American Naval Relations, 1917-1918* (Columbia, Mo , 1972), 48.

[21] *Hearings, 1920*, II, 1975; Sims' shipping figures, *ibid.*, I, 104; Cronon, ed., *Daniels Diaries*, Nov. 21, 1917; T. Royden (Br. member of Inter-Allied Shipping

Committee) and J. A. Salter (of Br. Ministry of Shipping) to Wilson, n.d., July, 1917, Wilson Papers, Sers. 2, Box 165.
[22] Sims, *Victory at Sea*, 9.
[23] Sims to Secretary of Navy (Operations), Apr. 14, 18, and 19, Sims Papers (the Apr. 19 cable is also in Wilson Papers).
[24] Arthur J. Marder, *From the Dreadnought to Scapa Flow* (London, 1969), 4, 160-66; Br. War Cabinet minutes, Dec. 26, 1916, Mar. 2, May 1 and 10, 1917, CAB/23/1 and 2; Jellicoe to Admiral Sir Frederick T. Hamilton, Apr. 25, 1917, Papers of F. T. Hamilton, National Maritime Museum, Greenwich, Eng., HTN/117 MS 57/060; Jellicoe to Sir Edward Carson, Apr. 27, 1917, First Lord to P. M., May 1, 1917, CAB/24/12 (GT611), P.R.O.; Beatty to Jellicoe, May 7, 1917, Jellicoe Papers, 49008.
[25] Documents submitted by Sims, *Hearings, 1920*, I, 40-43; Sims to Daniels, Apr. 19, 1917, Sims Papers.
[26] Sims Papers; *Hearings, 1920*, I, 40-43.
[27] Sims Papers.
[28] Wilson to House, Apr. 6, 1917, R. S. Baker, *Woodrow Wilson: Life and Letters* (Garden City, 1927-39), VII, 3; House to Wilson, Apr. 8 and 22, 1917, Wilson Papers; Poincaré to Wilson, Apr. 16, 1917, *ibid.*
[29] Balfour's mission report to Lloyd George, printed for War Cabinet June 23, 1917, Lloyd George Papers, F/210/2/2.
[30] Cronon, ed., *Daniels Diaries*, Apr. 21, and 22, 1917.
[31] General Board to Daniels, Apr. 28 and May 3, 1917, GB425 SN721 and 724, ONRL.
[32] Mayo at *Hearings, 1920*, I, 588.
[33] Balfour mission report to Lloyd George, printed June 23, 1917, Lloyd George Papers, F/210/2/2.
[34] Tables submitted by Pratt and Daniels, which agreed, *Hearings, 1920*, I, 1235-37; II, 2941; Cronon, ed., *Daniels Diaries*, Aug. 27, 1917.
[35] *Ibid.*, May 1, 1917; *Hearings, 1920*, I, 1235-37; II, 2941.
[36] *Ibid.*, II, 1849-50, 1959, 1970-71, 1884, 1894, 1943.
[37] *Ibid.*, 1864-68, 1930, 1982-93.
[38] *Ibid.*, 1904.
[39] Balfour mission report, June 23, 1917, Lloyd George Papers, F/210/2/2; Department of the Navy Memorandum (confidential), "Anti-submarine Warfare," no addressee or signature (except illegible initials), Wilson Papers, Sers. 2, Box 159.
[40] Baker to Wilson, May 27, 1917, Wilson Papers; Seymour, ed., *House Papers*, III, 53; Joffre to Baker, Aug. 21, 1917, N. D. Baker Papers.
[41] Baker to House, July 18, 1917, N.D. Baker Papers.
[42] Gen. John J. Pershing, *My Experiences in the War* (New York, 1931), II, 54-59; Field Marshal Sir William Robertson, *Soldiers and Statesmen, 1914-1918* (London, 1926), II, 238-39.
[43] The Russian Civil War minimized raw material and food shipments from Russia to the Central Powers.
[44] Lansing to Wilson, Apr. 28, 1917 (with Taussig's letter to him of April 16), Wilson Papers; Tariff Commissioners William S. Culbertson and Edward P. Costigan to Wilson, May 9, 1917, *ibid.*; Baker, *Wilson*, VII, 71.
[45] *Hearings, 1920*, I, 594.
[46] Northcliffe to Lloyd George, June 20 and July 17, 1917, Lloyd George Papers, F/41/7/8 and 10; Foster to W. V. Long (Secretary of State for Colonies), Oct. 2, 1917, *ibid.*, F/32/4/102.
[47] McAdoo to Wilson, May 16 and Apr. 30, 1917, Wilson Papers.

[48] Balfour to Wilson (through Spring-Rice), July 1, 1917, Wilson Papers; W. H. Page to Lansing, July 5, 1917, *Foreign Relations, 1917*, Supp. 2, I, 535-36, 543-45; Page to Lansing, July 20, 1917, Wilson Papers, Sers. 5A; Colby to Wilson, July 21, 1917, Baker, *Wilson*, VII, 179.

[49] Lansing to Elihu Root, June 27, 1917, Baker, *Wilson*, VII, 129; *ibid.*, 168, 180; McAdoo (through Lansing and Wilson) to Spring-Rice, July 13, 1917, *ibid.*, 153-54.

[50] Sims to Pratt, Nov. 16, 1917, Sims Papers; Sims to Benson, Apr. 30, 1917, *ibid.*

[51] Br. War Cabinet minutes for Oct. 12 and 19, 1917, CAB/23/4.

[52] J. A. Salter, *Allied Shipping Control: An Experiment in International Administration* (Oxford, 1921), 358-67; Joseph S. Tulchin, *The Aftermath of War: World War I and U.S. Policy Toward Latin America* (New York, 1971), 41-2; Burton J. Kaufman, "United States Trade and Latin America: The Wilson Years," *The Journal of American History*, LVIII (Sept. 1971), 361.

[53] Wilson to Baker, Apr. 11, 1917, N. D. Baker Papers, Box 4; Emmett to Sims, May 19-June 25, 1917, *passim*, Sims Papers.

[54] R. R. M. Emmett to Sims, May 19-June 25, 1917, *passim*, Sims Papers; FDR to Daniels, July 12, and Oct. 29, 1917, Daniels Papers.

[55] Cronon, ed., *Daniels Diaries*, Feb. 9, 17, and 21, 1920.

[56] Sims, *Victory at Sea*, 204-39; *ibid.*, 207-08.

[57] Churchill to Wilson, dated by archivist "ca. July 1917," Wilson Papers, Sers. 2, Box 165.

[58] *Hearings, 1920*, I, 1235-36, 1545, 1551; Pratt to Sims, May 6 and 27, 1917, Sims Papers.

[59] Sims to Daniels, for Operations, May 1, 1917, Sims Papers.

[60] Sims to Daniels for Operations, May 25, 31 and June 15, 1917. Sims Papers; Sims to Benson for tugs, May 24, for revenue cutters, July 3, 1917, *ibid.*, Sims to Daniels personally for all types of craft for convoying, July 3, 1917, *ibid.*; Cronon, ed., *Daniels Diaries*, Apr. 21 and May 2, 1917.

[61] Buckler to House to Wilson, May 24, 1917, Wilson Papers.

[62] Benson to Sims (over Daniels typed signature), June 20, 1917, Sims Papers.

[63] Sims to Secretary (operations), June 21, 1917, *ibid.*

[64] Sims to Benson, June 22, 1917, *ibid.*

[65] Benson to Sims, June 24, 1917, *ibid.*

[66] Secretary of Navy to Secretary of State, June 23, 1917, copy received by Sims July 10, 1917, *ibid.*, Sims to a "My dear Admiral," July 11, 1917; Sims to Benson, Sept. 1, 1917, *ibid.*

3

THE CENTRAL POWERS' RISING PROSPECT FOR VICTORY

July-November 1917

T HIS ALLEGED POLICY of "most hearty cooperation" well suited Wilson's intentions toward the "Associated Powers" whom he refused to call his allies. On July 1, however, Balfour sent a message; taken with Buckler's, it helped move him to action. The President got on well personally with the Foreign Secretary, especially after Balfour let him know that he anticipated that the President would rank as the twentieth century's Lincoln. The Foreign Secretary cabled that "shipping losses continue to exceed replacement . . . . Available tonnage, leaving out America's [potential?] contribution, will ultimately be inadequate to secure a proficiency of foodstuffs, oil, fuel, etc." If only the United States would consent to help with convoying, however, there would be hope of salvation.[1]

Moreover, the evidence suggests that the President's physician and frequent golfing companion, Rear Admiral Cary T. Grayson, who had links with Navy Department headquarters, had been filling the President's ear with pro-Sims and pro-convoy arguments. On July 2, Wilson wrote Daniels: "As you and I agreed yesterday, the British have done absolutely nothing constructive in the use of their navy. I think it is time we insisted upon plans of our own, even if we render some of the more conservative of our naval advisers uncomfortable."[2] The next day, he informed Daniels that the institution of the convoy system was such a plan which he intended to pressure the British into adopting. One passage virtually paraphrased Balfour's recent appeal: "I do not see how the necessary military supplies of food and fuel oil are to be delivered at British ports in any other way than under convoy." Another said, "I am not at all satisfied with the [supposedly negative] conclusions of the admiralty with regard to the convoying of groups of merchantmen." Probably setting the stage for a later version of how the Atlantic convoy system came into existence, Wilson instructed Sims (in a passage from which the reference to convoying was deleted when the cable went out), "Report to me, confidentially of course, exactly what the Admiralty have been doing . . . and add . . . your own comments and suggestions . . . without regard to British judgments . . . . In particular, I am . . . referring to convoying."[3]

By telling the President that the British "have just inaugurated it and we are ready to cooperate with them," Daniels stopped this from going out with its passages about the convoy system. He added a grumble that, as Mayo's fleet needed anti-submarine craft in case a long-range U-boat came over, "the British should make a greater effort to supply a larger number of either destroyers or other small craft for convoy through the danger zone." Besides, Sims already had 35 anti-submarine craft, and 8 armed yachts were enroute to him, Daniels protested.[4] This seemed to satisfy the President. He did not instruct Daniels to send the 200 craft which the General Board thought were vital. Wilson probably decided that Sims and the British could do enough with what they had to make the convoy system work sufficiently well to stave off an Allied collapse. At this point, he intended to do no more than this minimum necessary to avert a German victory. Presumably, if the Reich's defeat should prove unavoidable, this must be accomplished not by Entente forces assisted by those of the United States, but by American forces assisted by those of the Allies after they and the Germans had debilitated each other.

Daniels took his cue from the President's draft cable to Sims; he ignored Sim's influence in getting convoys started and glowed to Wilson: "You have no doubt observed with some satisfaction that they have all come around to your original proposition [actually at best a groping suggestion along with a number of others which were most unfeasible] that merchant ships should be convoyed. When you proposed it, I took it up with the General Board, Benson, Mayo, and the British and French Admiral [*sic*] who nearly all . . . opposed it. But they have now adopted it. All wisdom does not come from trained naval officers and your point of view is now adopted. Sims looks for the best results . . . . "[5] Presumably, Sims, too, had followed the President's lead. Daniels, in 1922, altered his diary for February 1917 to make Wilson the author of the principle of convoy when Cabinet members had suggested it and Wilson had declined to order it. In May 1917, presumably influenced by the plea of the Balfour mission and Sims's correspondence that he had read on convoy, Wilson had opened up his options about a future decision by telling his Cabinet that he favored convoying, but that he was "without confidence" in his opinion.[6]

In mid-July the President and Daniels sketched their anti-British portrait of Wilson as the father of transatlantic convoy for later use. The President then confided to the Secretary that, in phrasing the cable that had gone to Sims, he had "been more foxy than you thought." Wilson explained that he had couched it so that Sims's " 'partisans' " could not claim that " 'Sims is original. If he had been given his way he would have . . . achieved success. Now [thanks to Wilson's "foxiness"] he has advised only what the [ineffective] English are doing, etc.' " Wilson repeated the gist of this denigration of Sims to Sir William Wiseman on July 13, saying that it was he himself who had "always favored convoying."[7] Daniels later took this line in the 1920 Senate Committee Hearings, where he asserted that Wilson had been the originator of the convoy principle (see note 50, this chapter).

Sims interpreted the edited version of the President's message to him as a rebuke for letting the Admiralty do his thinking for him; he half expected his dismissal.[8] On the other hand, Wilson reassured Daniels about his request for a direct reply from Sims by summoning the Secretary to open Sims's still sealed answer. Nevertheless, Admiral Grayson was soon making arrangements for Sims to notify the President in code (unknown to Daniels or Benson) if Sims had any more strategic proposals that the Navy Department refused to accept. Presumably Wilson sought to prevent credit to Sims or the British which might diminish his influence over a peace conference. Perhaps, too, he was worried that Daniels and Benson tended to lean so far in an anti-British direction that they might let the Allies go down and permit the Germans rather than himself to impose the peace settlement. Grayson sent word that if Sims cabled a key word ("safe") to the physician, Wilson would then direct Daniels to give him all of Sims's correspondence with the department.[9] Presumably the President would explain to Daniels that he wanted to make certain that Sims was doing his own thinking. Sims, however, got the ex-White House aide who brought him the instructions from Grayson to put them in writing; he then sent Benson a copy to assure him that he did not intend to operate behind his back.[10]

One wonders why, in March 1917, the President did not present the Allies with the ultimatum that they renounce their war aims and accept his peace terms, or he would refuse to ask Congress for a declaration of war and halt the export of war materials to them. Or why, when Balfour and Viviani arrived soon after the American declaration of war, did he not tell them that he would give no naval or military help to their struggle for survival, that he would husband war needed supplies at home for an independent American course in the war, and that he would leave the war as soon as Germany agreed to abandon her U-boat campaign?

Wilson felt compelled to enter the war to respond to the U-boat challenge in order to uphold the nation's right to prosper through seaborne exports; to get a seat at the Peace Conference; and to make it feasible to fight on a serious scale if this became necessary to prevent a German victory. The President's insistence on the right to export goods to both of the warring coalitions had lain behind his rejection of William Jennings Bryan's arguments against his proposed warning to Berlin over the sinking of the munitions-bearing *Lusitania*. On March 16, 1917 (even though relations with Germany had been severed) Washington responded to a Mexican protest (as previously noted) against American exports to the Entente by reaffirming its stand that it had the right to sell to both sides.

Germany's U-boat campaign, on the other hand, threatened to halt America's ongoing exports and to plunge the nation into a depression by defeating the Allies. Once the 1917 U-boat campaign was announced and several American ships had been torpedoed, it also seemed necessary to the President to declare war to keep political control at home. The U-boat counter-blockade hardened the determination of the pro-war faction; it weakened the resolve of the pacifist and isolationist groups; and it made it likely that the uncommitted would go over to the interventionists as time passed. The President, in his war message of April 2, 1917, stressed the provocation of the new U-boat warfare that sent "vessels of every kind, whatever their flag, their character, their cargo . . . to the bottom without warning . . . . " From June 14, 1917, however, his public addresses stressed the Reich's economic and territorial objects as reasons why "we were forced into the war." In that speech, he charged that the Berlin authorities had incited Austria's ultimatum that had begun the war as a step in Germany's "plan which compassed Europe and Asia . . . from Hamburg to the Persian Gulf the [German] net is spread." The Turks were "serving Germany." The Kaiser's government offered peace only on the unacceptable condition that the Reich be allowed to keep the vast economic empire it was building that would signify "an immense enlargement of German industrial and commercial opportunities." Not only would Berlin's control over the resources of Europe and the Turkish Empire's oil resources in Iraq and the Arabian Peninsula virtually exclude Americans from commercial access to them, one inferred, but Wilson added that the Germans planned to dominate Persia. Two months later he added Russia to the domains sought by Germany. In April 1918, he offered to negotiate peace with William II's government if Germany's "civilian statesmen" would thrust aside her militarists' purpose of erecting an "empire of gain and commercial supremacy, an empire . . . hostile to the Americas . . . . " A few days later, he told foreign press correspondents that the German people could keep their monarchy, but when the American delegation entered the peace conference chamber, it would tell both the Central Powers and the Allies that they would "get nothing as to territory."[11]

Certainly, however, Wilson foresaw that the peace settlement would transfer some territory. He intended to use his seat at the Peace Conference to insure that the League of Nations held sovereign powers over most of the territories that were transferred, and that the League guaranteed Americans equal access to the markets and raw materials of these lands, regardless of which nation acted as its custodial agent over them. Moreover, the League would prevent the Royal Navy from constricting American economic expansion. In May 1916, he had sanctioned a message to London implying that he could not join the Allies because, if Germany were defeated, "Russia, Italy, and France would then be more concerned as to the division of spoils than they would for any far-reaching agreement . . . [about peace]." At that time, he wrote House that the United States "must insist upon her rights of trade and upon freedom of the sea . . . against Great Britain, with the same . . . firmness she has used against Germany." He continued that the peace settlement must establish a league, "a universal alliance to maintain freedom of the seas . . . [and] a virtual guarantee of territorial integrity and independence" (doubtless he meant the latter to apply against the several powers' sphere of influence in China and against both the British and the Germans in Middle Eastern lands such as Persia). In his "Peace Without Victory" speech of January 1917, he called for riparian rights to the sea for landlocked nations "where this cannot be done by the cession of territory." This, he implied was part of his grand design for Americans to have unintimidated access by sea to the markets of every nation: "the paths of the sea must alike in law and in fact be free." On March 5, 1917, he restated this anti-British goal: the seas "should be accessible to all on equal terms."[12] As Armistice Day approached, he told the British liaison representative (to Colonel House), Sir William Wiseman, that American would find it unacceptable if Britain annexed Germany's African colonies outright. They should be "held in trust" under the League of Nations. He was going to get "equality of trade opportunities everywhere" embodied in the peace settlement, he added. As for the Royal Navy, Lloyd George had inferred from Wilson's Fourteen Points Address of January 8, 1918, that he intended to get it put under the League's control. At the Peace Conference, when Lloyd George mentioned that a South Pacific island (Nauru) which the Empire was to acquire from Germany had "very valuable" phosphate deposits, Wilson insisted "that the policy of the open door would have to be applied. He drew attention to Article 28 of the Covenant of the League of Nations which provided for 'equal opportunities for the trade and commerce of other members of the League.'" Now he explicitly told Wiseman that the League should acquire control over Britain's navy.[13]

The President also chose to work at getting the Allies into "our hands" while the war lasted because he dared not present Balfour and Viviani an ultimatum over peace terms in April-May 1917. He may have worried that if they rejected one, and he halted exports to the Allies in fulfillment of it, the United States would plunge into a depression. Wilson had been bluffing when he had warned the Allies in late 1916 that if they defied his demand that they "put up for collateral the 'hundreds of millions of our own and foreign securities' which they still held" (in the context of his impending call for a peace conference) he could stimulate American exports "in other directions." The Allies would have diverted their ships from the American routes to more distant ones to try to get war supplies (despite the decrease of total space available that the greater time and distance would inflict). Lansing had warned the President in September 1915 of the consequences of a halt to the Allied buying: "the result would be restriction of outputs, industrial depression, idle capital and idle labor, numerous failures, financial demoralization and general unrest and suffering among the laboring classes . . . . " On March 5, 1917, Walter Hines Page had cabled Wilson: "Perhaps our going to war is the only way in which our preeminent trade position can be maintained and a panic averted.

The submarine has added the last item to the danger of a financial world crash."[14] Besides, the Allies had, in response to the Wilsonian pressure of November-December 1916, made counter threats, which escalated those they had made earlier in 1916.

In May, the President had called for a league of nations to enforce the peace settlement. British Foreign Secretary Sir Edward Grey had retorted that under the circumstances, a Wilson-sponsored peace conference would lead to an "inconclusive or disastrous peace accompanied, perhaps promoted, by . . . friction between the Allies and the United States over maritime affairs." The French ambassador (Jules Jusserand) was more blunt. If Wilson's call for peace detached "one or more" of France's Allies from her side, "Russia, Japan, and Germany would . . . drift together in an alliance after the war and attack the United States." America would then get no "sympathizers" unless she "more actively took the part of the Allies." The possibility of such an anti-American combination loomed up larger in January 1917, when the Washington Cabinet discussed the prospect that Russia might soon make a separate peace and House told Wilson that the Tsar's "bureaucracy have an entente with Germany."[15] Soon the Zimmerman Note jarred public emotions about a potential German-Japanese alliance.

When Wilson had tried to bring financial pressure to bear against the Allies in November 1916, the British Ambassador, Sir Cecil Spring-Rice, reported an easing of the constriction after he had countered that if the American squeeze against war supply credits forced the Entente to make peace, there would "be a new alignment of the policies of England and France" and "the Monroe Doctrine will no longer receive the sanction that it enjoys [from Anglo-French naval power]." He had also claimed that "the Mexicans have openly threatened that they can at any time make an alliance against America with Japan." From Rome on January 15, 1917, Ambassador Thomas Nelson Page had reported a "widespread movement by Italians to divide themselves, France, . . . and Latin America from the United States by stressing commonly-shared Roman Catholicism and Latin ideals." These Italians asserted that they would rescue the Latin Americans from their apprehension that the United States "will so overshadow them as to menace their liberty."[16]

In February, Wilson had informed Lloyd George that even if America declared war against Germany, he would, in effect, continue to work for a peace without victory for the Allies. The Prime Minister took this as a threat over American support for the Allies war effort. Lloyd George at first balked at the President's insistence that, to facilitate a peace conference, Italy was to get virtually none of the Austrian lands promised her by the Treaty of London. If Britain agreed to this, Italy would leave the war as soon as she learned of it. The Prime Minister, however, soon saw merit in appeasing the President over conditions for convening a peace conference. He assured Wilson that he wanted America "in the war not so much for help with the war as help with the peace." Alas, "most of the present belligerents . . . that win

will want some concrete gain . . . . Even Great Britain, who wants
nothing for herself, will be prevented from returning the German
colonies. South Africa and Australia will not permit . . . [it] ." So "the
President's presence at the peace conference is necessary for the proper
organisation of the world." Although the Prime Minister still balked at
renouncing the Allied goal of independence for the "subject" peoples
of Austria-Hungary and the probable loss of "Italy as an ally" that
would ensue, on February 21 Walter Hines Page reported that his
attitude "had completely changed" (owing not only to his desire to
please Wilson, but to the prospect of the maritime and military
advantages of Britain that would derive from bribing the Habsburg
Kaiser out of the war).[17]

This improved British stance brightened the outlook for the
Wilson-House effort of April-May 1917 to get a peace conference with
the Central Powers going.

The President's determination to postpone maximum naval and
military commitments to the "common cause" against Germany was
partly rooted in his hope that the German liberals and socialists might
gain sufficient influence to bring about peace negotiations with him.
Alternatively, the German government and high command might decide
that complete victory would prove too costly to achieve and would
themselves become willing to negotiate. Whether or not Washington
altered its naval construction program to prosecute that war and send
Sims more anti-U-boat craft hung largely on the likelihood of early
peace negotiations.

During the Balfour and Viviani visits, Wilson and House renewed
their previous efforts to induce the British and French to agree to
accept, in effect, the President's peace without victory, without
annexations, without indemnity goals in order to get a peace
conference underway.

Wilson gave House the task of inducing Balfour and his executive
secretary, Sir Eric Drummond, to state their minimum terms for a
conference with the Germans to discuss Berlin's peace terms. Balfour
replied that these hung "largely on the condition of the U-boat warfare
and also upon the condition of Russia, France, and Italy." The British
agreed that "if Turkey and Austria are willing to break away from
Germany, or were willing to force Germany to make peace [the Reich
realized that it could not win the war if Austria left its side] . . . certain
concessions should be made to them," presumably at the expense of
the war aims of the other Allies.[18] Moreover, there would be "no
insistence that the makers of war should be punished before a
settlement should have even been tentatively discussed." Obviously, it
would have been most awkward to insist afterwards. The two Kaisers
and the Austro-German military and naval leaders, whose forces were
then more victorious than the Allies' forces, would refuse to accept the
later settlement. Besides, although in March, House had lauded the
President as one of the chief architects of the Romanovs' downfall
through his inspiring public utterances, he now held that, as Russia was
going from bad to worse, it would be better not to seek the removal of

William II. Above all, the German Emperor was popular with his people; to demand his overthrow would weaken the chances of getting peace negotiations underway.[19]

The British initially balked at House's insistence that the Central Powers were not to be asked to withdraw from the lands they had conquered in the east. Reluctantly, they agreed that only a demand of a German withdrawal to the 1914 borders in the west would be adequate to convene a peace conference (although this would have left Alsace-Lorraine in German hands). Balfour agreed to help keep the number of Entente delegates to the peace conference at a minimum. The British were not too discontented with the American terms. Drummond cabled Lloyd George that Washington had agreed that London could keep its conquests in the Levant, as "we must fulfill our undertakings to the Arabs."[20] By then in control of the Sultan's domains in the Arabian Peninsula and most of Mesopotamia (oil-rich Iraq), the British lacked only Palestine to complete their own territorial program. True, Africa was not discussed, and subsequently Wilson would demand that the British give up their claims to German colonies there. But virtually all of William II's African colonies were now in Anglo-French hands, and mostly British at that. Thus the President proposed a return to the *status quo ante bellum* only in the west; in the east, Germany and Austria-Hungary were likely to be awarded limited gains on the basis of a partial *uti possidetus* agreement which would apply as well to Britain.

Before he left Washington, however, Viviani threw cold water on Wilson's proposals: France would not consent to any such approach to peace, he told the President. Soon, too, London, Paris, and Rome dissented from the Wilsonian program. Lord Robert Cecil (Minister of Blockade) stated that Britain would fight on until Germany agreed to pay indemnities to the Allies; the French Foreign Minister, Alexandre Ribot, proclaimed that France would fight on until the Reich agreed to cede Alsace-Lorraine; the French and Italian legislatures passed resolutions declaring that their respective irredentist claims were non-negotiable; Italy declared a protectorate over Austrian-occupied Albania. Wilson discussed the British and French intransigence with his Cabinet on May 29; Daniels noted that "all agreed" that these demands for an "indemnity . . . [and] for Alsace and Lorrain [*sic*]" were "most unfortunate." But the President said that he could not afford to denounce these British and French aims yet; he would wait until a peace "settlement" to insist on "what was right." Although later in that year, he told his Cabinet that he wanted a plebiscite held to decide the fate of Alsace-Lorraine, he had to act to prevent a Senate resolution that spring calling for such a vote (which the Germans were too likely to win). And on June 5, Colonel House advised him that publicly he should use phraseology that avoided dampening "the hopes of France for Alsace-Lorraine and of Italy for the Trentino." House added that "England will not be offended" by such indefiniteness. Indeed, Balfour had expressed to House discontent at Italy's treaty awards and ambitions.[21] By this uneasy Anglo-American accord, Russia, too, was

Standing, from left, are Admiral Benson; Prince Arthur, Duke of Connaught; Club Chairman Brittain; and Ambassador Page. Seated are Admiral Sims and an unidentified man. Photo courtesy of William S. Sims II and the London News Agency, Limited.

deprived of the gains promised her by the Treaty of London. This cleared the way for Wilson's subsequent claim to American protectorates over the Middle Eastern territories it had awarded to the Tsar. Indeed, the President would try to improve on this at the Peace Conference by seeking a mandate over France's promised land in Syria (and, with less hope of success, over either Britain's claims to all of Palestine or oil-rich Mesopotamia).

Both during the war and at the Peace Conference, the United States' relations with the Allies were strained by Wilson's ambivalent stance toward taking provinces from the Central Powers if they were defeated. In December 1917, the French worried about the possibility that Wilson would require some Levantine mandates. They were apprehensive that the superior efficiency of large American corporations in the vicinity of their own family-run enterprises would drive French entrepreneurs bankrupt. These French apprehensions would swell into outrage when, at the Peace Conference, Wilson demanded to know by what right Britain and France presumed to dispose of the fate of the Syrians. Lloyd George rejoined that he was willing to give them independence (instead of awarding them to France). The President replied that that would not do: the Syrians required "guidance, and some intimate superintendance." His solution, an American mandate over them, promised to alienate France permanently from the United States and to wreck Anglo-French relations in the Levant (as Lloyd George agreed to let Wilson have them if a Gallup Poll-style plebiscite turned out in America's favor).[22]

The President objected more determinedly to letting France, Italy, or Japan acquire protectorates than he did to the lesser evil of letting Great Britain do so on several grounds. Although British merchants would gain subtle advantages even from mandates under the aegis of the League (and talk of instituting an imperial trade preference policy throughout the Empire was growing toward the end of the war), Paris, Rome, and Tokyo practiced exclusionary practices in lands they controlled. The natives, the President anticipated, would riot or revolt against French or Italian rule which would be harsh to them and dangerous to profits of prospective American merchants and investors (this point is discussed in Chapter 7). The British were far less likely to incite chaos. Above all, they had conquered most of the lands in question by the end of 1917, and the remainder by Armistice Day. Possession, Lloyd George would then reason, was nine-tenths of the right to determine their fate. Until the Paris Peace Conference, Wilson hoped to win British help against the territorial ambitions of the French, Italians, and Japanese, and Franco-Italian support against Britain's maritime goals (to this end, House reported encouragingly from Europe in December 1917: none of the Allies "like each other"). In April-June, of that year, the United States completed and launched two more dreadnoughts with workers who had not yet been diverted to anti-U-boat construction.[23]

In July 1917, Pratt's special committee on naval construction policy largely convinced Daniels and Wilson that anti-submarine craft would have to be given building priority over capital ships to diminish the risk that the Allies would be defeated. Pratt proposed that the first through fourth priorities be given to anti-U-boat craft: submarine chasers, destroyers, scout cruisers, and submarines; fifth to battleships; and fourteenth (last) to battlecruisers. On July 13, both the President and the Secretary took up Pratt's cue. Wilson implied his agreement with the General Board's reasoning that America's ability to fight alone against Japan or Germany or both would be enhanced by a shift to anti-U-boat building, and with Pratt's reasoning that it was too late to expect to catch up to Britain's capital ship strength before the ongoing war ended. "In the future," Wilson explained to Sir William Wiseman, (perhaps with an eye to fanning doubts about the advantage that George V's dreadnoughts gave Britain over the United States), naval warfare would be largely fought with great numbers of destroyers and submarines; therefore any delay in the building of capital ships (by

America) would not be " 'very important from a strategic point of view.' "[24] Despite this rationalization, Wilson would join Benson at the Peace Conference in pressing Daniels and Congress for a great additional program of capital ship construction, in the face of the fact that the only navy capable of seriously challenging America's battleship firepower would be Britain's. (A more complete discussion can be found in Chapter 7.) Even in July 1917, Wilson dismissed the notion that Japan's navy was capable of attacking America's West Coast (though not the Philippines) as "absurd." His remarks to Wiseman were undoubtedly meant to instill the notion that by postponing capital ship building, the United States was gaining anti-submarine craft that would give its navy a better ratio of them to dreadnoughts (if a confrontation with the Royal Navy ensued) as well as more submarines that could torpedo Britain's capital ships and merchant ships.

Thus, even if the President had to wait to get the Allies into his hands over peace terms, his partial immersion into the war at sea promised him a stronger hand against the British, the Germans, and the Japanese at the end of this war. On July 13, Daniels signaled the start of the three-month process by which the department and the Congress diverted the navy's shipyards to a primary stress on anti-submarine craft. That day he asked for $100,000,000 for additional destroyers, submarine chasers, and other anti-U-boat craft, although this money was also to be used "to speed up . . . construction of vessels of the regular program [i.e. heavier ships]." On September 1, he and McAdoo agreed to ask Congress for an additional $660,000,000, mainly for anti-submarine craft which Congress sanctioned the following month.[25]

The Allies' reaction to Wilson's April-May 1917 peace conference efforts encouraged American naval expansion. Wilson's May 1917 peace conference terms to Balfour envisioned some Russian territorial concessions to Germany and Austria. He was determined, however, to insure that Russia remained sufficiently independent of the Germans so that the Slavs' vast resources did not give the Reich overwhelming future power. On the other hand, Russia must be kept open to potential American commerce and investment opportunities; but she must not be propped up in such a way that she carried out the postwar provisions of the Paris Economic Pact. The President continued to call for peace without annexations, saying that this would encourage the Allies' liberals, socialists, and pacifists to fight on for a peace without victory. He ignored appeals that this was demoralizing the very elements in Italy and Russia who were willing to fight. In January 1917, T. N. Page had cautioned him that his speeches were helping to demoralize the Italians. Now, in May 1917, his ambassador to Russia, David Francis, cabled that "phrases uttered by you are being used by radical socialists . . . to force the provisional government . . . to remove the chief incentive for offensive operations . . . . [they say] what is the use of Russia continuing the war . . . if she cannot be compensated for the enormous expenditure of life and money which a vigorous prosecution of the war would entail." A similar cable from an expert on Russia, William E. Walling, failed to move Wilson. "Immediate renunciation of no annexations no indemnities programme by President may save Russia. Nothing else will."[26] Russia continued to flounder.

The condition of the French and Italians and, above all, the deterioration of Russia's armed forces combined with the U-boat tolls, forced a gloomy outlook upon the London War Cabinet. On July 31, it decided that victory was "not likely to be realized." Only the British were doing any serious fighting against the Germans on land and sea, and only they were likely to do so in the foreseeable future. At the impending inter-Allied conference, however, they thought it better not to divulge their prognostication to their partners. To do so would make the others "conclude that the *status quo ante [bellum]* was the best that could be hoped for," as Balfour put it, "and that it would be better to reach this status now," than after additional sacrifices. The London War Cabinet called upon Lloyd George to find out (when feasible, one presumes) whether President Wilson would be willing to carry on the struggle against worse-than-ever odds if only the two English-speaking great powers were left in the lists against the Teutonic powers. Yet Americans who shared Wilson's hope for a compromise peace joyfully welcomed the Reichstag peace resolutions of July. But in that month, Wilson wrote House that "England and France *have not the same views with regard to peace as we have* [italics the President's] by any means. When the war is over we can force them to our way of thinking, . . . but we cannot force them now . . . ."[27]

In his June speech, Wilson had spoken of Germany's progress towards achieving a state of invincibility. He had implied that she might not reach it. By July, however, the State Department had become convinced that the Berlin authorities intended to retain the French and Belgian iron and coal mines they were exploiting, harvest the oil deposits they had acquired in "Central [*sic*] Europe," and irrigate lands in the Ottoman Empire from which cotton would flow to stem the effects of the British blockade.[28] In July, 1917, House proposed a debate over peace terms between the *New York World* and the *Berliner Tageblatt* to build popular support for a compromise peace. But the President cautioned him of "deep dangers" in this plan.[29] No doubt he felt that the Allies would discern his hand behind the debate, that one or more of them would lose heart at seeing its own war aims dismissed in the exchange of views and would make a separate peace, or that they would unite against him at the peace conference and afterwards.

Before Wilson and Colonel House could resolve their difficulties about the prospective *World-Tageblatt* discussion, Pope Benedict XV issued a peace appeal which aroused such reactions in the Allied and American capitals as to render it stillborn. Lansing advised the President that "unwittingly or . . . [otherwise,]" the Pontiff "has become an agent for Germany in this matter." If the several Allies and Wilson were agreed on this much, they were by no means united on the reply which the President made.[30]

From his reply to the Pope, the President drew some satisfaction from listening to Jusserand "go up in the air" over Wilson's implicit condemnation of the Allies' economic war aims. House congratulated

Wilson for keeping the door open to peace negotiations. The Colonel helped to prop it open by drawing the attention of prominent American Catholics to certain passages so that they would stress them to the Vatican and "Catholic Germany and Catholic Austria" would take note of them.[31] This attitude hardly justified all-out aid for Sims. The Pontiff's terms, however, were unacceptable. As Wilson had done in May, Benedict XV now called only for an evacuation of Belgium and France to Germany's 1914 boundaries; new borders in the East were to be settled at a peace conference. The difference was that the Pope went too far, in Wilson's eyes, toward the implication that the German hegemony from Riga to Macedonia was to be expanded toward the Urals: a "return to the *status quo ante bellum* . . . . [as] proposed by His Holiness . . . would . . . result in abandoning the new-born Russia to . . . [control by] the German Government." Wilson did extend an olive branch for reasonable German terms. He denounced, moreover, those who aimed to impose "economic restrictions meant to benefit some nations and cripple or embarrass others." "Cripple" doubtlessly applied to the Allies' intentions towards Germany, and "embarrass," to their terms for the United States. The President promised that all of the warring powers would be accorded "participation upon fair terms in the economic opportunities of the world — the German [and American] people of course included." He would tolerate "no punitive damages," or "dismemberment of Empires," or "selfish economic leagues," he assured Berlin and Vienna.[32]

The Allies realized that greater American naval and military aid would be sent only if they could convince Wilson of the innocuousness of their own postwar intentions. In Rome, Foreign Minister Baron Sidney Sonnino had recently disavowed any selfish Italian aims; he had linked his noble renunciation to "the help of the United States" which he hoped to get in fighting the war. The Italian legislature, however, spoiled his intended effect on Wilson by heaping scorn on him, thinking his repudiation was sincere. The London War Cabinet soon decided on a more subtle approach. They would not renounce their expansionist purposes, but their war aims would, "with advantage, be allowed to fall into the background." Both London and Washington had, for some months, allowed the President's stance against British navalism to do so, although he would make "freedom of the seas" a mandatory commandment among his Fourteen Points of January 1918. His own adoption of the British blacklist system against the remaining neutrals had, however, left this point in some confusion. So, had it been generally known, would the Navy Department's sentiment in favor of an American use of unrestricted submarine warfare if the Allies went down and left the United States stranded.[33] Perhaps this helped to explain Benson's tardiness and stinginess in sending Sims submarines. Perhaps, too, Benson was husbanding his submarines for use against the British in a possible future war, as outlined by the Navy General Board at Armistice time. (Further discussion can be found in Chapter 7.)

In the summer of 1917, the General Board was convinced that American naval chances of victory in the present war, as well as one against a possible future anti-American coalition would be enhanced by shifting the construction emphasis towards anti-submarine craft, scouting vessels, and cruisers. The navy was out of balance, "top-heavy" from its long stress on capital ships.[34] Benson, however, never thought so, either during the war or the Peace Conference. It would not be the fate of Germany's two hundred destroyers or other craft, but the division of her twenty-odd battleships that would exercise him during the Armistice and peace talks (along with the likelihood that the British would get the lion's share of the Reich's battle cruisers as well).

During the spring and summer of 1917, Sims's messages from London had harped on the necessity of suspending the dreadnought program in favor of anti-U-boat building. The combined Anglo-American total in capital ships would give an ample margin of safety over Scheer's fleet; at least it would if Benson were willing to let some dreadnoughts join Beatty's Grand Fleet. The British had virtually halted capital ship construction in favor of anti-U-boat vessels and cargo ships. Sims kept protesting that the Department's miserliness in sending him the anti-submarine craft meant that convoys could not be started in the Mediterranean. No convoy protection for outbound ships from Britain or France was possible with the resources which the Allies and he had. Enemy U-boat construction was increasing.[35]

Yet two additional motives stayed the administration's hand. One was the ambition of acquiring the maximum of foreign markets while the war lasted. At the August 16 Cabinet meeting, the President decided that construction of merchant ships should take priority over the building of anti-U-boat craft to prosecute the ongoing war. Daniels' diary reveals Wilson's rationalization. The question raised was "shall we build merchant ships or destroyers? McAdoo rather thought the first. W[ilson] said much would depend on how long the war would last. We are building 117 [slowly], and the proposed 150 could not be secured until 1919 and later. Then it would be a top-heavy [*sic*] Navy whereas the merchant ships would get in the trade and that was the chief need."[36] Few foresaw that the war would end before 1919, but the President would adhere to this attitude of placing trade above aid to the Allies even during the great 1918 German offensives when he declined to take merchant ships out of profitable trade routes to send troops to France. (Additional discussion can be found in Chapter 5.)

In May and June 1917, Pratt had written Sims that the department was worried about the domino effect which the weakness or collapse of one or more of the major Allies might cause. Even a "draw, or a doubtful victory . . . [might animate] Japan . . . [to] combine [with other anti-American] powers to cause trouble." Pratt held that, as neither the British nor the Americans had treated the Japanese as equals, one could not blame them for looking out for their own interests. Their leaders were confident that they could get along well with a victorious Germany; they believed that the Germans respected them for their industrial and military prowess. The Mikado should be encouraged to send troops across Siberia to bolster the eastern front and thus "offset Russian weakness."[37] Pratt reminded Sims that "there are mighty few [Americans] like yourself . . . and myself who are Anglo-Saxon to the bone and realize that England has carried the bag long enough." But if Sims wanted more of the American naval craft afloat and more anti-submarine craft to be built, he would have to help persuade the British to sign a treaty which they would be reluctant to accept. All officers at the Navy Department, he assured Sims, were agreed that efficiently to fight the present war, capital ship construction ought to be postponed. "However, such a policy may leave us with our guard down in case of future complications . . . . This is where you come in . . . in your diplomatic way . . . to make safe the future . . . well being of the entire Anglo-Saxon race. Even were a forced peace to result, England's Fleet must never go elsewhere but to join our own, and such portion of it as we might need . . . ought to be at our disposal." [38]

Through Balfour, Colonel House was also seeking this treaty. But Sims was more trusted by the London government than was the President's alter-ego. If Sims expected the conversion of his country's shipyards to an emphasis on antisubmarine construction and the receipt of the four dreadnoughts for which he was asking, he would have to persuade the British to turn over as many dreadnoughts — for American use against one or more possible future enemies — as the United States would have built had it not turned to anti-U-boat construction. In effect, Sims and House were to induce London to promise that after this war, if America found itself likely to fight Japan, the Royal Navy would have to turn over to the Navy Department the number of dreadnoughts which the United States would have built, had it not suspended capital ship building in order to prosecute the war against Germany. If the war should last three more years, and the United States would have completed five new battleships in those three years, Britain would be obliged to let the United States have five of her newest when Washington declared the nation to be in danger. [39] Benson's view notwithstanding, the United States intended to strengthen its naval position through alteration of its building program, and make Britain pay it for achieving this greater potency.

On July 2, the discouraged Pratt informed Sims that the limited destroyer construction authorized was being delayed by the administration's failure to coordinate the allocation of materials and manpower between destroyers and merchant ships. Sims hinted to Pratt on July 28, that he had struck a snag. Although the Prime Minister had informed him "a few days ago that the required assistance would be given," he was now promising only that he would "take the matter up" with his Cabinet. Sims added that as Lloyd George was "overcharged" with work, one could not "be sure that it will be done right away."[40]

The treaty was never signed. The London War Cabinet felt that the American efforts were likely to incite a breach in the Anglo-Japanese alliance and to increase the chances of a Central Power victory. Balfour gave the principal arguments for rejecting House's and Sims's proposals. For too long, His Majesty's Government had treated Japan as "a mere convenience." On the other hand, the Tokyo government had reasonably well fulfilled the obligations which the alliance imposed upon it. The U.S. President would never accede to London's counterproposal that Japan be made a party to their proposed pact, even though this would give Washington all the security it needed against the two naval powers Wilson avowedly feared: Germany and Japan. Neither would Wilson assent to a Japanese-sponsored Monroe Doctrine for East Asia which would recognize the Mikado's right to the primary position in the Far East and thus reduce Japanese-American tensions. Moreover, Australia and New Zealand would profoundly resent such a step by Britain as jeopardizing their relations with Japan while the Royal Navy was preoccupied with the war against the Central Empires.[41]

Balfour added that the secrecy Wilson insisted upon was unlikely to be maintained. The French, Italians, and Russians would draw the worst inferences from having been excluded from such an Anglo-American arrangement. So would the U.S. Senate, which would probably assert that its constitutional rights had been violated. Thus the House-Sims proposition would probably result in an angry Senate and people who would be loath to help during the present war; in the continental Allies' suspicion that Washington and London were up to something at their expense; and in a Japan so incensed that she might well make a separate peace, if not an alliance, with Germany. The United States offered no adequate inducements to offset these dangers. At Jellicoe's prompting, the Americans were urged "that destroyers would be of more use to them than capital ships in a war with Japan."

David F. Trask has observed that Wilson did not encourage House to seek the capital ship transfer treaty. Perhaps House (like Sims) was so alarmed at the likelihood of a German victory that he sought the anti-Japanese pact more as an offering to the President on behalf of stepped-up naval aid to the Allies in Europe than from a conviction that Japan posed the formidable threat to the United States that the requested agreement and the delay in sending Sims the anti-submarine craft and battleships he wanted had inferred. Sims wrote Pratt on June 7, 1917, that America would have nothing to fear from the Japanese "after this war is over for many years to come . . . . our battlefleet must soon hopelessly outstrip theirs." Pratt urged Benson to let part of the navy yards' facilities then devoted to battleships turn to merchant ships because "the needs of our allies are immediately imperative" and "in case this war terminates successfully, the merchant ships . . . will be . . . most useful . . . in furthering the ultimate good of the country." Pratt neglected to press for submarines for Sims, his June 7 study held (as previously noted) a more persuasive point for Benson: "augmenting our submarine Fleet" instead of continuing capital ship building would be useful against Britain in case of a postwar confrontation with Britain.[42]

The vitality of Japan's threat in the summer of 1917 may have owed much to its attractiveness as an excuse for minimizing support for the Allies against the Central Powers. In December 1916, (as previously noted), the Vatican had sent word to the President that, if he needed a diplomatic excuse for halting the export of war supplies to the Allies, he could say that his tensions with Japan (and Mexico) required him to husband America's resources at home. As matters turned out, the consummation of the famous Lansing-Ishii agreement of November 1917 temporarily eased Japanese-American stress.[43]

By July, Sims had launched a series of missives to induce the Navy Department to send him some dreadnoughts. The British wished Benson to send four coal-burning dreadnoughts to give the Grand Fleet a more comfortable margin of safety. They sought to retire five or six older battleships and to use their crews on newly launched anti-submarine craft for which they lacked trained men. Four of Beatty's leviathans had by now been taken from him so that they could guard the English Channel against a possible sortie by units of Scheer's fleet. This left the new British margin at twenty-four to Scheer's nineteen. Worse yet, Beatty would have to cope with a possible surprise challenge by all of the High Seas Fleet with an inferiority of anti-U-boat vessels to protect his major ships against torpedo attack.[44]

In Washington, Mayo chafed at the passive role his fleet was forced to play in the war. The Commander-in-chief prodded Benson to let his entire fleet stand alongside of Beatty's. Ignoring the department's June 23 declaration of its war policy, he wrote Benson in October that it ought to draw up one.[45] Sims, however, did not want the whole fleet; the British had ample coal for the coal-burning dreadnoughts, but as to oil-burning warships they could barely supply their own. Nevertheless, Benson refused to send any. He had three objections. He sought to keep the fleet out of a second Jutland. In his opinion, the Admiralty might arrange the deployment of the combined forces so that the American dreadnoughts would bear the danger of the most exposed position if Scheer chose to give battle.[46] Thirdly, before they gave any more cooperation, he and the President intended to acquire at least equality with the British in directing the course of the naval war. Their ultimate goal was to dominate the Allied naval effort. Thus Wilson would complete his four-pronged control of the Entente if the war lasted long enough: the American army, navy, treasury, and his own moral might would be the instruments of his dominion.

Pratt had begun to hint to Sims of this naval ambition in May. Sims's high standing with the British and French was to be employed to get Washington's "European policy carried out . . . by a man thoroughly in touch with and satisfactory to the Allies." Although "England's naval policy dominates the policy of the entire Allied nations . . . . if the war does not end soon, the United States interest is going to be a very big one." Therefore "we should not . . . accept their policy without a look in ourselves." In May Captain Pratt had also hinted that Sims should inveigle himself a seat on the Admiralty Board. "There should be a seat . . . for one of our own . . . men of unquestioned ability . . . who has the confidence and the policies of his own Department at his finger end, with the power to make definite decisions . . . you . . . [are the man]."[47]

Pratt had also written that he had been advocating "putting the army on the other side immediately and the use of dreadnoughts [as troop transports] escorted to put them over." He agreed with Sims that there was no doubt that "we will have England's fleet back of us at the finish . . . [so] we should throw ours into the game where they [*sic*] will count." He was pressing for accelerated submarine production to acquire a force to hold in "reserve in order if things do not go just right of doing as Germany with our submarines exactly what she has been doing . . . ." However, Sims should be sent as many as Benson could be induced to let go over.[48]

By July, the administration had found an additional means by which it might gain control over Allied naval strategy. In exchange for a paramount influence, it might be willing to risk throwing its warships "into the game where they will count." Daniels informed Wilson that Mayo wanted "to go to Europe." The President began prodding the Navy Department to devise a means by which it could obtain "equal control" with Whitehall over Allied operations. Wilson told Daniels that Sims was not to get his four dreadnoughts until the Admiralty agreed to a "conference to determine a joint program — we are asked to send and send, but not a conference where we have [an] equal voice." On August 16, Daniels and Benson brought Mayo to the White House. Daniels chronicled the President's ambitious instructions. "Mayo said that he hoped that the President would not expect too much. No, but he expected plans by which America could lead and become the senior partner in a successful naval campaign." Mayo must have figuratively gulped. Five days earlier, on the deck of his own flagship, Wilson had exhorted his junior officers to go over his own and Benson's heads, if one of them thought he had a plan which would, in effect, enable the American navy to take the lead from the British in a campaign of assaults on the Reich's home sea bases. If such an assault scheme were rejected by the admirals, the officer should take his case directly to his President. "I am willing to sacrifice half the navy Great Britain and we together have to crush that nest [of U-boat bases], because if we crush it, the war is won." With these words, Wilson would supposedly risk reducing his sea power close to the state of Japan's without the British naval treaty, despite the fact that every reasonably well-trained naval officer knew that "guns afloat were no match for guns ashore."[49]

No officer came forth with such a plan. Benson fruitlessly sought one for months. Mayo was more impressed by the disasters which had overtaken earlier naval assaults, particularly at the Dardanelles, in which a combination of ground guns and mines had turned back the aggressors after they had lost capital ships for nothing. Sims countered that the British had tried similar enterprises; "blood and tears" had been their only reward. When, at the White House, Wilson repeated his willingness "to make great ventures," Mayo took fright and said so. The President rejoined that he "of course wished no policy that would mean suicide." One suspects, however, that the President had no great expectations that anyone would present him with a feasible plan for such a campaign. He was presumably responding to the discontent among naval officers over the meagerness of the American contribution to the fighting. His call for a daring attack on Germany's U-boat bases was probably intended to shift unwelcome attention away from the Navy Department's policy onto the shoulders of the allegedly unimaginative British and Sims. Indeed, Daniels was to contrast this bold presidential speech to Mayo's officers with the Admiralty's and Sims's alleged timidity in fighting the war at the 1920 Senate Committee Hearings. Then Wilson was to instruct Daniels "to print a large number" of copies of his speech for public dissemination.[50]

In October the General Board warned that an attack upon the Reich's submarine bases was certain to prove a costly fiasco. The best that the department could come up with was the Roosevelt-Redfield mine barrage (about which Benson and Daniels were still skeptical) now that a promising mine had been developed. Sims, the British, and Benson agreed that it ought to be tried; Daniels told the President that it might not prove very effective, but it was all there was to offer. Work on it began. As it was not completed by Armistice day, one can say only that it seemed promising.[51] In September 1917, Benson told Sims he was not going to send any dreadnoughts until "very much stronger arguments are produced . . . [and] a plan of operation of the combined allied naval powers" was forthcoming that gave America a strong voice in control of their use.[52]

Benson may also have been resentful of the Admiralty's refusal to divulge useful information to American naval intelligence, either in London or Washington. This was an outgrowth of Anglo-American commercial competition and of the Admiralty's dislike of Benson's intelligence section's man in London. One result of Benson's deficient intelligence reports was that he long worried under the mistaken impression that the British intended to turn over five of their capital ships to the Japanese at the war's end as a reward for their naval help against the Central Powers.[53]

However, Benson had no cause to be vexed with Sims for his role in the intelligence quarrel. The Navy Department sought information about firms, banks, and shipping companies with possible German connections in the United States and Latin America. This trespassed on territory that Whitehall wished to keep unknown to British trading rivals. In 1917, the London Cabinet took steps to prevent British mining and oil investments in Latin America from passing into American hands. Yet Sims's intervention at the Admiralty did elicit information which Benson's office found highly useful.[54]

In October, Mayo reported his London findings to Benson. It would be detrimental to American interests to change "even the personality" of its naval commander in the war zone. Mayo urged that Sims be sent his dreadnoughts and all possible anti-U-boat craft, including submarines and gunboats. They were needed for convoy work; Mayo pointed out that the figures showed that merchant ships out of convoy were being sunk at twenty times the rate of those in one. Still, all Benson promised Sims was that, should the United States declare war against Austria, he would probably send him five destroyers for use in the Adriatic. He did not improve on his earlier messages that a few American submarines might arrive in European waters.[55]

The Army-Navy baseball game on July 4, 1918. King George V congratulates the captain of the Army team. Central News, Ltd., photo.

At the end of October, the President decided that House and Benson would go to London and Paris to investigate the Allies' condition. The moment seemed propitious for extracting their consent to an equal or paramount American voice in the Entente's naval effort. The Allies' plight had gone from bad to worse since the departure of the Balfour and Viviani missions. The President noted in October that in France "there lies near the surface . . . a very considerable revolutionary feeling" against the war and social inequalities. He knew from her entreaties for American help with coal and food that Italy was in dire straits. In August House had cautioned him that "if we add [sending and supplying] a large American army in France [to the shipping tonnage needed to keep the Allies going], the French and Italians will be in a worse plight regarding coal and other necessities than they were last winter. Will they bear the strain? I doubt it . . . ." And that month Sims had warned the Navy Department that "129 German and Austrian divisions were, until recently, on the Russian Front." Now, however, he feared that "Russia will give way entirely." Much of this Teutonic power seemed about to be freed for use in the west where France was "war weary" — who knows how close she is to the breaking point?"[56]

Benson had barely set foot on English soil when the Bolsheviks overthrew Kerensky's pallid republic and asked Berlin and Vienna for armistice terms. And on October 24, five days before he sailed, the battle of Caporetto, a paralyzing calamity for Italy, began.

On October 29, Daniels bid Benson Godspeed. The Secretary noted that he went with "WW's . . . instructions . . . 'all possible cooperation but we must be free' " (of joint plans which would leave the United States Navy in a junior relation to that of George V, one infers).[57]

Upon receiving "assurances" from Whitehall, presumably that they would not be placed in a discriminately dangerous position, Benson cabled Daniels from London to send Sims his four dreadnoughts. They came. A fresh pro-Sims report from Churchill to Wilson no doubt facilitated their sailing.[58] The Admiralty, however, balked at Benson's suggestions for assaulting the Reich's naval bases. Jellicoe informed him that plans were being laid only for naval attacks upon Ostend and Zeebrugge in Belgium. Even these U-boat havens offered minefields, enemy submarines, small surface torpedo firing craft, land guns, and treacherously shallow approaches in which surface ships could get stuck in range of the enemy's shore batteries. It remained to be seen what the Americans could do to help against these bastions. Benson did agree that Sims's destroyers could be used to aid the Grand Fleet if Scheer again threw down the gauntlet.[59] Evidently alarmed at the prospect of the American navy's being left alone to cope with Central Power naval might, he also told Sims that he would in the future be more generous in dispatching him anti-submarine craft for convoy and patrol work. [60] Shipping losses had somewhat declined since August; but sinkings still exceeded launchings each month, and most of the vessels lost were inbound ones laden with war-needed cargoes.

The President had not entirely abandoned hope of a compromise peace. He instructed House's inquiry experts "to study the just claims of the larger states like Russia, Austria, and Germany herself"; yet that same November he was digesting Pershing's memorandum concerning the likelihood of "Britain and ourselves being left to carry on the war without material aid from any other power."[61]

For some weeks before Caporetto, Thomas Nelson Page had been urging the President that an American declaration of war against Austria would boost Italian morale, give him more influence over Italian policy, and enhance future Italo-American commerce. The President reluctantly decided that these considerations were convincing. He had no intention, however, of sending any troops to Italy or the Balkans. Furthermore, the phrasing of his Austrian message to Congress left the Italians as mistrustful as ever of America. This distrust continued to hamper Sims's Mediterranean efforts. The President assured Vienna that he did "not wish in any way to impair or re-arrange the Austro-Hungarian Empire." Then how were the Italians to obtain the chief objects for which they had entered war — the Trentino, Istria, and Dalmatia — if this Empire were not to be impaired? The President hinted that he was trying to coerce Germany into a negotiated peace by saying that, if Berlin did not accept his terms soon, "it might be impossible . . . to admit Germany to the free economic intercourse" of the postwar world. He removed most of this sting, however, by turning his fire by implication onto the Allies' Paris Economic Conference: "The wrongs committed in this war cannot be righted by similar wrongs against Germany and her allies." No victors were going to be allowed to implement their "covenants of selfishness . . . . " He called on Reich's leaders to abandon goals which prevented the German people from sharing "the comradeship of the other peoples of the world."[62]

Notes on Chapter 3

[1] Page cables to Wilson, June 20 and 25, 1917, Wilson Papers; Balfour via Br. embassy to Wilson, July 1, 1917, *ibid.*

[2] Wilson to Daniels, *ibid.*, July 2, 1917, *ibid.*

[3] Wilson to Daniels, July 3, 1917, *ibid.*

[4] Daniels to Wilson, July 3, 1917, *ibid.* As has been noted, the Grand Fleet was allowing the majority of its destroyers to be used for anti-U-boat work. It had as few as 51 to cope with a possible surprise battle with the High Seas Fleet's potential of 100 U-boats and 200 destroyers, so Sims informed Wilson on July 11, 1917, *ibid.*

[5] Daniels to Wilson, July 14, 1917, *ibid.*

[6] Lane to George W. Lane, Feb. 9 and 25, 1917, Anne W. Lane and Louise W. Wall, eds., *The Letters of Franklin K. Lane, Personal and Political* (Boston and New York, 1922), 237, 239-40, summarizing Wilson's anti-convoy position on Feb. 6 and 23. See E. David Cronon's remarks on Daniels' suspicious reference to the *Lane Letters* with respect to his entry on convoying, supposedly on Feb. 25, 1917, in Cronon, ed., *The Cabinet Diaries of Josephus Daniels, 1913-1921* (Lincoln, 1963), 106, note 3, and entry for May 4, 1917.

[7] Cronon, ed., *Daniels Diaries*, July 16, 1917; W. B. Fowler, *British-American Relations 1917-1918: The Role of Sir William Wiseman* (Princeton, 1969), 244.

[8] Sims to Page, Aug. 17, 1917, Sims Papers.

[9] Cronon, ed., *Daniels Diaries*, July 24, 1917; Lt. P. H. Bastedo to Sims, Sept. 9, 1917, Sims Papers: "Mrs. Grayson . . . . told me that the President had said . . . that he would like to see any plan put into effect that Admiral Sims believed would . . . do away with the submarine menace, regardless of whether the plan were favored by . . . our Navy Department . . . . " Rear Admiral Grayson confirmed this to Bastedo, *ibid.*

[10] Sims to Benson, Sept. 10, 1917, Sims Papers.

[11] *PPWW*, V, 7, 61, 94, 201; Lord Burnham to Balfour, July 23, 1918, with text of Wilson's April 8 statements, Lloyd George Papers, F/15/8/7.

[12] R. S. Baker, *Woodrow Wilson: Life and Letters* (Garden City, 1927-39), VI, 200; *ibid.*, 213; *PPWW* IV, 412; *ibid.*, V, 4.

[13] W. H. Page to Wilson, Mar. 17, 1918, Wilson Papers; "Notes of an Interview with the President at the White House," Oct. 16, 1918, in papers of Sir Eric Geddes, ADM/116/1806, P.R.O.; Council of Four minutes, May 6, 1919, 180.03401/146, National Archives Microfilm Publications, *General Records of the American Commission to Negotiate Peace, 1918-1931* (of Record Group 256) (Washington, D. C.), Microcopy No. 820, roll 113. Hereafter this collection is referred to as GRACNPM 820.

[14] Wilson also demanded this collateral to guarantee the highest level of American capital for postwar rehabilitation investments — Baker, *Wilson*, VI, 378; Richard Hofstadter, *The American Political Tradition and the Men Who Made It* (New York, 1948), 254; *ibid.* 270.

[15] Baker, *Wilson*, 225-226; *ibid.*, 227; House to Wilson, Jan. 20, 1917, Wilson Papers.

[16] Spring-Rice to Lord Hardinge (Undersecretary for Foreign Affairs), Dec. 6, 1916, to Balfour, Dec. 16 and 22, 1916, Balfour Papers, 49740; T. N. Page to Wilson, *Lansing Papers*, I, 749.

[17] Lansing to W. H. Page, Feb. 8, 1917, Lansing MSS, Vol. 24; Page to Lansing, Feb. 11, 1917, *ibid.*; Page to Lansing, Feb. 21, 1917, *Foreign Relations, 1917*, Supp. 1, 56.

[18] Charles Seymour, ed., *The Intimate Papers of Colonel House* (Boston and New York, 1926-28), III, 56.

[19] House to Wilson, Mar. 17, 1917, Wilson Papers; Seymour, ed., House Papers, III, 56, 58.
[20] Baker, *Wilson*, VII, 79-80, Drummond to Lloyd George, May 21, 1917, Lloyd George Papers, F/60/2/16.
[21] Baker, *Wilson*, VII, 180; Cronon., ed., *Daniels Diaries*, May 29, Dec. 6, 1917; House to Wilson, June 5, 1917, Wilson Papers: Seymour, ed., House Papers, III, 48-9.
[22] Sir Mark Sykes to Balfour, © Dec. 18, 1917, Lloyd George Papers, F/51/4/14; minutes of Council of Four, May 22, 1919 180.03401/22 ½. GRACNPM 820.
[23] The Inquiry to Wilson, Jan. 21, 1919, Wilson Papers, Sers. 5B; David F. Trask, *Captains and Cabinets: Anglo-American Naval Relations, 1917-1918* (Columbia, Mo., 1972), 181-82; Cronon., ed., *Daniels Diaries*, Apr. 24, June 30, 1917.
[24] Quoted in Warner R. Schilling, "Admirals and Foreign Policy, 1913-1919," Ph. D. diss., Yale University, 1953, 106; *ibid.*
[25] USNSF, U file: Diary of . . . Daniels, July 13 and Sept. 1, 1917.
[26] Page to Lansing, Jan. 29, 1917, who sent it to Wilson Feb. 28, 1917, Wilson Papers; Francis to Lansing, May 11, 1917, who sent it with Walling's appeal to Wilson on May 17, *ibid.*, Sers. 5A. Only after weeks of delay would Wilson send even an observer to Paris where the Allies were trying to devise means of saving Russia — Baker, *Wilson*, VII, 290; *ibid.*, 69, 76-77; House to Wilson, July 23, 1917, Wilson Papers, on how shabbily the Russian ambassador had been treated when he "had gone the round of Cabinet officers . . . he says it is not true that Russia is making demands upon us for railroad equipment looking to after the war conditions." The ambassador got no American shipping space for any supplies.
[27] Br. War Cabinet minutes, July 31, 1917, CAB/23/3; Paul M. Warburg to Wilson, marked "July 1917," Wilson Papers, Sers. 2, Box 164; Baker, *Wilson*, VII, 180-81.
[28] *PPWW*, V, 63; Spring-Rice to Balfour on recent conversations at State Department. July 27, 1917, Balfour Papers, 49740.
[29] Baker, *Wilson*, VII, 180-81.
[30] Lansing to Wilson, Aug. 20, 1917, *Lansing Papers*, II, 44; House to Wilson with Br. intelligence report, marked by archivist "1917?", Wilson Papers, Sers. 2 Box 172; see also Dragan Živojinović, "Robert Lansing's Comments on the Pontifical Peace Note of August 1, 1917," *The Journal of American History*, LVI (Dec. 1969), 560-63.
[31] Wilson to House, Sept. 2, 1917, Baker, *Wilson*, VII, 253-54; House to Wilson, Aug. 15, Sept. 1, and 4, 1917, Wilson Papers. House's advice of Aug. 15 said that it was not as important to beat Germany "to her knees" as it was to get peace terms that would allow Russia to become "a virile republic." Besides, Germany would inevitably become more democratic "within a few years of peace."
[32] *PPWW*, V, 93-96.
[33] T. N. Page to Lansing, July 31, 1917, *Lansing Papers*, II, 36-38; Br. War Cabinet minutes, Aug. 20, 1917, CAB/23/3; Pratt to Sims, Apr. 30, May 6 and 27, 1917, Sims Papers.
[34] Seymour, ed., *House Papers*, III, 70-73; General Board Reports GB 420 SN 598, Apr. 20, 1917, and GB 420 (no SN), Aug. 29, 1917, Subject: Naval Policy, Building Program, ONRL.
[35] Sims to Operations, Apr. 19, May 8, June 27, July 21, 1917, Sims Papers; Sims to Wilson, July 11, 1917, Wilson Papers.
[36] Cronon, ed., *Daniels Diaries*, Aug. 16, 1917. Between Apr. 6, 1917, and Nov. 11, 1918, only 44 destroyers were launched in the U. S. — Seymour, ed., *House Papers*, III, 74, note.
[37] Pratt to Sims, May 6 and 15, June 7, 1917, Sims Papers.
[38] Pratt to Sims, June 7 and July 2, 1917, *ibid.*

[39] Drummond told House on May 14 that his treaty proposal had been sent to Lloyd George and an answer was expected in a "day or two," Seymour, ed., *House Papers*, III, 66ff. See Trask, *Captains and Cabinets*, Chap. 3, for a fuller account of House's role in these negotiations.

[40] Pratt to Sims, July 2, 1917, Sims to Pratt July 28, 1917, Sims Papers.

[41] Br. War Cabinet minutes, May 22 and July 3, 1917, CAB/23/2; Balfour's exposition on the treaty, June 22, is Appendix 2 of July 3 minutes (also to be seen as GT 1138, CAB/24/17, P.R.O.).

[42] Trask, *Captains and Cabinets*, 116; *ibid.*, 113; Pratt to Benson, June 7, 1917, USNSF, UB file.

[43] T. N. Page to Lansing, Dec. 29, 1916, *Lansing Papers*, I, 744-45; *War Memoirs of Robert Lansing, Secretary of State* (Indianapolis, 1925), 290-302.

[44] Sims to Benson June 15 and July 21, 1917, Sims Papers; Sims to Wilson, July 11, 1917, Wilson Papers.

[45] Pratt to Sims, May 27, 1917, and *passim* through fall 1917, Sims Papers; *Hearings, 1920*, I, 598-600.

[46] Benson in *ibid.*, II, 1959.

[47] Pratt to Sims, May 6 and 27, 1917, Sims Papers.

[48] *Ibid.* On the 6th, Pratt described the U. S. Fleet as "interned" in its own waters.

[49] Cronon, ed., *Daniels Diaries*, July 24 and Aug. 16, 1917; *PPWW*, V, 82-88; Harold and Margaret Sprout, *The Rise of American Naval Power: 1776-1918* (Princeton, 1939, 5th Printing, 1966), 323.

[50] Cronon, ed., *Daniels Diaries*, Aug. 16, 1917; in his cable to Wilson of July 11, 1917, Sims had warned of the disastrous results sustained by the British and French in assaults by sea alone; *Hearings, 1920*, II, 2021-25: Daniels added here a claim that Wilson was the father of the Atlantic convoy system; Cronon, ed., *Daniels Diaries*, May 14, 1920.

[51] Any naval attack on a German North Sea base would be suicidal owing to heavy land guns, U-boats, mines, and aircraft guarding them, and Zeebrugge offered the additional hazard of treacherous shallows — GB 425-5 SN 778, Oct. 24, 1917, ONRL; Thomas G. Frothingham, *The Naval History of the Great War* (Cambridge, Mass., 1927), III, 236.

[52] Benson to Sims, Sept. 24, 1917, Sims Papers.

[53] Sims to Benson, Oct. 28, 1917, *ibid.*; Department of State agent E. V. Gillis informed Lansing on Feb. 27, 1917, that he had received a non-committal response from the British naval attache in Tokyo about the rumored after-the-war transfer of British warships to Japan, National Archives mf. 423, roll 2, *Records of the Department of State Relating to Political Relations Between the United States and Japan, 1910-29*, hereafter cited as USDSM 423; Benson told Mayo to find out what he could about this rumor in England, but Mayo's report of Oct. 1917 on his visit was silent on this matter. Since his report urged that Sims be sent the vessels he wanted, including dreadnoughts, and that Mayo himself be allowed to take most of the dreadnoughts and join the Grand Fleet, he presumably found no truth in the rumor — *Hearings, 1920*, I, 594, 602, 605. No such transfer was ever made; the British archives reveal no intention to do so.

[54] Benson's Director of Naval Intelligence, Capt. Roger Welles, to Sims, Sept. 15 and Nov. 9, 1917, Sims Papers; on Nov. 6 Welles deputy, Capt. Dudley Knox, wrote Sims that "the British are not frank with us . . . [in intelligence matters, owing to their] fears that after the war we are going to be an uncomfortably strong trade rival." On Sept. 14, the Br. War Cabinet sought means to prevent the sale of British-owned mining and oil properties in the Empire and in Latin America to Americans (minutes, CAB/23/5); on Oct. 8 and 9 it sought a means of protecting the British dye industry from any advantage certain American firms might gain

from connections with German firms (*ibid.*) The mining and oil stocks may well have been among those Wilson had in mind when he began his financial pressure against the Allies in late 1916.

[55] *Hearings, 1920*, I, 604, 600; Benson to Sims, Aug. 24 and Sept. 21, 1917, Sims Papers.

[56] Wilson to David Lawrence, Oct. 5, 1917, Wilson Papers; House to Wilson, Aug. 14, 1917. *ibid*; Sims to Pratt, Aug. 30, 1917, Sims Papers.

[57] Cronon, ed., *Daniels Diaries*, Oct. 29, 1917.

[58] *Hearings, 1920*, II, 1905; Churchill to Wilson, Oct. 22, 1917, Daniels Papers, saying that only 40 destroyers were guarding the Grand Fleet and it had only 24 dreadnoughts to Scheer's 19. On Nov. 12, 1917, Wilson wrote Daniels, *ibid.*, saying he had read Churchill's long letter "with close attention and a great deal of interest." This implied at least limited approval of its several recommendations. Wilson may have given Daniels verbal approval of the dreadnoughts based in part upon this letter before he sent it to him — Daniels acted at once on Benson's cable of Nov. 10, 1917. Cronon, ed., *Daniels Diaries*, Nov. 10, 1917.

[59] Benson at *Hearings, 1920*, II, 1852-53.

[60] Sims to Pratt, Nov. 6 and 16, 1917, Sims Papers.

[61] Baker, *Wilson*, VII, 359; *ibid.*, 350.

[62] *PPWW*, V, 134-41.

4

THE WAR IN

THE MEDITERRANEAN

B ENSON'S NOVEMBER 1917 visit to Sims's headquarters exposed
him directly to the persuasive powers of both Sims and the
Admiralty Lords, as well as to the enticing prospect of a strong
American role in the Admiralty's decision-making process. These alone
might not have sufficed to convert him to a policy of a more strenuous
American share in waging the war. But Benson became alarmed at the
sudden rise in the Central Powers' prospects of final victory. Russia
began capitulating to them at the same time that Italy was rendered
impotent.

At an inter-Allied naval conference in Paris in July 1917, Sims was
surprised at the magnitude of the mutual rivalries and suspicions which
were hobbling the "common" war effort in the Mediterranean. Rome's
Chief of Operation, Admiral Thaon di Revel, proved to be quite averse
to a "hearty cooperation" with his "partners."

Sims familiarized himself with the motives for their combat-chary
policies in the Mediterranean. These stemmed from the circumstances
in which the war had begun. The conflict had been precipitated by the
struggle of the Yugoslavs of Serbia to incite revolutions among the
Yugoslavs who lived under the Habsburg crowns of Austria-Hungary.
When Austria had gone to war, Russia had backed Serbia; in a larger
sense, this was a conflict for control of the Balkans between the
Slavs, on the one side, and the German-speaking Austrians and their
Hungarian partners on the other side. From the outset, however, Italy
intended to acquire as much Yugoslav and Italian-inhabited Habsburg
territory, and as much overall political and commercial influence in the
Balkans as possible.[1] In addition, Italy and Serbia had rival ambitions in
Greece and Albania. On the other hand, Rome was not much interested
in the Russian goal of detaching the Czech, Slovak, Polish, Ukrainian,

and Rumanian-inhabited lands from the Habsburg Empire. It feared an addition to Russian power.

These Latin ambitions and, above all, the longing to annex Austria's largely Italian-speaking provinces of the Trentino and Trieste had caused Rome to balk in 1914 at implementing its long standing Triple Alliance with Berlin and Vienna. Moreover, provision of this alliance stipulated that Italy would not be obliged to declare war against Russia and France if Britain's navy were ranged on their side.[2] Italy's neutrality declaration had helped save the French in the First Battle of the Marne in the summer of 1914. The French troops on the Italian frontier were rushed to bolster Field Marshal Joffre's reeling divisions. Rome's action had helped the Russians, too. Emperor Francis Joseph's Chief of Staff, Conrad von Hötzendorff, had been forced to leave some troops on the Austro-Italian frontier. Then, as Italy's neutrality had become more sinister, Conrad had been forced to shift more Austrian troops to guard the frontier, while endeavoring to cope with the Russians and Serbians.[3] From the outset, Berlin and Vienna had agreed that the containment of the Russians devolved primarily upon the Austrians. This plan had enabled the Germans to maintain about two-thirds of their troops on the Western Front. However, from time to time, the Germans had been forced to send reinforcements to the East when Russian drives threatened to break the Austro-Hungarian lines. By the time of Rome's announcement of hostilities (May 1915), the British and French had abandoned all intentions of launching an amphibious assault upon the Austrians' jagged coast. Although this would probably have forced the Germans to send help from France or from the Russian front, London and Paris had feared that they might lose more than they would gain: that Adriatic coast was an object of Italy's Balkan ambitions, and Rome was too likely to turn to Berlin and Vienna for an agreement that she would fight on their side if they would promise her France's Savoy, Nice, Corsica, and Tunis.[4] This would have added the Italian navy to the Austrian; the Allies' Mediterranean lifelines would have been endangered, the plight of the French and Russian armies would have been made worse.

In early 1915, Italy's astute Foreign Minister, Baron Sidney Sonnino, had been sensitive to the Allies desperation. On the day following the launching of the ill-fated British and French Dardanelles campaign to open the only good sea route by which to succor the Russians, as well as to drive Turkey out of the war, Sonnino had struck his bargain with the Entente. By the Treaty of London (April 26, 1915), much more than *Italia-irredenta* (the Trentino, Trieste, and Gradisca-Gorizia east of the Isonzo) was to be awarded to Italy if she helped the Entente win the war. The border of the Trentino was shoved north to give Victor Emmanual 300,000 German-speaking Austrians. In the Trieste-Istria region, Italy's borders were to be stretched to include a number of towns in which Austrian-ruled Yugoslavs constituted a clear majority. Worse, from a Slav viewpoint, most of Dalmatia, which today makes up the bulk of Yugoslavia's coastal region, was promised to Italy.[5] In a fruitless attempt to drive a wedge between the

Hungarians and the other Habsburg subjects, Fiume was left to the crown of Hungary-Croatia; to appease Slavdom's patron, Russia, a small strip of Austria's littoral was reserved for the Serbians. But the Serbian government remained outraged at these terms.[6]

The French also had disliked these concessions to the Italians. Paris had intended that France, not Italy, would replace the degenerating Russian influence in the Balkans.[7] If these were not enough seeds of discord for Sims to work around, the Pact of London had sown more in the Levant. As the British, French, and Russians had just divided among themselves all of the non-Turkish inhabited and oil-rich portions of the sprawling Ottoman Empire against their day of victory, the Italians were promised land in the southwestern quarter of the Turks' homeland in Anatolia. Balfour had sent the text of the Treaty of London, along with May 1916 Sykes-Picot Agreement (better delineating Anglo-French awards), to Wilson in May 1917 (House told Balfour, as noted, that these pacts were "bad, all bad").

After they obtained the Treaty of London, the Italians had worried that their partners intended to constrict their awards in Asia Minor. The boundaries of Italy's share had been left ill-defined, which would enable the British and French to agree at their leisure on the precise boundaries of their own awards. In addition to Constantinople, the Dardanelles, and adjacent coasts, this treaty gave Russia Turkish Armenia and territories adjoining it in Anatolia. Britain was to receive oil-rich Mesopotamia, a probable protectorate over Palestine, and a wide "sphere of influence" between the two areas. By the Sykes-Picot-Sazanoff agreements of March-April 1915, the British and French were free to arrange the rest of the Arabian Peninsula as they pleased, either as full-fledged protectorates or as autonomous, or independent, states.

Thus only Rome's future gains at Vienna's expense were accurately defined. As will be discussed, the naval policies of both the Italians and the French were strongly influenced by their rivalry with each other in the Balkans and in the Levant, as well as by their well-founded suspicions that both London and Washington hoped to minimize their gains in both areas. Despite her promise "to wage war in common against . . . the Entente's enemies" within thirty days, on May 23, 1915, Italy had declared war only against Austria. Not until August 28, 1916, would she reluctantly declare hostilities against Germany. The desire to keep trade channels with the Reich open, and the pro-German sentiment which had been stimulated by the thirty year alliance with Berlin, had caused this delay. Besides, Italy "had nothing to lose from a German victory over France and Russia — indeed, much to gain. France was her successful rival in the Mediterranean, Russia a possible danger in the Balkans and the Near East."[8] The tardy Italian entry into the coalition against Germany was prompted by the hope that more sorely needed war supplies would be forthcoming from the British and French.

The Italians and the three major Allies had added military and naval provisions to the Treaty of London. To prevent Austria from throwing her main weight against Italy, a military convention obliged the Russians to keep most of their troops arrayed against her, rather than against Germany (or Turkey); the Italians were reciprocally obligated. Another provision promised that "the Navies of Great Britain and France shall give their active and permanent support to Italy until the destruction of the Austro-Hungarian Navy or until the conclusion of peace." A naval convention had soon been consummated. London had agreed to a large loan, to finance Italy's war effort. France, Britain, and Russia had agreed to support the religiously excommunicated Italian government in excluding "a representative of the Holy See . . . [from] all peace negotiations . . . . " This partly stemmed from Berlin's half-threat to support Vienna's stand that sovereignty over Rome should be returned to the Pope if Italy joined their enemies.[9] All signatories promised never to enter into peace discussions with the enemy without the consent of each of the others.

Up to July 1917, the Italian Army had launched a series of twelve offensives that managed to tie down nearly half of the Austrian army. However, only a strip of eleven to fifteen miles of Habsburg soil was gained during these two and a half years.[10] At sea, di Revel, who held the Italian equivalents of both Benson's and Mayo's positions, had begun hostilities with twenty-three battleships to Austria's twenty. The navy had helped evacuate the disease-riddled remnants of Serbia's army during the winter of 1915-1916 when the enemy had driven the army through Montenegro and Albania to the sea. The internationally guaranteed neutrality of Corfu had been torn up as the Serbian army, then the French navy, had made it headquarters for their operations against the Austrians. Jealous and suspicious of this French action, the Italians had sent troops to Corfu to minimize Paris's influence over Balkan affairs. Meanwhile, in October 1915, Parisian-inspired Anglo-French landings had been made at Salonika. These had met with some Greek resistance. The French had subsequently persuaded the British to join them in a starvation blockade of Greece which, in December 1916, brought to power in Athens the French-sponsored Premier Eleutherios Venizelos. The advent of Venizelos had also brought Italian troops to Salonika to keep pace with their French rivals. By July 1917, other Italian troops were trying to maintain a toehold against the Austrians in Albania, in part to thwart French economic ambitions there.

The results of her naval engagements with the Austrians added to Italian anxieties. By August 1916, Victor Emmanuel's navy had lost four battleships, Francis Joseph's none. Nearly 60,000 tons of Italian warships had gone to the bottom; only 8,413 tons of Austrian naval craft had joined them.[11]

At the January 1917 London Naval Conference, the French had agreed that they would maintain at least eight battleships at Corfu to back up the Italian battle fleet; di Revel's capital ships, however, had by then taken sanctuary behind the great moles of Taranto Bay, where they continued to lie through 1917 and beyond. There they would await the disappearance of Habsburg naval power or the end of the war — unless their "allies" could pry them out.[12] Di Revel, like Benson, intended that his dreadnoughts should remain afloat for the influence they could exercise over the peace conference.

Roman suspicions of Anglo-French intentions in the Levant also encumbered Sims's and British efforts to persuade di Revel to do more to help against the U-boat campaign. In December 1916, Minister Without Portfolio Leonida Bissolati-Bergamaschi had told the head of the British military mission to the Italian Supreme Command, General Sir Charles Delme-Radcliffe, that he would like to work out a way of using the Italian navy more actively. He had urged that British, rather than French, troops be sent to bolster the Italian Alpine Front against the Austrians, as Franco-Italian relations were "not so cordial." This probably meant that he distrusted the British less than the French over Rome's war aims. Bissolati had lamented, however, that he could not take steps to improve the Italian naval endeavor until the "cooling in the relations between Italy and her Allies owing to the claims which Italy is making concerning Asia Minor, etc., not being fully satisfied" had been ameliorated. [13]

Rome's distrust of Wilson also impeded Sims's efforts to unite the Allies behind an aggressive policy towards Austria. As the United States formally entered the conflict, Rome's envoy in Washington, Count Macchi di Cellere, advised Sonnino that "the contribution of America, fatally useful to the Allied cause, is a usurer's mortgage on the peace conditions which the vaunted, but not true, disinterestedness only serves to conceal. Wilson's ambition to dictate peace . . . [had impelled him to enter the war] to exert the desired influence at the peace conference." [16] Indeed, after several conferences with Italian admirals, Sims informed Benson that Rome feared that President Wilson would make a premature, compromise peace at their expense; "they dread the influence of America on European politics." [15]

These Italian apprehensions were not groundless. In February 1917, the President had pressured Lloyd George to drop his call for the dismemberment of the Habsburg Empire and secretly to discuss peace terms with the Austrians. Wilson's January 'peace without victory' speech had offered Vienna's enemies nothing; worse, it had left the door open for modest Austrian gains. The death of the eighty-six year-old Francis Joseph, in November 1916, had loosened some of the bonds of loyalty which had held the several nationalities of the Empire together. The new sovereign, Charles, had sensed this and might prove willing to make peace for limited acquisitions in return for small concessions. The wearing strain on his peoples of the massive Russian drives, fighting the Italians, and conquering Serbia, Montenegro, Rumania, and Albania had been compounded by the harrowing effects of the Allied blockade. Hunger stalked Vienna. When informed of this, Wilson had addressed the British Prime Minister. Lloyd George had momentarily balked. The American peace proposal, however, had two merits. It might elicit maritime and financial aid from the icy President; Britain's generals and admirals were pressing him for relief from the strains which Austria's war effort imposed. In addition, peace with Vienna would virtually halt Mediterranean submarine sinkings. Perhaps the removal of the Dual Monarchy's forces from the lists would tip the balance so that

Russia and France could stay in the war.[16] On February 8, Page had told the fiery Welshman that, despite the unrestricted U-boat announcement, the President was "trying to avoid breaking with Austria in order to keep the channels . . . . with her open so that he may use her for peace [in Berlin]." London had been requested to disavow "the peace terms recently stated by the Entente . . . that . . . they would insist upon a virtual dismemberment of the Austro-Hungarian Empire . . . as the large measure of autonomy already assured to these older units of the Empire [except for Austrian Poland] is . . . sufficient . . . . " Wilson had informed Lloyd George that an American declaration of war would not impede his departure from it as soon as Berlin met his terms; he did "not doubt that Austria can be satisfied without depriving the several Balkan states of their political *autonomy* [italics added to stress the fact that these by-then-conquered states had been politically independent in 1914] and territorial integrity." The President had candidly stated that "the effort of this Government will be constantly for peace even should it . . . [declare war]."[17]

Lansing had then assured Charles' ambassador-designate to Washington, the Habsburg-true Pole, Count Adam Tarnowski, that the United States would gladly "act as intermediary in obtaining a definite assurance from the Allies that they would preserve the integrity of the Austro-Hungarian Empire . . . excepting Poland." This would have dashed all of Italy's war aims; but it presumably would have allowed a Habsburg to mount the throne of the union of Russian and Austrian Poland, as agreed to by Vienna and Berlin in December 1916.[18]

Meanwhile, the Emperor-King Charles, encouraged by Washington's magnanimous attitude, had sounded out London and Paris. Lloyd George had by now adopted a more Wilsonian line; Charles could retain at least Austria proper, Hungary, and all of present-day Czechoslavakia. But Italy ought to get a modest something, particularly the Italian-speaking Trentino. Otherwise, she would never agree to the terms and would cry out that the British and French had betrayed her. Charles refused to agree to any concessions to Italy.[19] Still, the British and French (Ribot) premiers decided that they ought to attempt to get the Italians to abandon most of their terms. On April 19, 1917, they met with them at St. Jean de Maurienne. Concealing their negotiations with the enemy, Lloyd George and Ribot "talked vaguely of the advantages of . . . peace with Austria. Lloyd George pointed to Smyrna as Italy's reward [for giving up most of her claims against Austria]; Ribot tried to distract Sonnino from Smyrna [which he wanted for France's protégé, Venizelos] by offering him Koniah [also on the Turkish coast]. Sonnino . . . , however, agreed to take both. . . . Lloyd George and Ribot, not daring to confess that they were already negotiating with Charles, had to pretend that they had offered Smyrna and Koniah out of sheer goodness of heart."[20]

The wily Sonnino knew them better than this. "The Italians then pressed for a more formal agreement: and their allies were dragged along in order to conceal their double-dealing with Austria-Hungary. Besides, the British were afraid that otherwise the Italians might join with the French [and the Americans?] in refusing them Mesopotamia; they did not mind handing over part of Asia Minor, adjacent to the French sphere. The French acquiesced . . . Agreement was reached in August . . . by an exchange of letters in London."[21]

By 1917, French military intelligence officers in the Levant had ceased to cooperate with the British army and navy. Lloyd George had resolved to minimize French expansion there. His stance that the Italians had done nothing on land or sea to deserve their promised awards in Turkey only exacerbated Rome's suspicions. Why had the British refused for months the Italian offer of troops for the Levant with the rejoinder that the U-boats had left no shipping space for them? Lloyd George backtracked. He told the Italians that they need not contribute directly to the fighting in the East. Their overall performance in the common cause, however, would be the criterion for what they would get from the Ottoman Empire. He hoped that it would improve, he ominously told them.[22]

This British attitude fleetingly drove the Italians and French into a common front against Britain on the eve of Sims's July naval conference with these naval powers. For the moment, the French promised to support Sonnino over his promised lands in Turkey; Sonnino agreed to a free hand for the French in Greece. There the British (and the Italians) had long painfully chafed under the arrogance of the Allied theater commander, General M. Sarrail, whom Paris claimed it had to retain, as he was the protégé of the powerful French Left. His "invention of the Albanian Republic of Kuritza," which contained "rich copper and coal mines for French investors," infuriated the Italians. Lloyd George was convinced that the general was seeking to advance purely French interests while only the British troops were doing any hard fighting in the area. But when, in June 1917, he moved to demand Sarrail's removal, Balfour dissuaded him: the U-boat campaign might doom the inter-Allied expedition to decimation and surrender; it would be better if a Frenchman rather than a Briton were in supreme command of such a catastrophe.[23]

These inter-Entente tensions and the lack of a unified military and naval effort worked against the Allies' war campaign. However, as long as Italy and Russia remained in the war, they helped save each other as well as France from ultimate defeat.

Knowing enough of this background to be wary, Sims actually made his debut, in the negative sense, into French naval affairs by journeying alone instead of accepting Jellicoe's invitation to go with him to Paris in May 1917. The principal purpose of the conference was to find more effective anti-submarine measures — at least from the British point of view. The British had earlier considered asking the Japanese to loan or sell them some capital ships to give the Grand Fleet a more comfortable margin of safety for a possible second Battle of Jutland. Balfour, then First Lord of the Admiralty, had overridden the proposal; it was likely to elicit a face losing rejection from Tokyo; it would advertise the Admiralty's apprehension of a possible defeat. In 1917, when the London War Cabinet did inquire of the Japanese, ships

were refused.[24] Meanwhile, at the January naval conference, the British
had sought French and Italian assent to the removal of older British
battleships from the Mediterranean; they would be retired and their
crews used to man newly-launched craft to cope with the German
U-boats. Di Revel and the French Chief of Naval Staff, Admiral
Ferdinand-Jean-Jacques De Bon, had strenuously objected. Eventually
De Bon had subsided somewhat, but the Italians had raised such a
clamor that now, in July, Jellicoe dared not ask their consent to the
removal of the last of his Mediterranean battleships. Thinly veiled
threats that Italy would collapse or leave the war before this fate
overtook her had greeted his January proposals. The French had
promised to keep at least eight battleships at Corfu to help offset the
partial withdrawal of British battleships. The Italians had been forced
to accept this compromise, but they were leery of it. This had left some
British cruisers and destroyers at Malta and Gibraltar, and four light
cruisers and two submarines in the Adriatic to bolster di Revel's units
against potential Austrian cruiser or destroyer raids on Italy's east
coast.[25] Whitehall also maintained an ineffective anti-submarine barrage of small boats in the Straits of Otranto. These small boats were
intermittently attacked by Austrian surface ships. Only a few old
British destroyers tried to protect them; the Italians and French so far
declined to help prevent their loss.[26] The French had all of their large
warships in the Mediterranean, but they were divided between Toulon
and Corfu. The Italians held their capital ships at Taranto, while most
of their destroyers remained passively at Venice and Brindisi, awaiting
supposedly imminent Austrian attacks on these or other cities which
might precipitate revolution in Rome, so di Revel insisted.

Therefore, the thirty-four Italian destroyers in the Adriatic could be
used neither to protect the British barrage at Otranto nor for patrol or
convoy duties with merchant ships. Pressed, the French unenthusias-
tically agreed to try to provide a vague "few" destroyers from
somewhere for convoys.[27]

Jellicoe, Sims, and De Bon concentrated on prying Italian destroyers
loose. De Revel insisted that his destroyers "must be husbanded" from
rough seas to meet "the danger of a high sea action between the
Austrian and Italian fleets." Sims rejoined that in such a high sea action
the Italians could not expect to join their destroyers to their battleships
before the battle began; they were stationed impossibly far apart.
Between them, Sims went on, the Italians and French in the Adriatic
and at Corfu, just south of the Otranto Straits, had exactly twice the
Austrian destroyer strength — forty-four to twenty-two; surely they
could spare some for the barrage. Moreover, Sims's own destroyers were
"available at any time for . . . offensive duty in connection with a high
sea action." Besides, Sims told di Revel, the Italians would still be far
better off than Beatty; the Grand Fleet "could probably not count on
more than 50 destroyers against about 140 German destroyers" if
Scheer threw down the gauntlet again. Di Revel's destroyers, sent to the
barrage, would make better scouts and would also be in a position to
join far more swiftly the battleships at or coming from Taranto.[28]

Admiral Sims awaits the arrival of President Wilson at Brest, December 1918.
Photo courtesy of William S. Sims II and the London News Agency, Limited.

Di Revel remained immovable. As his battleships did not venture from the Taranto shelter even for navigation or gunnery exercises, he had small expectations that if he let them engage Emperor Charles's fleet, they would perform any better than in the disaster-filled past.[29] At the January conference di Revel had pleaded that the loss of any additional ships might get him lynched by irate compatriots; now, he repeated that he dared not chance the loss of "even a single destroyer." Italy's morale was too shaky. An attack on a weakly defended point on the Austrian coast was proposed. Although Sims increasingly pressed for this, the Italians vetoed it as too risky to themselves.

As a result of this conference, Sims pressed Benson on the need to achieve unity of command and effort among the Allies and Americans everywhere that the war was being waged. All endeavors "against the enemy, both military and what might be called a 'shipping campaign' are really dependent upon America's support, and. . . a closer coordination of effort . . . . " Thus he implied the need for a declaration of war against Austria, and a unified naval command in the Mediterranean. From February 1 through July 29, since the launching of the enemy's campaign of unrestricted U-boat warfare, 3,800,000 tons of ships had been sunk; 2,264,000 of British; 1,517,000 of Allied, neutral and American (in that order). Sims and the Entente had insufficient war craft to convoy ships in the Mediterranean or outbound from northern ports. Yet as the limited number they had were committed to convoying, they could not hunt submarines, nor could they launch an amphibious assault against the Austrian coast. [30]

Sims hoped that the strengthening of the powers of the "Allied War Councils" would bring pressure to bear on reluctant admirals such as di Revel and Benson. American participation and a broadening of American functions would tend to give the U.S. an independent moral persuasive force which could minimize the baneful influences of national interests and ambitions. A more efficient endeavor against the enemy should follow. He advised Benson that "the Allied War Councils . . . should be supplied immediately, and should be kept supplied with more definite information about America's plans and intentions." This could not effectively be done "by long distance communication . . . [but] only by sending responsible representatives to Europe . . . [to] join in the coordination of all branches of war activity." [31]

By the time of the next Mediterranean Conference, Sims felt that his influence had suffered a partial eclipse among the Allies. Washington's reluctance to do more to help with naval and merchant shipping burdens and other differences accounted for this. Reporting on this London conference of September 4 and 5, 1917, he told Benson that "few things are discussed freely with me." With America's neutral position towards Austria, Bulgaria, and Turkey in mind, Sims himself urged that the United States send more anti-U-boat vessels to northern waters so that Jellicoe could send additional British craft to the Mediterranean "for trade protection." [32]

Sims surmised that, while the Italians were determined not to attack anywhere on Austria's coast for fear of humiliating results, they were equally resolved that no Allied-American expedition should venture there, lest Rome lose her claim to control of the future of Dalmatia and more. Sims supported the British effort at this September gathering to acquire effective direction of the protection of traffic in the Mediterranean. Nominally, their Admiral at Malta (Sir Somerset Arthur Gough-Calthorpe) had got this power in July; he was supposed to coordinate his activities with the titular Allied commander in this sea, the French admiral at Corfu. But the Italians ignored the Frenchman, and the British forces at Gibraltar were officially out of his control. The French destroyers at Corfu were but "nominally" available to Calthorpe. [33]

In November 1917, American Naval Intelligence found that the total of Allied, neutral, and American U-boat losses exceeded world construction by 50 percent. [34] The proportion of cargo space being sunk in the Mediterranean was now larger than before the northern routes got partially effective convoy protection. Even if this screen could be extended to southern waters, the Germans had won a small victory by forcing their enemies to adopt the convoy system. Available cargo space was reduced by delays in assembling for sailing, in keeping to the speed of the slowest ships, in zig-zagging to confuse the U-boats, and in the impossibility of unloading as rapidly as before, now that so many vessels arrived in port at once. The system's overriding merit was that the ships arrived. The Entente's and Sims's need for more anti-submarine craft, however, would continue to prevent achievement of minimum possible losses through the end of the war. Some ships left their convoy for ports while the majority of the caravan continued under escort to a more common destination, and U-boat torpedoes often struck them down. Neither were there spare escorts to save ships which fell behind their train before they reached haven. [35]

In the fall of 1917, the British advised the Italians to ask Washington's help with coal and food, and ships to deliver them. By the eve of Caporetto, however, London had abandoned hope that the Americans could aid Italy. France was nearly as badly off. There was ample coal in Britain, if only it could be carried to them. Including the 720,000 tons of German shipping seized by the United States, that country had some 4,000,000 tons of shipping. But no American ships appeared at Cardiff for loading coal. If more ships did not reach the Italians and French soon, they might well be forced to capitulate, as the Russians also appeared likely to do the same. Then, "our Allies go out of the war and America never comes into it," Sir Joseph Maclay starkly summed up for the War Cabinet. Colonel House expressed similar misgivings to Wilson. Balfour cautioned his Cabinet colleagues that "the Italian Government have been justly frightened by the food riots . . . [which they] suppressed only after great loss of life." This meant that British ships could not be spared for Pershing's army and "the Americans must give us assistance in wheat in addition to bringing over their own troops." But Maclay reported that America's cargo ships were too devoted to more profitable and safer commerce with Latin America to render aid to Italy. [36]

As fear of revolution and dictatorship spread from Petrograd to Rome and Paris in late 1917, the British cabinet hoped that the United States would use part of the 430,000 tons of idle Dutch ships it was about to requisition in American ports to carry coal to Italy. But by March 1918, the British had abandoned hope that the Americans would use their seized Dutch ships to help Italy. Moreover, the French had not carried out their part of the bargain to send a substantial fraction of their somewhat increased domestic yield of coal to the Italians; nor had they allowed the British to use French rails to send them more from Welsh collieries. Instead of sending France their own railroad cars to carry their own troops and supplies to the front from port, the Americans were tying up British and French cars which could be taking coal to Turin. Instead of keeping their agreement to use six designated American ships for troop transport, they were using them in profitable trade "while we carried their troops in our steamers." The British cabinet concluded that the Americans had provided "very little assistance in the solution of our problems." [37]

The strain added by Pershing's army had further forced the reduction of British imports; more industries were closing down. Exports were falling; so were the incomes from them. Food rations were being cut still farther. British farm machinery lay idle for want of fuel, excaberating the food shortage. However, the War Cabinet ordered British coastal vessels, which carried coal to heat and light the Kingdom's cities, to carry coal to Genoa. Nevertheless, hunger and frost stalked the homes of Italy and France. [38]

In the summer of 1917, Count Luigi Cadorna, commander of Italy's army, assured his British and French partners that Italy would attack the Austrians before snows closed the Alps to an offensive. In September, however, he grew wary. His troops appeared to be demoralized by clerical and socialist denunciation of Italy's participation in the war. U-boat-inflicted sufferings were aggravating war weariness. Rebellious workers had been conscripted and sent to fill his ranks in the Caporetto area. Cadorna informed his Allies that he would await and repulse an expected *modest* Austrian offensive, then counter-attack. Disgusted, Lloyd George and the new French Premier, Paul Painlevé, ordered the artillery they had loaned him for his vaunted offensive back to the Western Front. [39]

With little inkling of the Austrian power massed against him, mostly during the night, Cadorna was unprepared for the overwhelming artillery and gas bombardment which launched the enemy avalanche through the Alps on October 24. While fourteen Austrian divisions feinted an attack in the Trentino, thirty-one Austrian and six German divisions struck from the Carnic and Julian Alps. Their goal was limited: to drive the Italians back to half-way between the starting line and the Piave. These divisions (with superior artillery), however, hurled the forty-seven Italian divisions of the 2nd and 3rd Armies all the way back to the Piave. By November 12, not counting the dead and wounded, Cadorna had lost 275,000 men as prisoners; 400,000 to flight; and vast quantities of artillery, ammunition and food abandoned to the invaders. The general now counseled the new Prime Minister, Vittorio Orlando, whom the catastrophe had brought to power, that "we are faced with an incurable moral crisis." The decision to ask the enemy for terms was not his, but Orlando's, he concluded. [40]

Orlando and the retained Foreign Minister, Sonnino, however, decided that "Italy would starve or freeze" if they surrendered: the blockaded Central Powers were too needful of food and coal for themselves. [41] Cadorna was dismissed. His successor, General Alfredo Diaz, resolved to hold the south bank of the Piave. Although the Austrians were now entrenched only sixteen miles from Venice, heavy snows clogged their supply routes through the Alps. These fresh exertions, their frightful losses to the Russians, and their privations from the Allied blockade left the Austrians almost as exhausted as the Italians. Besides, Diaz's men stiffened their resolve at the news that twelve British and French divisions were arriving to help them stave off collapse. The Italians held onto the Piave, but their potential for offensive action against serious resistance had been extinguished.[42]

Soon Rome breathed somewhat easier, and London and Paris more fearfully; four of the six German divisions in Italy entrained for France to join the 39 divisions that Hindenburg and Ludendorff were moving from defeated Russia to add to the array they were massing against Field Marshal Douglas Haig. Lenin's departure from the war made Lloyd George and the new French Premier whom this and Caporetto helped raise to power, Georges Clemenceau, anxious to keep Italy at least nominally in the struggle. Even passive roles by Diaz's and di Revel's forces were deemed vital to averting a fatal shift of power to the Central Powers. London and Paris also sought to keep a Rumanian force in the field. Rumania's army helped Vienna with an excuse to Berlin for leaving the nearly 1,000,000 troops it had in Russia and Rumania there, instead of shifting them to the Western Front. Similarly, the slightly more than 1,000,000 Austrian troops on the Italian Front must be kept tied down there.[43]

The Rumanian Government, however, had lost faith in the Allies' power to win the war and to reward it at the peace table. It appealed to Wilson. If the President would underwrite the awards by which the Entente had induced Bucharest to join them in 1916, King Ferdinand would try to make his way into the Ukraine with the tattered remnant of his Army. But instead of promising that Transylvania, Bukovina, and the Banat would be transferred from Emperor Charles's crowns to Ferdinand's, Wilson merely promised his "hearty cooperation" in enhancing the "fraternal good will" between the American and Rumanian peoples. He did say that at the peace conference he would do what he could to see that Rumania continued to exist "as a free and independent nation." The British concluded that the President's attitude, in January 1918, had precipitated demands from Rumanian leaders for surrender to Vienna and Berlin.[44]

During Caporetto, Sims first advised the Navy Department that Italy needed more naval assistance and that America's neutrality with Austria meant that it should "be based on a British force [such as the one at Gibraltar] so that the latter may, when we relieve some of their vessels, render further assistance to the Italians." As the magnitude of the disaster grew, however, he advised that a declaration of war against the Dual Monarchy was desirable "so that we will have greater liberty of action" as American warcraft operating out of Gibraltar "may contact Austrian submarines any time." Sims reported that Benson, then in London, was alarmed at the worsening position of the Allies.[45]

Stronger urgings for a declaration against Austria gushed from Thomas Nelson Page's pen in Rome. The Allies' continuation of the war might be at stake. The reliable Swedish envoy to Italy (Baron de Bildt) informed him in November that Berlin was prepared to offer peace terms which included face-saving sops to Italy, France, and Britain. Only America had the power to tip the balance against a Latin decision to accept fractions of the Trentino and Alsace-Lorraine and a British one to be satisified with Mesopotamia and Palestine in return for an implied free German-Maygar hand in East and Central Europe, including Russia. Such a peace "would be equivalent to recognizing the Central Empires as wholly victorious," Page warned. Italians were bitter that the United States was not even formally at war against Austria; their poor morale and the future of Italo-American commercial relations would be enhanced by a declaration against Charles.⁴⁶

The day following Page's alarming cable, Lansing advised the President that he could find no excuse for a declaration of war "on Austria as far as hostile acts are concerned." Wilson had to make do with his indictment of Austria as a vassal of Germany. Turning the tables on Wilson, Lloyd George's most powerful Cabinet colleague and confidant, Alfred, Viscount Milner, now confided to House that London had erred in being so obdurate toward Germany's offers to negotiate peace. America should "keep her ears open and listen to every peace whisper and of course let all the Entente countries consider any offer," he urged.⁴⁷ Perhaps he sent this message primarily to frighten the President out of his 'one-third speed ahead' war policy, although his note should be read in the context of the serious misgivings entertained at this time by Lloyd George about the advisability of continuing the fighting. To let the Allies make peace under these circumstances would not only exclude the President from a dominant role at the peace conference; it would also leave Germany in so strong a position as perhaps successfully to reverse the trend toward America's rise to eminence in international commercial and investment markets. And, quite possibly, Germany would work in partnership with Japan.

Presumably the Sultan of Turkey, Mohammed V, remained free (in contrast to Charles) of the taint of German domination. Wilson made no allusion to Turkey in the December 4, 1917, speech to Congress against Austria. Even in the stark days for the Allies of the following April, when Sims and the Inter-Allied Naval Council recommended an American declaration of war against Turkey and an ultimatum of one to Bulgaria if she did not make peace with the Entente, Wilson refused to make so much as a verbal attack on Constantinople or Sofia. ⁴⁸ Certainly he was not going to do anything which would enhance the British or French position against the Sultan in his oil-rich provinces.

Although apprehensive that American and British war supplies would not be sufficient to keep Italy afloat, Sonnino told a secret session of the Chamber of Deputies that it was "necessary to recede from certain [territorial] claims." He and Orlando were outraged at the President's war message on Austria to Congress: the war was to result in "no annexations, no contributions, and no punitive indemnities" for anyone. At the Inter-Allied Naval Conference of February 1918 in Rome, Sims was probably not much surprised to find that the French had become as intransigent as the Italians against his proposals. Both Wilson's Austrian war message and his Fourteen Points Address of January 8, 1918, avoided even a firm commitment to the transfer of Alsace-Lorraine and *Italia irredenta*. Lloyd George's attempt to wrest the initiative from Wilson by delivering a war aims speech just before his own angered the President. The British aims were also ennobled by altruistic principles. They embodied, however, no reference to "freedom of the seas" and they were only somewhat more generous of phrase towards the Mediterranean Allies. Hence Sims, by now convinced that he and the British must stand united in persuading di Revel and De Bon to accept their policies, got nowhere. Wilson served notice that he would rally the common peoples of Europe against their leaders if their governments sought to achieve their expansionist aims. [49]

From the time of Ray Stannard Baker, accounts of Wilson's motives in proclaiming his Fourteen Points have stressed the President's concern over the damage to the struggle against Germany wrought by the Bolsheviks' publication of the Treaty of London and other greedy Allied pacts. Doubtless, however, he was also worried that Bolshevik indictments of his own war aims were undermining his support among the peoples of Europe. In November-December 1917, Trotsky and *Izvestia* charged that Wilson had entered the conflict to continue the policy by which Americans had "made money from the blood of the peoples of unfortunate Europe" and because "America could not permit the victory of either" the Allies or the Central Powers. In fact, "America is interested in weakening both coalitions and strengthening the hegemony of American capital," Trotsky asserted. The President's expression of friendship for the Russian people was but a tool in his endeavor to insert American capital into Russia at the expense of German and British capital. Washington was "sufficiently satisfied by the exhaustion of the Allied countries and of Germany." [50]

Wilson studiously divided his fourteen planks into two groups: those mandatory and those desirable. Germany was assured of the "absolutely impartial adjustment of all colonial claims," but she "must" evacuate Russia and Belgium. Freedom of the seas in peace and war, open covenants openly arrived at, and the formation of a League of Nations were also mandatory. But his imperatives gave way to negotiable "shoulds" as to the evacuation of France, the "readjustment" of Italy's frontiers "along clearly recognizable lines of nationality" (which would cost her most of Istria and Trieste, the German speaking Tyrol, and all of Dalmatia, in addition to her claims in the Levant), and the evacuation of Serbia, Rumania, and Montenegro. Even his "should" on Alsace-Lorraine was worded so that the door was left open for a plebiscite which would confirm or rescind its 1871 transfer to Germany, and the Inquiry (the American experts on the economic and political aspects of the peace settlement organized under Colonel House, with Wilson's approval) had concluded that the Germans would win an overall vote or, if balloting were by subdivisions, the best parts. As for the Ottoman Empire, its non-Turkish nationalities "should be assured . . . an . . . opportunity of autonomous development," but Wilson did not say under whose supervision. He did state that the United States harbored "no jealousy of German greatness and there is nothing in this program which impairs it." Neither was he going to be a party to any "hostile agreements of trade" against her. These passages implied his and Benson's aim during the Armistice negotiations to maintain Scheer's fleet as a potent, independent force to help offset the effects of British sea power and to reopen trade between America and Germany.

Orlando rushed to London to demand Lloyd George's assurance that neither Wilson's nor his own speech had shattered the writ of the Treaty of London. Lloyd George retorted that "England is not in the habit of repudiating her engagements." But the Italian press clamored to know why the American President exempted Austria from his rubric on the self-determination of peoples while he "rigidly" applied it to Italy. It also waged "a campaign to impress the Yugoslavs to having Italy take the lead . . . and primacy among the peoples of Southeastern Europe."[51]

Sims found, in February, the Italians were as intransigent as ever. Sonnino explained their obstinacy to the Allied Supreme War Council on February 1. His partners could hardly expect di Revel "to venture into the Adriatic" with his fleet where (the Foreign Minister asserted) Austria held the advantage, when "Italy came into this war with this object" of achieving definite security in the future through the cession of Trieste and Dalmatia. "The last speeches of Mr. Lloyd George, President Wilson, and M. Pichon [Clemenceau's Foreign Minister] . . . rather left . . . [Italy's war aims] out in the cold."[52]

Even the anti-Government, anti-war newspaper *Stampa* indicted Wilson for his supposed violations of his own freedom of the seas doctrine and called for an international solution to the "question" of the Panama Canal. On the other hand, the stands of London, Washington, and Paris against Italy's aspirations, along with the moral malaise, the U-boat-inflicted sufferings, and Caporetto, were aiding the rise of Benito Mussolini's new "pro-war 'fascio' " movement. By April 1918, Ambassador Page was counseling Wilson that even Italy was moving toward joint sponsorship with Britain and France of the independence of all Slavs, Rumanians, and Italians under Charles's crowns.[53]

By June it was obvious that, if the President did not soon announce his own patronage of these independence movements, the Allies would be able to depict him as a moral laggard. Lansing and House persuaded him to change his position through a unilateral declaration. It would cost him little; "Austria is already at the breaking point," House assured him. Indeed, Vienna's 1918 offensive to knock Italy out of the war had been stopped by the flooded Piave. Wilson's belated declaration was designed to leave him free of "the jealousies and differences" among the Allies in pursuing American interests in the Balkan settlement.[54]

Fortunately for the Allies, Caporetto, Lenin's defection, and Germany's improved prospects frightened them into agreeing to the formation of their Supreme War Council. As David F. Trask states, "the Supreme War Council was pre-eminently a political organization designed to concert inter-Allied strategy. Since it brought together the most important political and military leaders of the Allied and Associated Powers, it provided an unusual opportunity to resolve issues which required joint consultation." The Prime Ministers of the three principal Allies usually represented their governments. In theory, the military representatives of each of the Allies were disinterestedly to advise all of the political heads; in practice, they spoke for their own national interests. Although the Council's existence did something to limit rivalry and cross purposes, "its principal function . . . was to prepare joint recommendations on grand strategy, which were referred to the various governments for their acceptance, rejection, or modification." General Tasker Bliss, the American military delegate, joined with his Allied counterparts in informal discussions on planning and strategy. They then presented any recommendations agreed upon to the several Prime Ministers.[55] Wilson, however, usually refused even to send his deputy, House; he feared that House would become a prisoner to unacceptable Entente political, military, naval, or economic goals. Indeed, he publicly rebuked House for implying at the Supreme War Council's inception that America's participation in its military and naval councils carried with it an American sanction of the Allies' political war aims. Bliss himself was careful to defer "punctiliously to both General Pershing and the War Department," rather than act as an impartial expert.[56]

As Benson's man in Europe, Sims joined the other Chiefs of Naval Operations as a member of that Council. The inter-Allied Naval Council was being formed while Benson and House were making their November-December 1917 visits to London and Paris. Its functions paralleled the Military Council's. Just as in practice Pershing, with Wilson's support, ignored first the Supreme War Council's and then Generalissimo Foch's desires when he chose, so Benson did the Naval Council's. Indeed, he and his British, French, and Italian opposite numbers framed the wording of the Naval Council's responsibilities and authority so as to leave themselves free to do so. On December 3, Benson cabled Daniels the functions and scope of the embryonic Naval Council. It was to recommend "the best division of forces employed" to the several heads of governments. "The object of the Council [was] to watch over [the] general conduct of naval warfare and coordination of action at sea." It was to submit any recommendations it might have upon these "for the decision of the governments."[57]

In practice, the rival Allied and American Mediterranean naval policies remained uncoordinated and largely unaffected by the creation of this inter-Allied body. In northern waters, the British Admiralty, with Sims's full cooperation, continued to direct the naval efforts as if the Allied Naval Council did not exist. And Sims complained both to Benson and to his European counterparts that joint discussions between the navy, military, maritime transport, and political councils were required to determine the feasibility of such proposals as his own for an amphibious assault on the Austrian coast and the Anglo-French one for an expedition to Archangel. In fact, of the few joint army-navy meetings held, nothing significant was accomplished except, in October 1918, the Armistice terms.[58]

The Allied Naval Council recommended that a newly-arrived

number of American wooden sub-chasers be assigned the task of "hunting submarines in the Mediterranean." Instead, Benson ordered that they convoy merchant ships. Sims protested that, when possible, Benson should follow the Council's recommendation; in this instance experience had demonstrated that too often these vessels found even the Mediterranean too rough to keep track of the merchant ships they were supposed to be protecting. Benson replied that Sims could assign most vessels where he wished.[59]

In mid-February 1918, Sims summarized for Benson the inter-Allied Naval Conference (on February 12) held in Rome. As yet no American vessels were protecting the Otranto barrage; the French now joined the Italians in openly refusing to assist in this mission. "Winter in the Adriatic" would be too severe for their vessels and crews. Sims's admission that he hoped a strengthening of the Otranto barrage would bring about a battle with the Austrian fleet only served to harden the Latins' resolve to resist his proddings.[60]

Sims waxed eloquent about the advantages of making an amphibious attack on some of Austria's less strongly defended off-shore islands. He volunteered that he would induce his Navy Department to contribute battleships. Di Revel remained unimpressed. Since August 1916, when di Revel had decided to avoid another naval fight with Austrian ships, he had been forced to risk his warships to assist the Army. The results did not justify Sims's optimism. Between September 1916, and December 1917, the Italian ratio of losses to Austrians' had improved only to the point that 25,531 tons of di Revel's warcraft had gone to the bottom in exchange for 7,373 tons of the enemy's.[61]

Doubtless di Revel knew what the American ambassador and Sims himself were reporting to Washington about the state of affairs in Italy. Page assured the President that the internal forces working to demoralize Italy out of the war, which had done so much to cause the nation's losses at Caporetto, were as virulent as ever. "The disentegration of the 2nd Army was caused by Papal and Leninist socialist propaganda to refuse to fight," he informed Wilson. Since then, only the pacifist section of the socialist press had approved the President's Fourteen Points speech (the clerical press avowed that the Pope's peace proposals were better). The majority of Italian periodicals were demanding the full realization of Italy's territorial aims which, they said, "your expression eliminates." Page cautioned that "some of those [Italians] in control are against us." Most Italians were so dispirited from the results of the fighting and the continuing coal and food shortages, they believed that a fresh enemy drive from the north would bring on the final "collapse of everything." Page reluctantly admitted that some in the government in Rome believed that Italy's true interests lie rather with the forces of . . . order, as represented by the Central Empires . . . . this element certainly has no sympathy with America." There was an "all-pervasive" assertion that the Americans "are exploiting the situation for our own purposes." The Italians held that the Americans were "really only doing enough to establish themselves as a great creditor nation with a view solely to our commercial advantage hereafter. . . ."[62]

Sims knew all this. He assured di Revel that he sympathized with his view that some of his destroyers would have to remain at Venice and Brindisi to discourage Austrian raids on east coast cities. But he refused to accept di Revel's assertion that morale was so terrible that Austrian retaliation against the east coast for an assault on an inadequately defended part of the enemy's coast would result in revolution. In other words, he believed that di Revel was exploiting the morale problem to gain leverage against American and British naval strategy. Sims informed Benson that the February 1918 naval conference demonstrated that the Italians were resisting any aggressive naval action primarily because they distrusted Wilson, Lloyd George, and Clemenceau. The "springs of opposition are fed by concern for the condition of affairs when this war is over." The Rome government not only feared that the President would make "a compromise peace" when it suited his interests to do so, it dreaded that "United States' assistance would lead to 'meddling' in European politics." The Italians were jealous and suspicious of French intentions. The result of all this was that no expedition was to be allowed against Austria until the Italians "are sure that they can do it alone and be a success."[63]

In March, Sims appealed to First Sea Lord Admiral Sir Rossyln Wemyss for more backing at the impending inter-Allied Naval Council meeting. The First Sea Lord gave it, but the French paid only lip-service to Sims's renewed proddings. Clemenceau awaited the day on which a French-dominated landing could be attempted. Whitehall thought that the Italians had been so sobered by Caporetto that Rome would release its anti-U-boat craft into the control of a British admiral who would then supervise the protection of Italian shipping. Rome's admirals, however, insisted that a devastating American naval attack was imminent; the British must rush some of *their* warships to Venice and Brindisi to help fend it off; the main railway to the front was in danger of being cut. Eventually, the British did manage to pry a few Italian cruisers and smaller craft out of the fleet's shelter in Taranto Bay for merchant ship convoy duty. In April-September 1918, however, an Allied (mainly Anglo-American) barrage of surface craft and mines was laid down across the Otranto Strait. This virtually halted Austrian submarine operations in the Mediterranean and slowed German operations there during the last weeks of the war.[64]

In the spring of 1918, the London Admiralty and Sims resolved to try to reduce the high merchant ship losses in the Mediterranean, as well as to bring about more effective overall action against the enemy by creating what they dubbed an admiralissimo. He would exercise control over all Allied and American naval forces in that Sea. In April, Sims sought to persuade the several admiralties to agree that Jellicoe should be made admiral-in-chief in the Mediterranean. He reported that the Italians were so antagonistic towards the French that they would welcome the supercession of the nominal French commander by an English admiralissimo. In mid-May, the resentful French gave him the misleading impression that they would agree to the creation of a unified command under Jellicoe. Di Revel told an inter-Allied Naval conference that he would move his Fleet from Taranto to Corfu to join the French warships there as part of the new unified endeavor. This would create a Latin Grand Fleet to give battle if the Austrian fleet came out; it would also release some British and French warcraft so that they could move east to guard against the possibility that the Germans would man and use ships of the Russian Black Sea Fleet.[65] Since Lenin's formal surrender at Brest-Litovsk on March 8, these vessels were theoretically available to the enemy — provided that crews could be found to man them.

In late May, however, Sims found that the whole program of unification was headed for fatal shoals. Clemenceau, never anxious to implement this admiral-in-chief project, seized upon Rome's new attitude to justify his outright rejection of the entire arrangement. The French Tiger angrily informed Lloyd George that Orlando was entirely to blame for the Entente's failure to find the means of interdicting the potential egress of "the Russian Fleet in the Black Sea," as well as for forcing France to decline to give the "powers to the admiralissimo as had been done in General Foch's case." Clemenceau could no longer consent to an English admiral-in-chief because "Admiral Thaon di Revel's dreadnoughts are quietly at anchor at Taranto where they never come out . . . for . . . battle exercises, still less for maneuvres, which is sufficiently explained by the Admiral being assured that he will not be attacked." Moreover, the creation of the unified command was contingent upon moving the Italian fleet to Corfu. Clemenceau was not going to countenance di Revel's scheme of including five Italian dreadnoughts in this move, when only four of the eight French battleships at Corfu were dreadnoughts. This was an Italian trick to justify naming one of di Revel's admirals as commander of the Latin Grand Fleet by virtue "of a preponderance of first-line battleships." He demanded of Orlando that only four Italian dreadnoughts be sent; Orlando responded with a refusal to send any. Clemenceau then warned that he would stop the use of French rails for transporting coal to Italy; he requested that Lloyd George threaten to refuse to send any more by sea until the Rome government ceased "systematically" trying to wriggle "out of all its obligations" to the other Allies. Lloyd George, however, declined to use strong measures against Orlando.[66]

Sims's endeavors to save this project got little support from Washington. Its only chance of success lay in Anglo-American solidarity and some American pressure on the Italians and French. Yet Daniels and Benson refused to back up Franklin D. Roosevelt's attempt in July to press Rome to accept Jellicoe; indeed, Daniels ordered the Assistant Secretary of the Navy, who had gone to Rome after visiting Sims and the London Admiralty, to backtrack. The Italians and the French were then informed that the United States was not supporting Jellicoe's candidacy or anyone else's. Because Sims in June had pointed out to Benson that the Italians were making the inter-Allied Naval Conference "a farce" and that neither the French nor the Italians would ever accept an admiralissimo of rival Latin nationality, obviously Washington preferred that no admiral-in-chief be created — unless and until the

Allies would accept an American officer for the position. If the war continued into 1919 or 1920, it seemed possible that the Allies would accept an American admiralissimo. In the summer of 1918, nearly all Allied and American leaders thought that the war probably would continue for a few more years. At Pershing's headquarters, it was anticipated that, by the summer of 1919, he would replace Foch as generalissimo. Sims may have unintentionally encouraged the Navy Department in a parallel expectation. In July 1918 he asked Benson to appoint a flag officer in the Mediterranean for his modestly growing force, even though as yet it was but 5 percent of the total arrayed against the enemy there.[67]

Meanwhile, no British admiral was to be trusted with the overall command. On the eve of Caporetto, Colonel House had advised Wilson that "the English naturally want the road to Egypt and India blocked and Lloyd George is not above using us to further his plans." Above all, the fate of the oil-rich lands of the eastern Mediterranean might be adversely affected by a strategy devised under a British admiral-in-chief. Wilson was irritated by Roosevelt's assumption "to speak for the Government"; Ambassador Jusserand was reassured that he had had no authority to do so.[68] Thus, the program for the unification of command and endeavor was dashed onto the rocks of the four Mediterranean "partners'" rival ambitions and mutual distrust.

The war in the Mediterranean area demostrated that the naval and military power and the morale of belligerents lacking coal and iron deposits (such as Italy and Turkey) were the most susceptible to debilitation from surface or underwater interdiction of their imports. The suspicions of Rome and Paris that neither Lloyd George nor Wilson intended to allow the course of the fighting to help them acquire the Levantine lands promised them by the Treaty of London were added to fears of disastrous results of naval losses upon morale. The two English-speaking leaders were even tepid in their support for the restoration of Alsace-Lorraine and *Italian irredenta*. As a result of these four-power antagonisms, the submarine losses in the Mediterranean remained unnessarily high. The total effect of shipping losses led Sims to advise Benson as late as October 1918, that the Italians were justly afraid to launch an attack on their northern front; the lack of cargo space meant that they could not sustain an attack if the Austrians offered serious resistance.[69]

Notes on Chapter 4

[1] Victor S. Mamatey, *The United States and East Central Europe* (Princeton, 1957), 23-24.

[2] Albert Pingaud, *Histoire diplomatique de la France pendant la Grande Guerre* (Paris, 1938-40), I, 50; A.J.P. Taylor, *The Struggle for the Mastery in Europe, 1848-1918* (Oxford, 1954, reprinted 1957, 1965), 522; Ronald Seth, *Caporetto, the Scapegoat Battle* (London, 1965), 25-27; Girard Lindsey McEntee, *Italy's Part in Winning the World War* (Princeton, 1934), 2-3.

[3] McEntee, *Italy's Part*, 4; Barbara Tuchman, *The Guns of August* (New York, 1962), 297-99, 304.

[4] Seth, *Caporetto*, 37-39; Sims to Benson, Feb. 15, 1918, Sims Papers.

[5] Text of Treaty of London sent by Balfour to Wilson, May 18, 1917, Wilson Papers.

[6] *Ibid.*, Taylor, *Struggle for Mastery*, 544, 545; Mamatey, *East Central Europe*, 25.

[7] Milner to Lloyd George, Nov. 3, 1917, about France's Balkan "policy of indefinite grab" and her "schemes of future exploitation" of the area, Lloyd George Papers, F/38/2/20.

[8] Taylor, *Struggle for Mastery*, 547-48; Mametey, *East Central Europe*, 24.

[9] Seth, *Caporetto*, 39 including note; the Russo-Italian army and the Anglo-French-Italian naval pacts are summarized in Pingaud, *Histoire diplomatique*, I, 298: the naval terms called for the deployment of the main Italian and French naval forces in the Adriatic, an Italian to command the active, a Frenchman the reserve fleet positioned against the Austrians. In a general way, this was done. See also Paul C. Haplern, "The Anglo-French-Italian Naval Convention of 1915," *The Historical Journal* (Cambridge, England), 13, No. 1 (1970).

[10] Seth, *Caporetto*, Chaps. 4-6; McEntee, *Italy's Part*, 25-61.

[11] McEntee, *Italy's Part*, 85-87.

[12] "Minutes of Conference" of Allied admiralty representatives of Jan. 24-27, 1917, CAB/21/9, P.R.O.

[13] Delme-Radcliffe to Lloyd George, Dec. 15 and 25, 1917, Lloyd George Papers, F/56.

[14] Quoted in Mamatey, *East Central Europe*, 188.

[15] Sims to Benson, Feb. 15, 1918, Sims Papers.

[16] Mamatey, *East Central Europe*, 45-47, 59; U. S. ambassador at Vienna (Penfield) to Lansing, Jan. 25 and 27, Feb. 5 and 6, 1917, *Foreign Relations, 1917*, Supp. 1, 31, 34, 39; W. H. Page to Wilson, Feb. 20, 1917, *ibid.*, 56.

[17] Lansing to W. H. Page, Feb. 8, 1917, Page to Lansing, Feb. 11, 1917, Penfield to Lansing, Feb. 27 and Mar. 13, 1917, *ibid.*, 40-41, 62-63, 55-56.

[18] *War Memoirs of Robert Lansing, Secretary of State* (Indianapolis, 1925), 247-54; Mamatey, *East Central Europe*, 91.

[19] W. H. Page to Lansing, Feb. 20, 1917, *Foreign Relations, 1917*, Supp. 1, 56-57; *War Memoirs of David Lloyd George* (Boston, 1933-37), IV, 239-40.

[20] Taylor, *Struggle for Mastery*, 561 note.

[21] *Ibid.*

[22] Br. naval Commander-in-Chief East Indies and Egypt, Vice Admiral ? (signature undecipherable) to Jellicoe, Feb. 7, 1917, Jellicoe Papers, 49036; Lloyd George held that the only hope of preventing Russia's collapse and the sending of wheat and minerals from her to the Central Powers as well as German men and guns from the Eastern to the Western Front was to induce Austria to leave the war. War Cabinet minutes for Apr. 23, May 22, 24, and 29, June 14, 1917, CAB/23/2 and 3.

[23] Br. War Cabinet minutes for Apr. 10, June 6 and 14, 1917, CAB/23/2 and 3; Sir Rennell Rodd (Br. ambassador at Rome) to Balfour, May 26, 1917, Lloyd George Papers, F/56/1/38.

[24] Sims to Palmer, May 30, 1917, Sims Papers; Sims to Benson, July 30, 1917; *ibid.*; Balfour to Bonar Law, June 10, 1916, Balfour Papers, 49693; War Cabinet Minutes for Oct. 16, 1917, CAB 23/4.
[25] "Minutes of Conference" of Jan. 24-27, 1917, CAB/21/9. P.R.O.
[26] Sims to Benson, July 30, 1917, Sims Papers; Sims, with Burton J. Hendrick, *The Victory at Sea* (Garden City, 1920), 214.
[27] Sims to Benson, July 30, 1917, Sims Papers.
[28] *Ibid.*
[29] *Ibid.*; on June 13, 1918, First Sea Lord Sir Eric Geddes wrote Rodd that "di Revel declared ... that for eighteen months his battleships had never been out to sea, and that he therefore had them perfectly safe .... " FO/800/329, P.R.O.
[30] Sims to Benson, July 30, 1917, Sims Papers.
[31] *Ibid.*
[32] Sims to Benson, Sept. 11, 1917, Sims Papers.
[33] Sims to Benson, Feb. 15, 1918, *ibid.*; "Report of Naval Conference of the Powers United Against Germany, Sept. 4 and 5, 1917, Jellicoe Papers, 49034; Br. War Cabinet minutes for Sept. 21, Oct. 2 and 4, 1917, CAB/23/4.
[34] Capt. D. M. Knox to Sims, Nov. 6, 1917, Sims Papers.
[35] Sims weekly reports to Department of Navy, Aug. 24, Sept. 19, 1917, Jan. 8, Apr. 23, and Aug. 24, 1918, Sims Papers.
[36] Sir Leo Chiozzo Money (Government Shipping Controller) to War Cabinet, June 13, 1917, CAB/21/35, P.R.O.; War Cabinet minutes for Sept. 2 and 4, Oct. 19, 25 and 31, 1917, CAB/23/4; Balfour to War Cabinet, Oct. 27, 1917 (GT2412), Balfour Papers, 49499; House to Wilson, Aug. 15, 1917, Wilson Papers: the diversion of ships supplying the Allies to carrying Pershing's troops and supplies might well force France and Italy out of the war; an early negotiated peace would avert the gargantuan American expenditures of money and other resources which a graver weakening of the Entente would impose on the U.S. On Dec. 24, 1917, McAdoo warned Wilson that Italy was so short of food and coal that she was "threatened with famine and revolution." Wilson Papers. His solution was not to divert American ships, but to establish "an inter-Ally shipping board and bring the Italian plight before the British and French" (who were painfully aware of it).
[37] War Cabinet minutes for Nov. 14, Dec. 27, 1917, Jan. 16, Feb. 27, Mar. 19, 1918, CAB/23/4 and 5.
[38] Br. War Cabinet minutes for Dec. 27, 1917, Feb. 27, Mar. 19, 1918, CAB/23/4 and 5.
[39] Sims to Pratt, Aug. 30, 1917, Sims Papers.
[40] Seth, *Caporetto*, 137-38; 176-78.
[41] Br. War Cabinet minutes for Nov. 2, 1917, CAB/23/4; T. N. Page to Wilson, July 16, 1918, Wilson Papers, with a similar judgment.
[42] McEntee, *Italy's Part*, 73-76.
[43] In formulating his Jan. 5 speech, Lloyd George sought to sooth Austria so that she would not send "300,000 troops to the Western Front" while endorsing "the legitimate claims of Italy, Serbia, and Rumania" to keep them in the war. He observed that Germany, "now in her hour of triumph ... would never concede all that we are bound to insist on." War Cabinet minutes for Jan. 3 and 14, 1918, CAB/23/5; troop dispositions as of Dec. 31, 1917, by Br. Committee on War Policy, CAB/27/14, P.R.O.
[44] U.S. Minister to Rumania (Vopicka) to Lansing, Nov. 17, 1917, Wilson Papers; Lansing to Vopicka, Nov. 26, 1917, *Foreign Relations, 1917*, Supp. 2, I, 135; Wilson to first Rumanian minister to U.S., Dr. Constantin Angelesco, Jan. 15, 1918, *PPWW*, V, 163-64; House to Wilson with Milner's message, Nov. 3, 1917, Wilson Papers; Drummond to J. T. Davies (Lloyd George's executive secretary), Jan. 23,

1918, Lloyd George Papers, F/3/3/1.

[45] Sims to Benson, Oct. 28, 1917, Sims Papers; Sims to Pratt, Nov. 6 and 16, 1917, *ibid.*

[46] T. N. Page to Wilson, Sept. 26 and Nov. 19, 1917, Wilson Papers.

[47] Lansing to Wilson, Nov. 3, 1917, Wilson Papers; House to Wilson, Nov. 20, 1917, *ibid.*

[48] *PPWW*, V, 128-39; Sims to Pratt, Apr. 29, 1918, Sims Papers; Gen. T. H. Bliss to N. D. Baker, Apr. 27, 1918, to Wilson May 8, Wilson Papers.

[49] *PPWW*, V, 155-62.

[50] Francis to Lansing, Dec. 1 and 22, 1917, National Archives mf. 333, roll 1, *Records of the Department of State Relating to Political Relations Between the United States and Russia and the Soviet Union, 1910-29* (hereafter USDSM 333).

[51] Sir (James) Rennell Rodd, *Social and Diplomatic Memories* (London, 1925), III, 351; Wiseman to Drummond, Jan. 23, 1918, Lloyd George Papers, F/60/2/42, reporting Wilson had asked him if Lloyd George would recede from his position. The President did not wish to do so as he disapproved of Italy's war aims and her effectiveness in the war, Wiseman added. Pershing to Chief of Staff (Peyton C. March), Jan. 19, 1918, Wilson Papers.

[52] Sims to Benson, Feb. 15, 1918, Sims Papers; "Procès-Verbal of the 3rd Meeting of the 3rd Session of the Supreme War Council at the Trianon," Feb. 1, 1918, CAB/25/120, P.R.O.

[53] Page letters cited in note 51 above and Page to Wilson, July 2, 1918, Wilson Papers: the Italians continued to be "very suspicious of some sort of combination against them" led by France and supported at least to some extent by the U.S.

[54] T.N. Page to Wilson, Apr. 18 and June 11, 1918, Wilson Papers; House to Wilson, June 23, 1918, *ibid.*; Lansing to Wilson, May 10 and 18, June 21 and 29, 1918, *ibid.*; Lansing, *War Memoirs*, 261-62.

[55] Trask, *The United States in the Supreme War Council, American War Aims and Inter-Allied Strategy, 1917-1918* (Middletown, Conn., 1961), 38.

[56] Charles Seymour, ed., *The Intimate Papers of Colonel House* (Boston and New York, 1926-28), III, 223; Trask, *Supreme War Council*, 39-42.

[57] Benson to Daniels, Dec. 3, 1917, Wilson Papers.

[58] Sims to Benson, Feb. 28, Mar. 7 and 25, 1918, Sims Papers; Trask, *Supreme War Council*, 41.

[59] Sims to Benson, Mar. 7 and May 18, 1918, Sims Papers; Benson to Sims, May 6, 1918, *ibid.*

[60] Sims to Benson, Feb. 15, 1918, Sims Papers; Sims to Bayly, Feb. 15, 1918, *ibid.*

[61] *Ibid.*, McEntee, *Italy's Part*, 88-89.

[62] Page to Wilson, Feb. 5 and 26, Apr. 30, 1918, Wilson Papers.

[63] Sims to Benson, Feb. 15, Mar. 20 and Apr. 30, 1918, Sims Papers.

[64] Sims to Wemyss, Mar. 10, 1918, Sims Papers; Sims to Benson Mar. 20, Apr. 2 and 30, and June 14, 1918, *ibid.*; War Cabinet minutes for Nov. 8, 9, and 12, 1917, and Mar. 19, 1918, CAB/23/4 and 6; Sims, *Victory at Sea*, 229-31; Arthur J. Marder, *From the Dreadnought to Scapa Flow* (London, 1970), V, 32-35.

[65] Sims to Pratt, Apr. 29, 1918, Sims Papers; Sims to Benson, May 17, 1918, *ibid.*

[66] Sims to Benson, May 17 and 19, June 14, 1918, Sims Papers; Geddes to Lloyd George on an interview with Clemenceau, May 17, 1918, Lloyd George Papers, F/18/1/19; Clemenceau to Lloyd George, May 20 and 23, 1918, *ibid.*, F/18/1/20 and 21.

[67] Sims to Benson, June 14 and July 28, 1918, Sims Papers.

[68] House to Wilson, Sept. 18, 1917, Wilson Papers; Frank Freidel, *Franklin D. Roosevelt* (Boston, 1952), I, 364.

[69] Sims to Benson. Oct. 11, 1918.

5

U. S. LIMITS AID DURING THE GREAT GERMAN OFFENSIVES

November 1917 - November 1918

I F THE FRENCH WERE not as badly demoralized as their Italian allies when Benson arrived at Sims's headquarters in November 1917, they nevertheless clung to their policy of not taking the offensive until the British or the Americans had made the sacrifices necessary to break the German Army's powers of resistance.[1] Unfortunately for the British Army, the Americans were equally resolved upon a course of passivity with respect to Haig's and Petain's divisions. Although in November Sims got the impression that Benson was about to rush him the anti-submarine vessels and staff for which he had long agitated, he was destined to receive only a limited increase of forces following the Operations Chief's return to Washington. Indeed, throughout the war to Armistice Day, the Navy Department held to the course it had announced on June 23, 1917. Its policy was similar to those adopted by the Departments of War and the Treasury, to which they adhered virtually to the war's end. This policy called for only the minimum of American aid necessary to prevent the Germans from imposing their peace terms, then a three-pronged struggle to make Wilson's voice paramount on land, on sea, and in the world's countinghouses. This course was pursued, despite fears that Scheer would launch an offensive in northern French waters in support of the Hindenburg-Ludendorff drives. Secretary of War Baker had justified this policy in July 1917, it will be recalled, shortly after Daniels's statement of similar naval intent. By delaying a serious combat role until Pershing decided that his large, independent army was ready for battle, the United States would be able to conduct "a war of our own" which would give it "complete diplomatic and military independence" for leverage over the peace terms.[2] For the duration of the first two great German offensives of

1918, Pershing prudently behaved as if he would delay his combat debut until a German sector appeared to be vulnerable to an attack.

Just as Benson arrived in London, the President's Food Administrator, Herbert Hoover, tried in vain to change Wilson's military policy. Hoover advocated sending over only limited numbers of specialized American troops, without divisional paraphernalia, and placing them at the disposal of the British and French armies. This program might have enabled the British and French to break down German driving power more quickly when Hindenburg and Ludendorff struck; it might have enabled them to bring the war to an earlier end through Allied counter-attack. Two days before the Communist Revolution in Russia, Hoover urged Wilson to send only specialist forces to serve as auxiliaries to those of Haig and Petain. The program of a great independent American army in France with cargo space for all its divisional paraphernalia posed too great a threat to "both the armies and the civilian population of the Allies." It threatened to cause lasting damage to the democratic life of Europe. It so endangered the Allies' prospects for repelling the impending German offensive that they might give way, and "our army may be engulfed in the social cataclysm of Europe with its retreat absolutely cut off."[3] Whether or not Wilson foresaw the advent of the post-war dictatorships of Europe, he refused to budge from his settled war policy.

The Treasury Department pursued a similar policy of doing only enough to keep the Allies' heads above water. On January 16, 1918, for instance, the London War Cabinet was still cutting its purchases in America to below what it had programmed as essential. McAdoo had forced these cuts by reducing the British allocation of funds for January from $275,000,000 to $180,000,000. He had added that only by placing control of the needs of "the three western Allies" under himself would February see an easing of credit. Lloyd George and his colleagues sullenly agreed that they would furnish McAdoo all the information he demanded. Then Washington would "learn how much, perhaps too much, we had done for France." Civilian food rations, as well as the armed forces', were further reduced. These were the results, however, more of losses to U-boats than of McAdoo's stringencies.[4]

As the seemingly endless trek of German divisions moved out of prostrate Russia (until Ludendorff had ninety-two facing Haig's fifty-seven), no responsible Allied leader doubted that the influence of German liberals and socialists on behalf of a compromise peace was at its nadir. On the eve of the first German onslaught of 1918, the State Department advised Wilson that not since 1914 had the German people been so solidly united behind William II and his military and naval leaders. The Supreme Command anticipated that its U-boats, through their cumulative ravages, would help the Army force the Western Allies to the peace table. As Sims had predicted to Benson in October, the U-boats continued to withhold their fire from laden, inbound American troopships. Berlin hoped that this policy would elicit a continuation of the restraints on American efforts on behalf of the Entente.[5]

Through the great German drives and on into August, Sims

continued to badger the Navy Department for more warcraft and men. On August 26, the Acting Chief of Navigation, Laning, reproached him for this. Presumably Laning's conviction that the policy he had helped to carry out was correct was not as firmly set as this letter to Sims indicated; he later eagerly joined with Sims against Daniels and Benson at the 1920 Senate Committee Hearings. His justification for Benson's quick return to the course of June 23, 1917, upon his return from London was the most candid exposition that Sims had yet received of the Navy Department's failure to move beyond an "ahead half-speed" policy in anticipation of the 1918 German onslaughts. At the United States' entrance into the war, the Navy had had only sufficient personnel to man either all its anti-submarine craft for combat duty, or to keep its older battleships and auxiliaries manned and "use these officers and these men to build a truly great Navy[,] one that could actually [at some future time] deal some blows to the Huns. It was evident that [with] what we had then we could not win the war so . . . we took advantage of the enemy's inability to strike hard while we were building up our Navy [behind the screen of British anti-U-boat craft and the Grant Fleet]." Laning seemed to cast doubt on Wilson's and Benson's 1917 talk about the need to attack Germany's home bases: "to have wasted our strength to strike quickly when that strength was not sufficient to win would have been foolish." Of course, he added, "we recognize the importance of the work against the U-boats but we did not think that their extinction could alone win the war." Instead, Laning told Sims, the Department had been concentrating on the great navy of the future since "about the first week of July, 1917."[6]

In a speech on February 7, 1918, Daniels declared that America aimed to possess "incomparably the greatest Navy." Patently, this was not needed to fight the existing war against Germany. Laning's letter to Sims essayed a rebuttal of British indignation at the Department's use of sailors needed by Sims to man American troop transports. Navy crews, so American merchant seaman spokesmen charged, used three times the number of men that civilian crews did to perform the same functions. This threw some of them out of work. It also forced the British to reduce imports (now down to less than half of those of 1913) as more ships were required to transport the American Army. Moreover, the London War Cabinet was irritated by the Navy Department's policy of packing merchant ships in the Latin American trade with superfluous Navy sailors to "assist" resentful civilian crews. Sailors tied down on older battleships and auxiliaries in American waters were training men for crew duties on the greater postwar merchant marine and navy. In July 1918, Daniels noted that Cabinet members and "others" had consented to let the Navy train "men for merchant ships . . . 20,000 officers and 200,000 men . . . [of the Navy on merchant] coastwise and South American ships" and that Benson had gotten "full control" of merchant ships crew training for the Navy.[7]

Wilson refused to risk many American ships in the war zone to succor the Allies because he feared they would try to harm American commerce after the war. In his speech of September 25, 1916, he warned the nation about the postwar fate of American exports if there were insufficient American bottoms to carry them. A businessman

> who depended upon his competitors in the same market to deliver his goods to his customers ... [could expect the rivals] would deliver their own goods first and quickest .... Foreign vessels carry our goods where they, the foreign vessels, happen to be going ... only if they have room .... You cannot conduct trade that way ... we cannot lose any time in getting [our own] delivery wagons [ships].[8]

He acted in accordance with this logic in August 1917 when (as previously noted) he ordered that a higher priority be given to merchant ships than to destroyer production, and in April 1918 (as will be discussed) when he ordered ships kept in the Brazilian and Japanese trades instead of being diverted to carrying troops to France.

Upon his return home, Benson did send Sims enough officers so that he soon had a reasonably adequate planning staff. After Benson's arrival in London in early November 1917, during the last year of the war, the percentage of anti-U-boat vessels in commission sent to Sims rose from 21 percent to 27 percent.[9] Although nearly half of this modest accretion of warcraft was of rather ineffective wooden subchasers manned by college undergraduate volunteers performing their first duty at sea, additions of other types (he received nine of the seventy-nine submarines) enabled Sims to protect more ships with convoy. It also enabled him to take other anti-U-boat steps, to which attention will soon be given.

Despite the restraint in what was sent to Sims during those three periods, it is appropriate to say that the Navy Department advanced from its "ahead one-third speed" policy to one of "ahead half-speed," during November 1917-November 1918. It is true that it kept three-fourths of its ships at home. But in the fall of 1918, Benson feared that Scheer might, after all, break through the limited force of heavy British warships in the Channel and wreak havoc with Pershing's logistics, if not his troop transports. As a result, Sims received three dreadnoughts for the Channel just before Scheer did resolve to send out his ships. This gave Sims eight of the nation's thirty-nine capital ships. He also got three additional cruisers, giving him five out of thirty-one.[10]

Benson chafed at London's dominion over the world's cable networks. He was determined that the administration of post-war Africa should be internationalized under the League of Nations. Yet at the height of the great German offensives, he had to ask London and Paris to send a warship to restore order in America's semiprotectorate of Liberia; he had no bunkering facilities.[11]

During his November-December visit to London, Benson launched a plan to get a foot in the door of joint Anglo-American control over the naval course of the war. Had he succeeded, Sims might well have received more than the quarter of the Navy Department's anti-submarine craft which it was willing to send him up to Armistice Day. Benson intended that Sims sit on the British Admiralty Board. Through the Admiralty, Benson hoped to acquire influence over the war in the main naval theatre in the North. Through the inter-Allied Naval Council, he aspired to buttress this influence, as well as to gain some additional influence over the war in the Mediterranean. This would give him a voice to which the ratio of American anti-U-boat forces to Allied units in neither theatre seemed to entitle him. Even as late as August 1918, the American percentages of the total were rather modest:[12]

	Great Britain	France	United States	Italy	Japan
In the northern war theatre:					
Destroyers	80%	6%	14%	—	—
Submarines	78%	17%	5%	—	—
Other Patrol Craft	86%	11%	3%	—	—
In the Mediterranean theatre:					
Destroyers	27%	28%	2%	26%	7%
Submarines	13%	37%	—	50%	—
Other Patrol Craft	22%	66%	8%	4%	—

Such proportions encouraged the President's apprehension that an Admiralty seat was too likely to sink Sims into the position of a satellite of Whitehall's Civil and Sea Lords. Even had Wilson been willing to send a higher proportion of his warcraft to Europe, by the time Benson's proposal was submitted to him in late 1917, he had grown too accustomed to receiving sanguine assurances instead of anticipated outputs from his administrators for ship construction, aircraft construction, and other suppliers in response to his inquiries about production progress.[13]

Wilson was appalled at Benson's cable of November 25:

upon my suggestion British Admiralty invited Sims to attend daily meetings of their Navy Council . . . . At subsequent conferences with Sir Eric Geddes he suggested . . . making Sims an honorary member of British Admiralty Board. Jellicoe approved it. [Benson added that] while my whole effort over here has been to secure this condition [of joint Anglo-American planning of future naval undertakings], I feel that . . . approval of President is necessary before being acted upon.[14]

The President disapproved with "an emphatic *No.*" Sims, however, did not sense the depth of Wilson's opposition at once. In January, Benson cabled him of supposed concerns that the French and Italians would resent such a chair for him. Sims replied that Paris and Rome had assured Geddes of their approval. De Bon had even said that the French Admiralty might "do something of the kind" for Sims. Sims pressed upon Benson that it was "difficult" for the British admirals "to keep me in touch with everything" as "I do not have the privilege of listening to discussions on which decisions are based."[15]

Benson had come to England full of unformed plans for a daring offensive against Germany's U-boat bases. In the spring of 1918, however, the British launched assaults on Ostend and Zeebrugge without asking for, or receiving, American help. By then they grasped what lay behind the Navy Department's refusal of a seat for Sims; Wilson had rejected it, Daniels recorded, because "he would by such acceptance be tied up to English determination." Sims lamented that, had he been allowed his Admiralty place, he and his staff might have been able to convert the Ostend-Zeebrugge attacks from a partial to a complete success. But Benson had abandoned the project.[16]

Sims did receive additional staff officers. Churchill's long study of Sims's operations probably had won Presidential approval for this. In his October 1917 recommendations to Wilson, he had spoken of the need for strengthening Sims's hand. This would enhance his tacit alliance with the "younger and more imaginative" British Admiralty officers; he would thus be able to help the dynamic Geddes to overcome the complacent traditions which enveloped the senior Admiralty leaders. Among Sims's crews, "the opinion is unanimous that he is the ablest officer in our service."[17]

Benson, however, limited the expansion of Sims's staff. On his return to Washington, he brusquely ordered Sims to stop asking for so many of the Navy's talented officers for his staff and crews. Benson asserted that he needed many of them at home, but he did not specify for what purpose.[18]

The President and the Operations Chief were irritated at pro-Sims agitation in Congress. The President's disciple-biographer, Ray Stannard Baker, worriedly observed to himself in January 1918, that "a battle royal between Congress and the President is developing . . . as he has . . . not gained the people's confidence as an administrator." A Congressional inquiry into charges that Sims had not received adequate Navy Department support in warships or manpower had just been held. Because the House Committee lacked access to facts and figures and had a pro-Wilson majority, it had ended inconclusively. Sims was assuring the British that they were right to balk at bringing over entire American divisions and all their cargo-space-consuming paraphernalia. American machine gun units and infantry units alone were vitally needed to bolster the British and French armies at the Front. Theodore Roosevelt's ally and friend, the renowned General Leonard Wood, visited London; he assured the British that "whatever sacrifices they make for the purpose of giving us additional tonnage are only for the purpose of bringing over an unorganized and undisciplined mob," thanks to Presidential and War Department incompetence. London and Paris had serious misgivings about the abilities of American divisional and higher Army commanders. They considered American troops and junior officers, however, to be quite capable of being rapidly trained for combat, provided they were instructed and used as regiments and battalions by British or French divisions. To leave them under Pershing and his senior generals of dubious competence would mean that they could be withheld from the front when Hindenburg and Ludendorff struck.[19]

Anticipation of the great German offensive on land and the possible simultaneous offensive by Scheer in the English Channel brought only a limited increase of Sims's forces. Between November 1, 1917, and March 1, 1918, Benson's London assurances of increased aid raised Sims's total of anti-U-boat craft from eighty-six of the 412 in commission to 124 of 681. His percentage of the total in commission, however, fell slightly from 20.9 percent on November 1 to 18.2 percent on March 1.[20]

Despite the relative smallness of his gains, Sims was able to get certain measures underway before the Western Front erupted. He continued to improve on these during and after the German drives. In this fashion, the Irish Sea was virtually cleared of U-boats, and the complex North Sea and English Channel mine barrages were begun. Had the war gone into 1919, these barrages would have been completed and the U-boats confined to the North Sea.[21]

By the day the first formidable enemy land offensive of 1918 struck, Sims had received five American dreadnoughts, which raised Beatty's margin over Scheer to twenty-nine against nineteen. Because Scheer's heavy warships had sometimes successfully attacked ore ships in the North Sea, the American dreadnoughts in the Grand Fleet took their turn at escorting them. This angered Benson, who ordered their immediate commander reprimanded when he learned of it. When Daniels heard that one American dreadnought had been fired at with U-boat torpedoes, he hinted to Sims that he should halt this escort work.[22]

Then, at the height of the German land drives, Scheer almost created conditions for a second Jutland. On April 23-24, his battle-cruisers, accompanied by "the necessary support from the battleship squadrons," sailed out to destroy a convoy. Due to faulty intelligence, however, they found an empty sea and returned home. Neither Sims nor the Admiralty knew that when his ships reached haven Scheer decided that, for the remainder of the war, they would confine their activities to protecting the egress and return of the U-boats. Sims and Mayo, however, continued to worry that Scheer might decide to order his heavy units into the English Channel while the Grand Fleet was too far north to engage them quickly. They might wreak havoc with both the British and American naval forces in the area, as well as with cargo and troop-ships. Indeed, a desperate Scheer resolved in late October to attack the British with "the entire High Seas Fleet" supported by numerous U-boats by luring the Grand Fleet toward the Channel.[23]

The British mistrusted Pershing's intentions. At New Year's, 1918, Lloyd George weighed the consequences of the likelihood that Pershing would withhold his divisions from the battle line, leaving the British and French alone to face the great enemy blows expected in the spring. Russia was gone, Italy virtually prostrate, France in dubious condition. Perhaps the lesser of two evils would be to seek peace terms before the British Army was decimated.[24]

Wilson shared Lloyd George's conviction that the nation having the most powerful armed forces still intact during the peace negotiations would be most able to impose its peace terms. In the summer of 1917, the War Department foresaw that if Wilson could achieve a cease-fire before Pershing's Army entered combat, "our potential military force had become a strong card in any negotiations."[25]

Balfour unavailingly tried to reassure Lloyd George in the gloomy aftermath of Lenin's request for an armistice and of Caporetto. The Prime Minister erred in his conviction "that the nation among the Entente powers which possesses at the end of the war the largest army will have the most to say in determining the . . . [peace terms]." If Haig's men suffered frightful slaughter, such a "great diminution of our manpower . . . would not diminish the efficacy of the threat which we could . . . hold over the heads of unreasonable allies . . . of withdrawing from the Alliance. With or without . . . [a strong] Army, our abandonment of the Alliance would bring it to an end. Italy and France could do nothing, and America could not do very much . . . . " The French government, however, agreed with Lloyd George: he whose army was strongest at the peace table would have the strongest voice at it.[26]

A little afterward, Sims digested an observation of First Sea Lord Admiral Sir Rosslyn Wemyss (Lloyd George having finally rid himself of Jellicoe): Britain and the United States were the "milk cows" who suckled the other Allies. The outcome of the war, he believed, depended on Britain's continued control of the sea's surface and on her merchant marine's capacity for supplying the Allied and American armies.[27] Balfour meant that if Britain took her army, navy, and merchant marine out of the war, Pershing's and the other Allies' armies would either wither away from a lack of tonnage or be overwhelmed by Hindenburg's troops.

On New Year's Eve, 1917, Lloyd George considered the advantages of beating Wilson to the peace table. He instructed the British staff officers on the Supreme War Council to tell him whether they could "foresee a victorious end to the war? If so when and under what circumstances?" If not, could they "foresee such an improvement in the future military situation of the Allies as would induce the enemy to assent to peace terms more favorable . . . than those . . . likely to be obtained at the present . . . ? If the answer is . . . [yes], will the improvement be on such a scale as to justify the sacrifices involved in continuing the struggle?" And could they "suggest any means by which the enemy can be prevented from securing control of the resources of South Russia?"[28]

Haig urged that Britain seek a compromise peace. Let the Germans have a free hand to deal with Bolshevik Russia: "Our best policy," he replied, was "to strengthen Austria as against Germany, and to turn the latter in the direction of Russia for her future." As "the British Empire had already got a good deal out of this war" through its conquests in Asia and Africa, he could see little to be gained and much to be lost "by continuing the war for another twelve months." Not only would Britain "be much more exhausted and an industrial recovery . . . more difficult," but to continue the struggle would enable "America to get a great pull over us" in these rival fields. Furthermore, the United States

Admiral Sims at Admiralty House, Queenstown, 1918. Photo courtesy of
William S. Sims II and the Central News, Limited, London.

could not be relied on as "a serious national factor" in the fighting in
1918. Others also advised Lloyd George that the economic price
required for American troops, who would not make a timely combat
debut, was too high to pay.[29]

These considerations and his renewed goal of peace talks with the
Austrians animated Lloyd George to omit from his January 5 address
his usual exhortation for the crushing of Germany. The Habsburg
Monarch, however, let the current peace discussions with the British in
Switzerland lapse in favor of his renewed faith in ultimate victory on
the Western Front.[30] As has been noted, the British Prime Minister
painfully concluded that Germany, "now in her hour of triumph,"
would not agree to a minimum of acceptable compromises over terms.

On the eve of Wilson's Fourteen Points Address rejecting the Allies'
war aims, Theodore Roosevelt sent Rudyard Kipling his views on
Washington's war policy. The ex-President aimed to replace his archrival
in the White House; he had made peace with the Republican Party and
doubtless would have been its successful standard-bearer had he lived
until the 1920 Presidential election. The Rough Rider was far closer to
Sims and Pratt than to Wilson on the issue of naval and military

partnership with the Entente, as well as on postwar relations with Great Britain. His letter was circulated to the King and Cabinet in February, and provided additional incentive for refusing to divert more British shipping space to bring over entire American divisions.

Accompanying Roosevelt's letter was one of a similar tenor from a Boston Brahmin banker, a Mr. Ames, to the Wilson-House confidant at the London Embassy, Buckler. He, too, turned his letter from America over to Milner.[31] Both berated the President as an obstinate incompetent; they charged that the U.S. Army was woefully deficient in discipline, artillery, aircraft, and sanitation. The senior generals in charge were indifferent to or incapable of remedying matters. Roosevelt continued that "the delays and incompetencies which are robbing our intervention of three-fourths of its efficacy" were mainly the fault of the President who "is a cold and selfish hypocrite, a clever and adroit demogogue, and wedded to the belief that rhetoric is action." Despite Wilson's "entire inability as an administrator," he managed to convince himself after each of his speeches that " 'peace without victory' or whatever the moment's oratorical fervor has made him declare has become a fact . . . he is very great in *seeming* to win the war . . . but he is entirely willing to pose as the great peacemaker if this seems more personally profitable." Wilson would leave the war the moment that he profitably could do so; "he would eat all his past declarations [about a crusade for democracy, one infers] without even looking uncomfortable." His present attitude towards the subject nationalities of the Austrian Empire signified his "betrayal of the rights of small nationalities"; it also demonstrated that "he does not mean [to do] anything effective against the Mittel-Europa world menace."

On the other hand, Lloyd George's own stand on self-determination for the blacks in Africa was "a rhetorical and hypocritical flourish worthy of Wilson himself." Roosevelt did not know, however, that Lloyd George aimed to undercut the President over control of German Africa. The Prime Minister anticipated, with good reason, that a Wilson who had resegregated the Federal Government's offices (after they had been desegregated by Theodore Roosevelt) would not call for voting by the rank and file in Africa; recently, when quietly polled, the tribal chiefs had indicated their preference for the British. Lloyd George would keep the conquered German colonies despite the President's effort to induce the German authorities to talk peace over his Fourteen Points which included the "absolutely impartial adjustment of all colonial claims." Roosevelt, however, cast Wilson's peace effort in a reprehensible light: "just at present he [Wilson] is underhandedly endeavoring to urge . . . peace terms which, under the guise of high-sounding phrases, shall leave Germany substantially victorious; supreme over Russia, Central Europe and [blank] Asia . . . . "

As this writer has shown, however, Wilson was loath to make a peace which would leave Germany (or the Allies) in economic control of Russia. In this very speech, he demanded "the evacuation of all Russian territory" and "an unhampered . . . opportunity for the independent determination of her own . . . development." True, not much else was made a mandatory demand on Berlin, and he did not define of what Russian territory consisted. Russian Poland, he implied, "should" be detached from Russia. The Baltic provinces and Finland might remain German or Austrian satellites. In March, Walter Hines Page blundered by trying to excuse Lloyd George's slurs on the Fourteen Points to Wilson; he wrote that the Prime Minister had mistakenly assumed that they signified that Wilson aimed to render the British Navy impotent by placing it under League of Nations' control. As this was exactly what the President aimed to do, he and Lloyd George remained antagonistic towards each other for the duration of the fighting. Other American leaders, however, supported the President's peace without victory terms. Professor F. W. Taussig (Chairman of the United States Tariff Commission) wrote him in support of the Fourteen Points address: "We should not continue the war in order that France should get Alsace-Lorraine, or Italy the Trentino . . . . The Germans are entitled to get back their colonies . . . . We cannot insist upon the democratization of Germany . . . . Peace terms . . . of a draw will promote the change."[32]

Meanwhile, Pershing continued with his plans to avoid fighting the Germans until after they had exhausted themselves against the British and French. Then he would launch a great American counter offensive. His call for 100 American divisions in France by July 1, 1919, gave rise to anticipation at his headquarters that he, and no longer Foch, would by then be generalissimo over all Allied armies. Pershing was encouraged by his President's refusals first to the Supreme War Council, and then to Foch, to send his divisions into the fighting. This attitude encouraged the British to insist that Pershing's divisions be controlled by the Supreme Command or Foch.

On March 21, the most powerful artillery and gas bombardment ever yet exploded commenced the first great 1918 German offensive. Its focus was the southern section of the British-held front, near the junction of Haig's and Petain's armies. The British line reeled backward. Haig and the general to whom the now thoroughly frightened Allies and Americans gave control of all land forces in France, Ferdinand Foch, appealed to Pershing. He must send the four complete divisions (which he had had training in France for five to nine months and had nearly double the combat troops of four Allied divisions) into the breach which was appearing at this junction. These were far better trained than those the British had thrown into battle earlier in the war. Pershing refused. All he would do was send them into a quiet section of the French-held front to allow French divisions to move towards the threatening mass of German driving power, and let some engineers and other troops work well behind the British line to help prepare new defensive positions for Haig's retreating men. A mortified Sims cabled Benson; his wire was promptly laid on the President's desk. The officially-expressed British thanks for these dispositions of Pershing's men masked "bitter disappointment or worse . . . [that] American troops were not thrown in heavy numbers to help resist the German attack."[33]

The Secretary of War's biographer, Frederick Palmer, was serving as one of Pershing's staff officers. He subsequently concluded that, had Pershing accepted Baker's pre-March 21 suggestion that he position his completed divisions at this juncture of the British and French armies, the war would have ended earlier than it did. The British would have halted the German advance more quickly. Hindenburg and Ludendorff would have concluded that Pershing would throw the remainder of the 345,000 men he had when they launched their first drive into any breach. Instead, the American commander withheld his men until the end of May. Then he had 724,000 troops, but at the outset of June only two of his divisions gave battle. Even they would probably have been kept back, but by that time the Germans had abandoned their efforts to break the British line, and turned on the French. At Chateau Thierry, it looked too much as if Petain's *poilus* were breaking and running, and that only the sight of fresh American troops in battle plugging this gap could reenergize their will to fight. As this third German drive was near to exhausting itself, however, Pershing was able to continue to withhold most of his divisions until after the end of the fifth and weakest of the enemy offensives in July.[34]

Meanwhile, the London government suspended its policy against sending eighteen-and-a-half year olds into combat. Desperate British War Cabinet members suggested that the President be asked to send American dreadnoughts to the Grand Fleet so that Beatty could release Royal Navy sailors and marines for the fighting on the Western Front. The Admiralty, however, warned that Scheer might launch a naval offensive in support of Hindenburg's. Admiral Wemyss told the War Cabinet he "could not advise that the U.S. Navy was at present in a state of efficiency to replace fighting units" of Beatty's fleet. The Admiralty had released construction and dockyard maintenance men to the army. Wemyss' stand spared Lloyd George an American refusal.[35]

A few days later, Mayo urged that his fleet be allowed to stand beside the Grand Fleet. Instead of countering that a part of it could go over, Wilson rejected the notion outright, saying that he anticipated he would "come out of the war hating [the] English." He thus implied that his animosity toward Britain's rival war aims was a factor in his determination of how much naval support he would give the British against the Germans. Although Sims did volunteer his destroyers for battle "if the very worst came to pass in the Channel," the President's stance precluded ventilation of Sims's recommendation (first made a year earlier) that several dreadnoughts be sent across and based on Brest to guard against potential "raids by heavy enemy ships in the Channel out of reach of the British main fleet."[36] Hence, Washington would only send them in October 1918.

It was the militarily ambitious Pershing, not the party leader Wilson, who had (seven weeks earlier) first seriously raised the argument of "national sentiment" and predicted domestic "political opposition" to placing Americans under an Allied command. Five days later (on February 4), Wilson had seized upon this argument (which could also serve as an excuse) and given Pershing the orders he sought. His troops could receive the benefit of training from experienced Allied soldiers, but his trained men were not to be used (even under the direct command of their own brigadier or major generals) in combat unless an obviously imminent German breakthrough threatened to engulf both the Allied and American armies. Wilson ordered Baker to tell Pershing that "we . . . trust to his judgement upon all points of training . . . but . . . that nothing except a sudden and manifest emergency [shall] be allowed to interfere with the building up of a great, distinctly American force . . . acting under its own flag and its own officers." [37] To what extent domestic political concerns animated him and to what extent he used them as an excuse for delaying aid to the Allies is difficult to assess.

Nevertheless, the American people would have taken pride in the entrance of their men into battle alongside the British in March-April 1918. Frederick Palmer, a colonel under Pershing, afterwards wrote that "our own people, who had become used to the Allied wall as a fixture on the map, now saw it caving in . . . people in America were scanning each fresh newspaper edition for news that our troops were in the battle." The colonel pointed out that had Pershing sent his four trained divisions into combat at the outset of the first and greatest German offensive, "they would have been in action not as a part of either [the British or French] army, but as an American corps — an integral American force as large as the original British Expeditionary Force at Mons; larger than the five German divisions that . . . [stiffened the Austrians] at Caporetto." [38]

On April 1, Balfour admonished Wilson that Britain could only send more men to the front by conscripting men up to fifty years of age or "by ruining the few remaining industries which are not required for war." This got no American troops into battle. On April 9, House warned Wilson that Pershing's troops should be rushed into the firing line; if they were not, and the Germans broke through, Pershing's Army would be trapped. "Then there will be no end to the denunciations from such as Roosevelt . . . . " The President must consider "the effect upon your administration" of such a catastrophe. [39] Like Hoover and others (including Theodore Roosevelt), House seemed unaware of the supposedly overriding need for deference to patriotic emotions that required withholding American troops from the battle even under their own divisional commanders. Wilson, however, excused Pershing's passivity. He told Hurley that, were American troops to sustain losses comparable to those now being inflicted upon the British, "I dread to contemplate the . . . [reaction] of the American people." On the other hand, he was frightened that he could not get sufficient forces into France in time to take over the main burden of fighting the Germans when the British and French become exhausted. On April 3, he told his Cabinet that "unless we send over every possible man to support the Allies in their present desperate condition, ... defeat may require us to pay for the entire cost of the war to the Central Powers." [40]

Yet Wilson declined to reduce foreign trade. At his war council on that day, Hurley stated that American ships could transport "90,000 a month but this would require a reduction of imports and in [the]

Japan and Brazil trade." Wilson instructed him to "tell Great Britain how many we can send not taking out [the] Japan and Brazil tonnage and then ask England and France to furnish [the] ships for [the] balance."[41] After acrimonious negotiations and delays, the British did so. Sixty percent of the troops sent to Pershing during the great enemy drives were carried in British ships. (A further discussion is in Chapter 6.)

During the House mission to London and Paris in late 1917, the Allies had elicited an American promise of cooperation with the new Allied Maritime Transport Council. The Council had called on the Americans to agree "that neutral and interned tonnage obtained . . . by whatever country should be used . . . in direct war services . . . [by] being allotted to the most urgent war needs of any of the Allies." The Americans had provided figures that showed they had 3,620,000 tons of seagoing ships in the fall of 1917, but only 502,000 tons were entering the war zone, and they were "in private trade." This total excluded 750,000 tons of neutral ships the Americans employed in their own waters. The British stated that they had reduced their non-food and non-munitions imports from thirty-six to eight million tons since 1914, and America should provide the Allies with 1,000,000 tons of ships for troop transportation and other war needs in the next few months from new construction, from new neutral tonnage acquired, and from reductions in non-essential trades. The Allies challenged the Americans' statements that they could not divert some of the 1,750,000 tons of ships they were using in their Far Eastern and South American trades to serving Allied war needs because they instead needed to increase their tonnage in Asian and South American trades by 750,000 tons. The Americans had refused the Allies' request that they save time and space by letting the Japanese merchant marine provide 500,000 tons of shipping to carry part of the United States' Far Eastern trade so that America could divert 500,000 tons to carry war essentials across the Atlantic.[42]

On May 5, 1918, the Allies remonstrated in vain that Washington had not fulfilled its late 1917 agreement to the principle that "America, France, Italy, and Great Britain will all tabulate and make available to each other . . . the details of requirements for which tonnage is needed, and the tonnage available and likely to be available through new construction, etc. . . . to form the basis on which the general allocation of tonnage [of each nation] will be . . . [made] to the services most essential to the prosecution of the war." During January-October 1918, the Americans lost 139,000 tons of ships to U-boats; the British lost 1,617,000. The Americans gained 2,080,000 from new construction, the British 1,311,000. Counting acquisitions of foreign ships, the United States acquired a net gain of 2,233,000 tons; the British suffered a net loss of 680,000 tons.[43] Armistice Day saw the Americans with some 40% of Britain's tonnage, the world's second largest merchant marine, and an accelerated launching of new ships.[44]

The first great Hindenburg-Ludendorff offensive halted on April 5, with the southern reaches of the British line considerably bent, but not broken. The Germans gave Haig's army a three day respite before they drove against the northern stretch of the British line from April 9 to 29. On April 6, the President delivered a famous address which has been misleadingly called his "war till victory" speech. The logic of his phrases signified that Pershing should continue his waiting role and that Sims was not going to receive a majority of the Navy's anti-U-boat craft. Wilson did tell the Germans that, if they persisted in trying to break the front and in refusing to negotiate a compromise peace, he would eventually throw Pershing's divisions against them. Nevertheless, he avoided using "victory" in his speech. Immediately after his call for "force without stint or limit," he implicitly indicted both the Allies' and the Central Powers' war aims: this was to be "the righteous and triumphant Force which shall make Right the law of the world, and cast every selfish dominion in the dust." But he assured the Germans, he was "ready still, ready even now, to discuss a fair and just and honest peace" with them. He was prepared to "deal fairly with the German power, as with all others."[45] Still, in case the Germans mistakenly concluded that he was calling for their defeat or the overthrow of their government, Wilson two days later told foreign press correspondents in Washington that Burke's "idea of freedom" was his own; the German people were entitled to keep their time-tested Hohenzollern Monarchy. Furthermore, when the American delegates entered the peace conference, they would tell the delegates of both the Allies and the Central Powers, impartially: "Gentlemen of the Conference, we are here to see that you get nothing as to territory."[46]

It was a few days after this April 6 speech that Wilson anticipated that he would "come out of the war hating [the] English." He still had not got them sufficiently into his power. Recently, for instance, he had been unable to prevent Britons from purchasing shares in the great International Mercantile Company, which owned America's largest private fleet of ships.[47] His speech of April 6 alluded, indirectly, to additional grounds for minimizing the nation's combat role. Although Pershing told Foch in early April that he could use American troops in combat if needed, he soon rebuffed the generalissimo's attempt to do so; hence on May 1 Foch exploded at Pershing that his office was not "the empty decoration" that Pershing was trying to make of it.[48]

"Force to the utmost" meant that Pershing got an additional 700,000 men during the great enemy drives. He therefore had just over 1,200,000 when the last German offensive spent itself in mid-July. Two American divisions of about 22,000 men each, or nearly the equal of four British divisions, did some fighting alongside the Allies at the end of the third enemy drive; one of Pershing's divisions helped the mauled *poilus* halt the fifth German drive.[49]

For Sims, "force without stint or limit" meant that by the end of July the Navy Department had sent him 26.1 percent of all of its anti-U-boat craft in commission. This was an improvement over the 21.3 percent he had had when Benson arrived in London in November and the 18.2 percent he had had on March 1. The main component of this improvement was a large number of wooden subchasers manned by college students (too many navy sailors were preparing for the great future navy to allow a more professional manning of these boats). The November 1, March 1, and August 1 numbers of this type of boat in commission rose from 21 to 136 to 302, but none had been sent to Sims before March 1. These wobbly vessels composed 103 out of the 243 anti-U-boat craft sent him out of the navy's total of 932 on August 1; if only vessels manned by regular navy crews were considered, Sims had 22.2 percent of all anti-U-boat craft in the navy on August 1, just after the German offensives ceased. Similarly, his total of 264 out of 969 at the war's end (27.0 percent) was somewhat inflated by the presence of 121 of the navy's 299 semi-amateur craft. During the German drives, his share of the nation's destroyers rose modestly from 59 out of 70, to 66 out of 86; during the last months of the war it rose slightly more (though the percentage of the total fell) to 68 out of 107. Sims's tugs and minelayers totaled 16, 27, and 30 out of the 123 in commission at the end of these intervals; most of his additional professionally-manned craft escorted American troopships approaching and returning from Brest. His "converted yachts and other patrol vessels" totaled 27, 27, and 26 on the three dates, his gunboats 6, 6, and 5 out of 27 on November 1. He had 5, 5, and 5 Coast Guard cutters. Of submarines, which Sims wated to scout ahead of convoys, he suffered a slight decline of 11 to 10, to 9 out of 79. At Benson's insistence, five of these nine were kept patrolling off the Azores in waters seldom visited by U-boats or merchant ship convoys.[50] Probably this husbanding of submarines from the war zone is partially explained by an anticipation by Benson, Daniels, and Wilson of the General Board's Armistice-period warning about the possible need for them in a future war. The Board then held that it would be necessary to torpedo British merchant shipping as the Germans had done if Anglo-American tensions escalated into war. This will be discussed more fully in Chapter 7.

During the German offensives, Sims's cruiser strength rose from two to three, but only because one was reluctantly sent to Murmansk in May. Sims's battleship strength was held to five, all with the Grand Fleet. It was obvious by now that no great addition to Sims's forces could wrest much influence over the British at the peace table. On land, however, if the war continued into 1919, Pershing would have a fresh, relatively unbled, and numerically superior army to drive back the debilitated Germans, while the decimated British and French grudgingly lent what assistance they could. Only to save this American army from possible strangulation by sea did Benson send Sims three more dreadnoughts by October 1 to safeguard the English Channel.

To some extent, in 1918, Wilson may have used his tensions with the Mikado as an excuse for minimizing his help to the Allies against the Central Powers. Still, these tensions were substantial.

In his April 6 call for "force to the utmost," the President alluded to Japan and Russia. The trend of Japanese-American relations up to this point suggests that Wilson, in his speech, intended to frighten the Tokyo authorities out of adopting a more hostile stance. Far Eastern developments as well as those in the European Russia of 1918, incensed him against the British and the Japanese. For example, a joint proposal by the British and Japanese ministers to China over German and Austrian concessions in China prompted him, on August 8, 1918, to charge that they were "trying to scoop everything while the war is in course.[51] In April, one saw that the Japanese might yet take advantage of the other great powers' preoccupation with the war in Europe to acquire exclusive economic control over North China. American traders and investors would be squeezed out of all of China if the British and French, who had "spheres of influence" in Central and Southern China, joined the Japanese in excluding Americans. Britain and Japan had earlier seized all of Germany's holdings in China, the East Indies, and the Pacific. The greatest prize left for them "to scoop while the war" was "in course" was the Russian empire. In the West, the Germans and Austrians were in possession of Russia's richest, if chaotic, European provinces. Fears that this would enable the Central empires to offset the Allied naval blockade were exacerbated by terror that the Germans would break the Western Front unless part of their striking power was sapped by counter-intervention in Russia. The British and French hoped that this would encourage anti-Communist and anti-German forces to fight on. A landing in Siberia was also deemed necessary to prevent its resources from being supplied to the Central Powers. In June 1918, Pershing seconded the Allied appeals for full-scale intervention. The Germans appeared to be too likely to break through and trap his army without such a diversion.[52] But where Pratt and Sims wanted frank discussions, compromises, and a division of the world's trading and investment markets with London (and with Tokyo, in Pratt's case), Wilson was loath to enter into such negotiations with either rival power. Instead, he and his advisers mulled over the most effective means of seizing the economic initiative in Siberia from the British and Japanese.

Why did not the United States take a stronger stand in 1917-1918 against the Japanese threat to the Open Door in China? In persuading Tokyo to drop only the worst of its Twenty-One Demands on China in 1915, Washington's restraint had reflected its preoccupation with America's much larger markets in Europe and Latin America, and even in Japan herself. In 1917-1919, these markets remained too valuable to jeopardize by a confrontation with Japan. When, in May 1917, Lansing invited Kikujiro, Viscount Ishii, to Washington to work out a *modus vivendi* for the duration of the war over the Japanese-American rivalry in China, he knew that "neither the Americans nor the Chinese were prepared to defend [a treaty] against Japan." Moreover, Lansing and Wilson had reason to believe that as long as the Japanese refrained from a gross interference with Chinese-American trade, time was on America's side in her rivalry with Japan for commercial and investment markets in China. This was also true of the expansion of the navy and merchant marine. Lansing's subordinates at the State Department favored a relatively strong line with Ishii about the Open Door, one that would lead to an agreement that was deliberately vague in specifying the "special" rights that propinquity gave Japan in China while it postponed settling the fate of the Pacific Islands and Shantung to "the peace conference when American armed might was no longer [partially] diverted to Europe."[53] These purposes were achieved in the Lansing-Ishii Agreement of November 2, 1917.

By easing Washington's concern about China, this agreement left America freer to send more naval support to the Allies should that prove necessary to avert a German victory. Wilson was less worried about possible Japanese damage to the Open Door than he was about a possible German hegemony over Europe, Russia, and the Middle East; the Japanese were less worried about a possible German victory than they were about the rising military and economic power of the United States. As matters had stood in May 1917, neither Washington nor Tokyo was willing to send more than a fraction of its naval forces or merchant ships to the war zone. After nearly three years as a formal partner of the Allies against Germany, Emperor Yoshihito's Navy had only thirteen old cruisers and destroyers in European waters.[54] The United States and Japan were resolved to minimize the risk to their warships in case they needed them later for use against each other, and/ or against a victorious Germany or Britain.

The Lansing-Ishii negotiations had gotten underway in August 1917 as House's and Sims's hopes for the anti-Japanese capital ship agreement with Britain were dying. The United States had nearly three times as many dreadnoughts as Japan, but early in 1917 it had had only sixty-six destroyers to Japan's fifty-three. In May 1917, the General Board had urged that the Japanese be persuaded to rush twenty-five destroyers to European waters and 750,000 troops to the endangered Russian front. This would help avert a German victory while it created a hatred between the Germans and the Japanese that would virtually preclude a German-Japanese alliance. Lansing, however, had declined to mention this proposal to the Japanese. They would probably have rejoined that as the United States had more warcraft and manpower than did Japan, it should rush thirty-five destroyers and 1,500,000 men into combat.[55] Instead, Lansing had worked toward a compromise over China that would facilitate a possible increase in American warships in the war zone. He had known that he would hold an advantage in such negotiations: the Tokyo authorities feared the United States more than the Washington authorities feared Japan. In February 1916, the American ambassador at Tokyo, George W. Guthrie, had reported that the Japanese were alarmed that an Open Door would permit the Americans to use both their "surplus wealth accumulated during the war in Europe" and their inherently "superior resources" to oust them from the "predominant position" to which they were entitled in China. In August, Thomas Nelson Page had reported from Rome that the head of the Japanese delegation to the Paris Economic Conference had spoken of fears that the United States would attack Japan. Japan was therefore "making efforts to enter into closer relations with her European allies."[56]

There was evidence, it was true, that Japan was restless with her role vis-à-vis the United States or the Allies. Americans had reported from Tokyo in early 1917 that "none of the Japanese really like

England, they nearly all hate America, and mostly admire Germany" whom they wished to avoid offending "by actively participating in the war." In February, the valued part-time State Department agent E.V. Gillis reported from Tokyo that "it would take very little for Japan to go over to the side of Germany in case the latter had a marked success at any time." He added, however, that while she had sufficient merchant ships to attack the Philippines, she had not taken steps to acquire enough to transport troops and supplies to America's West Coast.[57]

Wilson and Lansing knew that the Japanese dreaded the probable outcome of a Japanese-American war. They cultivated that dread in Ishii. In April 1917, the American journalist John Callan O'Laughlin had reported that officials of the Japanese embassy had expressed fears of the "great war preparations" America was making. They feared the United States was raising an army to fight Japan "in the Pacific and the Far East." They wanted America to promise not to fortify the Philippines if she would not sell them to Japan. They feared that America's entry into the war would lead to Anglo-American coopera- tion "against Japan's ambitions in China and the Pacific." American officials "repeatedly reminded their guests [of the Ishii mission] of the growing power of the United States." Ishii was taken on a "courtesy" tour of Mayo's battle fleet. But the Viscount insisted that Japan was pleased by the American war preparations. When he remarked that Germany had thrice tried to entice Japan from the Allies' side, Lansing struck this potential bargaining lever from his hand: such German blandishments were "of no concern" to America as "Japan's loyalty as an ally and her reputation for good faith was [sic] too well established to be even suspected."[58]

A club that Ishii could not strike from Lansing's hand was Japan's partial economic dependence on the United States. Lansing had made the allocation of American steel to the Japanese conditional on their willingness to sell merchant ships to America. Ishii had been pressured into dropping his proposal for a Tokyo-dominated, Monroe Doctrine- style order for East Asia. But in May 1918, Washington heard that the Japanese frustration at the American design to make the United States their main source of raw materials had made them anxious to acquire the Russian half of Sakhalin Island, which had some iron ore, coal, and petroleum deposits. Their fear of Wilson was underscored by their declaration to the British and French, in March 1918, that they dared not send a military expedition into Siberia toward the Urals (as London and Paris were pressing them to do) without President Wilson's assent. Their troops might encounter serious resistance; Wilson might cut off exports vital to Japan's industries and the expedition's survival.[59]

Some American leaders had encouraged Lansing to compromise with Ishii on both moral and commercial grounds. In May 1917, Pratt had deplored the discrimination against the Japanese embodied in American immigration and land ownership policies. He held that by their efficient industry and high standards of personal character the Japanese had earned the right to some dominion over the mainland of

East Asia. He urged frank negotiations with the Tokyo authorities aimed at a detente over East Asia's markets and territorial arrangements. To a certain extent, in the fall of 1917, House had tried to convert Wilson to this outlook. China was sinking ever farther into a morass of banditry, warlordism, and anarchy which threatened to extinguish the profits of all advanced nations with interests in China. House recommended (unavailingly) that these "deplorable conditions" be alleviated by the establishment of three trustees for China: one selected by China, one by Japan, and one by the other powers concerned. But the President clung to his apprehensions of the "Yellow Peril," probably both out of genuine concern about a possible fusion of Sino-Japanese purposes as well as a desire to offer an excuse for limiting his aid to the Allies. In February 1917, he had told his Cabinet that "to keep the white race or part of it strong enough to meet the yellow race — Japan, for instance in alliance with Russia dominating China — it would be wise to do nothing . . . [against Germany]." In May 1917, he had given a softened version of this view as a reason for his opposition to "a fight to the finish" in Europe. [60]

In September 1916, the British had tried to take advantage of Japanese fears of the United States when their ambassador at Tokyo had suggested to his American colleague (doubtless with Japanese assent) an alliance between Tokyo and Washington "which would bring America into the quadruple group [with Britain, France, and Russia]." In the spring of 1917 (as previously noted), Wilson had declined London's counter offer of a similar alliance when the British cabinet had rejected House's anti-Japanese capital ship proposal. At about the same time, British naval officers in Washington were letting Benson know of their distrust of their Japanese allies. [61]

Lansing had reminded the Japanese in January 1917 that Washington had repeatedly recognized their special interests in Manchuria. But it did not want to extend this recognition to the rest of China. Lansing had therefore used a certain vagueness in consummating his pact with Ishii. The United States recognized only that Japan had "special interests in China, particularly in that part to which her possessions were contiguous." [62] Japanese-owned Korea abutted Manchuria. But did one count Japan's lease-held ports in China or the islands she owned outright off China's coast (including Formosa)? How did one apply the imprecise second meaning of 'contiguous' — near, in calculating the scope of Japan's special interests?

In December 1917, a spokesman for a group of American businessmen informed the State Department that they believed "their interests are safer under the aegis of some government other than their own [the Japanese]." They were forming a partnership with certain Japanese businessmen to create "the largest iron and steel company in Asia" which was to operate in both China and Japan. In January 1918, Washington was encouragingly informed that the British minister in China was working to prevent an exclusively Japanese patrol of the Yangtse. Although Chinese attacks on American gunboats on that river augered ill for American profits, the Wilsonian wartime policy toward

China and Japan saw a dramatic rise in America's share of Chinese imports. In 1914, it had been but 6 percent of the total; by 1921, it was to rise to 17 percent. However, this 1921 figure represented only 3 percent of America's exports.[63] In April 1918, as previously discussed, Wilson insisted that in the employment of American merchant ships priority be given to the Japanese trade rather than to transporting troops to France. A firmer policy toward Japan might have brought about more sales in China, but it also risked the possibility of fewer.

The policy of restraint toward Tokyo did ease Washington's concern about committing a modestly larger number of its warcraft to the ongoing war, including the four dreadnoughts sent Sims in December 1917. As the Allies accelerated their pleas to Wilson for intervention in Russia, however, the Japanese became alarmed at America's influence with the Allies. During the Lansing-Ishii negotiations, both men had sought to defer a Japanese-American argument over the Pacific islands and Shantung until a peace conference at which Wilson, and probably the Japanese, each anticipated support from the Entente. In April 1918, however, virtually the entire press of Japan violently denounced America's influence in the councils of the Allies and her influence in Siberia. They were alarmed at the outlook for Japan's future in China. The Americans were "working hard" to poison the Russians' minds against the Japanese in order to acquire the markets of Siberia for themselves, one newspaper charged. If they succeeded, the post war "Russian markets will be seized by the [now advancing] Germans and the Americans." Not surprisingly, the Japanese had limited their increase in naval support for the ongoing war to the replacement of one American cruiser (which had patrolled Hawaiian waters against no-longer-existent German surface raiders) and to the sending of one more anti-submarine craft to the Mediterranean.[64] They declined (it will be recalled) a British request for capital ships to help guard the English Channel against a possible outbreak of German capital ships.

The history of the Allied and American military invasion of Russia in 1918-1922 has received able treatment at the hands of other writers, particularly Kennan's.[65] However, a summary of the motives and effects of this intervention, some of which have been neglected, is necessary to account fully for Wilson's aversion to contributing to an Allied victory over the Central Powers. In addition, there arose an alarm in London during the German offensives in France that victory for the German and Finnish anti-Communist forces would result in new U-boat bases from which the enemy could torpedo vital Scandinavian ore shipments to Britain. Bases in the north of Finland and at relatively ice-free Murmansk would also provide a means for the longer range U-boats to circumnavigate the unfinished Norway-Scotland mine barrage into the western approaches of Britain and France.[66]

In the summer of 1917, at the time of the German advance on Riga and the acceleration of the internal disintegration of Russia, both London and Washington had wanted Japan (the only Allied power not seriously involved in waging the war against the Central Powers) to send troops across Siberia to help halt the Teutonic thrust and tie down enemy divisions. The British, however, had felt that the Americans, too, should land at Vladivostok and march westward. In London's view, the United States had not so extensively committed its military, naval, and merchant marine resources to the war in Europe that she could not do so either independently or alongside of Japanese forces. However, Wilson had balked. He had decided that there were not sufficient American ships to transport and maintain a large force in Russia, at least not without withdrawing some from profitable trade routes.[67]

The Bolshevik Revolution had brought a change in Wilson's view. To countenance a Japanese expedition in Siberia would allow them to acquire economic concessions because the Tokyo authorities would no longer need to obtain a central Russian government's consent. In the anarchy that had ensued, a local puppet, propped up by Tokyo's bayonets, could grant such concessions. On the other hand, the advent of Lenin and his peace-with-the-Central-Powers-program had foreshadowed the conditions surrounding the Allied fright at the great German drives in the West. In June 1918, Milner told Lloyd George that the German hold on Russia signified that the British, French, and American forces could not defeat the Central Powers, even assuming that France were not forced out of the war. The Reich's influence would continue to expand through Russia and Turkey into Asia. The American President would have to "be shaken out of . . . whatever half-way house he loves to shelter in" as an "associate" of the Allies, make a genuine alliance with them, and consent to bringing the full weight of Japan to bear so as to tip the balance against the Central Powers.[68] Doubtless neither Lansing nor Wilson had forgotten Jusserand's warning that, if the President's utterances about peace without victory helped to demoralize Russia out of the war, Britain and France would not even give him their sympathy if a German-Russian-Japanese coalition subsequently arose against America. At any rate, concern about Japan in 1917-1918 helped keep anti-U-boat craft as well as dreadnoughts at anchor in American waters. It was to result in Daniels's 1919 order, when the only great rival left in the Atlantic was the Royal Navy, that the Pacific Fleet was to be built up until it equalled the Atlantic Fleet in fire-power.[69]

In January of 1918, the Japanese Interior Minister, Baron Goto (soon to become Foreign Minister), informed the U.S. Ambassador, Roland S. Morris, that his people were appalled at the senseless slaughter in Europe. They drew consolation from President Wilson's calls for peace without a victor or a vanquished. Obviously, for reasons rather different from Wilson's, Goto shared the President's hope for an armistice which would preserve a balance of power in Europe. Morris, however, reported that the Baron represented the pro-German group which was gaining ascendency in Tokyo. Goto stated that the Cabinet wished to see France satisfied with some compromise over Alsace-Lorraine. Happily, Lloyd George's latest speech (January 5) omitted any restatement of his "intention to crush Germany." This was no doubt due to the benign influence of America's President. Now that the British showed marked signs of fatigue, Goto added, the continuation of the war rested upon the will of President Wilson. It was to be hoped that he would soon bring it to an end upon just terms acceptable to both sides.[70]

In February 1918, Wilson's Cabinet debated the question of intervention in Russia. The President wavered; "let Japan take the blame and responsibility" for intervention, he morosely declared. Lane, however, reminded him that this would give the Japanese a head start in the race for "our new land for development — Siberia . . . [and] we should have a front place at that table." Wilson procrastinated to London and Paris. The Allies were kept on tenterhooks for weeks about his consent to a unilateral Japanese march to the Urals or an intervention in which British, French, and American troops would enter Russia as well.[71]

In March, Sims recommended that the Navy Department send one cruiser to Murmansk for a limited time, as a token of its support for an inter-Allied intervention. Then the unleashing of the first two great German offensives led him to recommend that an expedition to northern Russia would be unfeasible for the time being. Even if the invaders could "come to terms with the local authorities in reference to the Allied stores at Archangel," the Germans would probably succeed in cutting the railroad from Murmansk to the interior. Sims agreed with the Allied Military and Naval Councils that cargo space was too critical to waste on an expedition of such doubtful results. Benson even more strongly opposed a diversion of American troops, cargo space, or warships to a Russian venture.[72]

In April, Washington (and Sims) received an alarming report from a State Department agent in Peking. "High Chinese officials inform me that Japanese are stating that if . . . [present German offensives] are successful, no dependence can be placed on the Allies for assistance to Chinese; and China must . . . throw in her lot with Japan."[73]

Part of the President's April 6 address on "Force to the utmost" should be read in the light of this background. He warned the Japanese that they were playing with fire by their tendency to accept and cooperate with German-imposed peace conditions. The Germans must agree to abandon their intent to exclude or discriminate against American trade and investment opportunities in Russia, the Levant, and Asia. He could not accept peace terms which allowed Berlin to "erect an empire of gain and commercial supremacy," an empire which would include even "the peoples of the Far East."[74]

By May, however, Allied badgering for intervention in Russia was becoming overwhelming. Wilson sought some device for acquiring control of it which would safeguard and promote America's economic ambitions in that country and frustrate the rival British, French, and Japanese goals. Commerce Secretary Redfield urged that American businessmen play a paramount role in a Washington-sponsored form of intervention. They would accompany a commission of economic experts who would endeavor to restore production and transportation in Siberia. Americans had "the opportunity and obligation to make our influence felt through commercial lines to the Russian people." Colonel

House, however, convinced Wilson that it was necessary to mask such commercial endeavors with a cloak of humanitarianism. The best way to intervene would be to send Herbert Hoover and his food relief people, along with some Red Cross and YMCA workers, into Siberia. Then Hoover would discover the conditions were so chaotic that he would appeal for "a safe and orderly field in which to work and you . . . [announce that you have] asked the assistance of England, France, Italy, and Japan, which they have generously promised" to protect this charitable enterprise. Of course, the Japanese would probably object, but "this program will place the Russian and Eastern situation in your hands . . . . " Redfield had to content himself with urging that the red tape be cut in the issue of export and import licenses for the anticipated trade which this expedition would bring.[75]

Nevertheless, the President was probably irritated when Lloyd George adopted a similar tack. British merchants were going into Siberia "to distribute goods . . . as relief . . . [and] not for profit." Later these would be sought. Meanwhile, London accepted Wilson's program by which the YMCA was to "dominate in Siberia" in the first stage. Although it was quickly obvious that troops would have to accompany instead of follow these agents of good will, the British were content to conform to the President's plan that "the economic mission" would wait and follow "after the military expedition" was well established. In July, Washington's permission for British participation in the economic profits of the venture relieved their suspicions that Wilson had "intended to restrict" these "to the United States."[76] At least, besides themselves, only the Japanese had asked to join in the commercial aspects. The Germans, of course, would have lost much ground here; it would be difficult for them to catch up if they lost the war.

On the other hand, the paucity of the military power which Wilson threw into Russia left him apprehensive about the advantages which the rival British and Japanese might acquire. He sent but 9,000 troops into Vladivostok, 7,000 into Murmansk. Even as Hindenburg's troops in the West faltered, the President suspected that the British were attempting "to rush him and to trick him" into abetting them in a scheme to restore "the old regime" in Russia. It was perhaps not so much a fear that a tsar would replace Lenin, as that the Allies aimed to create conditions conducive to the re-adherence of Russia to the terms of the Paris Economic Conference (with the Japanese avidly joining them) against American interests in Siberia and China which lay behind his apprehensions. Perhaps Wilson hoped that the modest scope of his intervention would be viewed by Lenin as sufficiently responsive to his recent hints that Wilson's non-intervention would be rewarded by admission of American goods and capital investments into the Soviet Union. However, soon after the Armistice, Daniels would bemoan the Japanese acquisition of utility franchises in Siberia.[77]

By early August, however, the Allied intervention and the beginning of the German retreat in France had relieved British fears that the progress of German-Finnish anti-Lenin forces would open up new

U-boat bases in the Far North. On the other hand, the intervention had served to aggravate Washington's hostility toward the British. For some weeks in the summer of 1918, Sims worried that he would be ordered to return the Grand Cross of the Order of St. Michael and St. George which the King had personally bestowed upon him. True, the President had raised no objection when Pershing and his generals had received similar awards from the French President. A July 1918 act of Congress authorized the acceptance of such awards, without excluding those from the British. Wilson, however, had earlier told Daniels that if Congress tried to override his opposition to "acceptance of naval honors . . . from Great Britain he would veto the bill." Finally, Sims received word that he could keep this one, but he must decline any more.[78]

On August 8, Haig's divisions broke the German line for the first time. As the Germans slowly retreated during the next three months, the morale of the Dual Monarchy, "deteriorated, largely as a result of the Allied economic blockade."[79] The morale of their lesser allies, the Bulgarians and the Turks, broke even more quickly; they were the first to sue for an armistice. Only after all four of the Central Powers had done so, however, did the Italians feel that they could launch successful military and naval attacks against the Habsburg forces. On October 21, revolution broke out in Vienna; the contagion quickly spread to Budapest and Prague. On the 24th, Diaz began a general offensive which was spearheaded by the British troops still in Italy. A few days later, an Austro-Italian naval armistice was signed.[80] Some hours later, however, two Italian frogmen sank an Austrian dreadnought. The Rome Admiralty excused this and other Italian attacks on Habsburg warships by citing the fact that the German-speaking Austrians were turning many warships over to detested Yugoslavs among their crews. The British, French, and American admirals at Corfu and Malta promised them refuge if they could escape past the hostile Italian warcraft.[81] Thus began the post-Armistice struggle between the French-backed Yugoslavs and the Italians over rival Balkan ambitions. However, Benson did rush Sims three dreadnoughts in October — not to help the British, but to guard against Benson's belated fear that Scheer might break into the channel and menace Pershing's supply lines. Scheer did, late in October, order the High Seas Fleet to thrust for the Channel. By November 4, however, his sailors were throwing overboard or killing the officers bent on carrying out his order. The rebellious crews were hoisting red banners emblazoned with the hammer and sickle over the Reich's dreadnoughts. On shore, news of this sparked radical risings in Germany's factories and cities. The Emperor fled to sanctuary across the Dutch border. The Berlin authorities rued the day they had smuggled Lenin back to Petrograd; the forty German divisions still in Russia were now deemed too contaminated with communist sympathies to be relied upon to halt the red tide inside the Fatherland itself.[82]

Notes on Chapter 5

[1] Premier Painlevé confirmed to Lloyd George that his government would not "call upon their troops for any further great and sustained offensive effort before it becomes evident that the enemy's strength has been definitely and finally broken." War Cabinet minutes for Oct. 7, 1917, CAB/23/4. See also note 2.

[2] Frederick Palmer, *Newton D. Baker* (New York, 1931), I, 231-32.

[3] Hoover to House, Oct. 26, 1917, Daniels Papers; Hoover to Wilson, Nov. 5, 1917, *ibid.*; Sims to Daniels, July 28, 1917, Sims Papers; Sims to Pratt, Aug. 18, 1917., *ibid.*

[4] War Cabinet minutes for Jan. 16, 1918, CAB/23/5; Lord Rhondda to Lloyd George, Dec. 4, 1917 and Jan. 7, 1918, Lloyd George Papers, F/43/5/44 and 48 stating that money recently promised by McAdoo had not materialized, so food purchases had to be cut. Hoover was telling him that unless all food purchases were made through one agency, presumably under American supervision, "he may cut them all off"; Hoover had warned that America "cannot finance our purchases beyond January."

[5] House to Wilson, Feb. 15, 1918, Wilson Papers; Poincaré to Wilson, Mar. 5, 1918, *ibid.*; State Department European expert William C. Bullitt to Wilson, Mar. 6, 1918, *ibid.*; Sims to Benson, Oct. 22, 1917, Sims Papers; Thomas G. Frothingham, *The Naval History of the Great War* (Cambridge, Mass., 1927), III, Chap. 30.

[6] Laning to Sims, Aug. 26, 1918, Sims Papers, in response to Sims to Laning, Aug. 17, 1918, *ibid.*

[7] E. David Cronon, ed., *The Cabinet Diaries of Josephus Daniels, 1913-1921* (Lincoln, 1963), Feb. 7, 1918; Graeme Thomson (Minister of Shipping) to Lloyd George, May 17, 1918, Lloyd George Papers, F/210/2/3; Cronon, ed., *Daniels Diaries*, July 12 and 16, 1918.

[8] *PPWW*, IV, 320.

[9] Documents submitted by Pratt at *Hearings, 1920*, I, 1235-36.

[10] Benson to Daniels, June 4, 1918, Daniels Papers; Frothingham, *Naval History*, 224-26.

[11] W. H. Page to Wilson, Mar. 17, 1918, Wilson Papers; Lansing to Wilson, Apr. 8, 1918, on Benson and Liberia, *ibid.*

[12] Sims' figures at *Hearings, 1920*, I, 159; Geddes to Lloyd George, Aug. 26, 1918. ADM/116/1809, P.R.O. with Sims current figures: the U.S. had 3 percent of the total naval strength in waters about the British Isles, 6 percent of the total Allied and American strength in the Mediterranean.

[13] Examples are Hurley's assurance to Wilson, early Dec. 1917, Wilson Papers, Sers. 2, Box 171, that a program for building 6,000,000 tons of merchant ships in 1918 was "well underway" (about half that got built); Secretary Baker to Wilson, Dec. 19, 1917, *ibid.*, on the supposedly excellent state of aircraft production.

[14] Benson to Daniels, Nov. 25, 1917, Daniels Papers.

[15] Cronon, ed., *Daniels Diaries*, Nov. 26, 1917. Benson to Sims, Jan. 9, 1918, Sims Papers; Sims to Benson, Jan. 10 and 31, 1918, *ibid.*

[16] Cronon, ed., *Daniels Diaries*, Jan. 31, 1918; Sims to Benson, Apr. 19 and June 4, 1918, Sims Papers; Sims to Pratt, Apr. 29, 1918, *ibid.*

[17] Churchill to Wilson, Oct. 22, 1917, to Daniels who cabled it with Wilson's comments on it to Benson Nov. 12, 1917, Daniels Papers. Wilson wrote that he had read "it carefully and with a great deal of interest" — probably meaning that, up to a point, favorable action on it should be taken.

[18] Benson to Sims, Dec. 22, 1917, Sims Papers.

[19] R. S. Baker, *Woodrow Wilson, Life and Letters* (Garden City, 1927-29), VII, 509-10; Sims to Bayly, Jan. 24, 1918, Sims Papers; minutes of War Cabinet

meetings in Jan.-Mar., 1918, *passim*, CAB/23/5 and 6; Robert Blake, ed., *The Private Papers of Douglas Haig* (London, 1952), 315.

[20] Documents submitted by Pratt, *Hearings, 1920*, 1235-36.

[21] Sims to Benson, Feb. 28, Mar. 7, July 28, Aug. 17 and 30, 1918, Sims Papers.

[22] Pratt deliberately neglected to send the reprimand: unpublished Pratt autobiography (© 1939), NHFC, chap. xiv, pp. 21-2; Cronon, ed., *Daniels Diaries*, Mar. 13, 1918.

[23] Frothingham, *Naval History*, III, 171-72, 213-14, 272; Arthur J. Marder, *From the Dreadnought to Scapa Flow* (London, 1970), V, 170-71.

[24] Minutes of Special War Cabinet meeting of Dec. 31, 1917, CAB/23/13, P.R.O.

[25] Palmer, *Baker*, I, 347.

[26] Balfour to King and Cabinet, Nov. 24, 1917, Lloyd George Papers, F/160/1/14; War Cabinet Secretary Sir Maurice Hankey to Prime Minister, Aug. 28, 1918, *ibid.*, F/23/3/10 with a report of what the French were saying.

[27] Sims to Capt. J.R.P. Pringle (senior American officer in Ireland), Jan. 17, 1918, Sims Papers.

[28] Minutes of Special War Cabinet meeting (a session to which Lloyd George invited but a few select advisers) of Dec. 31, 1917. CAB/23/13, P. R. O.

[29] Field Marshal Jan Christian Smuts to Lloyd George, Jan. 21, 1918, Lloyd George Papers, F/45/9/9, reporting his interview with Haig on this matter: Hankey and Sir Thomas Royden (shipping adviser to the War Cabinet) warned of permanent damage to Britain's economic life from "sacrificing imports *now* in order to bring over U. S. troops." They thought that the tacit understanding "that the U. S. Government will make good tonnage later is open to grave risks." Clement Jones with this report to Lord Curzon, Jan. 3, 1918, CAB/21/55, P.R.O. Lloyd George almost acted on their advice: in a draft cable to House of Jan. 15 (not sent), he stated that he was not going "to bear the great additional sacrifices which diversion of shipping would entail for the sake of . . . [American military] assistance . . . at a distant date." Lloyd George Papers, F/210/2/3. He probably withheld this as he decided against seeking a negotiated peace at that time.

[30] *War Memoirs of David Lloyd George* (Boston, 1933-37), V, 367.

[31] Roosevelt to Kipling, Jan. 7, 1918, and Ames to Buckler, Jan. 24, 1918, both printed and circulated to King and cabinet Feb. 19, 1918, CAB/21/41, P.R.O.

[32] Page to Wilson, Mar. 17, 1918, Wilson Papers; Taussig to Wilson, Jan. 30, 1918, *ibid.*, Sers. 5 A.

[33] Palmer, *Baker*, II, 129-30, 133-34, 147; War Cabinet minutes for Mar. 25, 26, and 27, 1918, CAB/23/6; Sims to Benson, Apr. 2, 1918, Sims Papers.

[34] Palmer, *Baker*, II, 135, 212; Gen. Peyton C. March to Wilson, Dec. 30, 1918, Wilson Papers, Sers. 5B, with monthly troop strength in France figures for 1917-1918.

[35] War Cabinet minutes for Mar. 23-Apr. 5, 1918, *passim*, CAB/23/6.

[36] Cronon, ed., *Daniels Diaries*, Apr. 15, 1918; Sims to Benson, Apr. 2, 1918, Sims Papers; Sims to Sec. of Navy (Ops.), Apr. 14, 1917, *ibid.*

[37] Pershing to Baker, Jan. 30, 1918, Palmer, *Baker*, II, 116; Wilson to Baker, Feb. 4, 1918, N. D. Baker Papers, Box 8.

[38] Palmer, *Baker*, II, 133-34.

[39] Balfour to House (through Wiseman), Apr. 1, 1918, Balfour Papers, 49692; House to Wilson, Apr. 9, 1918, Wilson Papers.

[40] Baker, *Wilson*, VIII, 64.

[41] Cronon, ed., *Daniels Diaries*, Apr. 3, 1918.

[42] J.A. Salter, *Allied Shipping Control: An Experiment in International Administration* (Oxford, 1921), 288-89, 294, 302.

[43] *Ibid.*, 359, 361, 366-67.

[44] *Ibid.*, frontpiece chart.

[45] *PPWW*, V, 198-202.

[46] Lord Burnham to Balfour, July 23, 1918, Lloyd George Papers, F/15/8/7, enclosing text of Wilson's Apr. 8 speech to foreign correspondents.

[47] Hurley to Wilson, Jan. 25, 1918, Wilson Papers, agreeing with Wilson that there was no legal ground on which they could prevent the sale to War Cabinet on shipping losses to November 1917, Lloyd George Papers, F/35/2/33.

[48] Procès-Verbal of 1st Meeting of 5th Session of Supreme War Council, . . . Abbeville, May 1, 1918, Lloyd George Papers, F/210/2/3.

[49] Palmer, *Baker*, II, 154, 218-22, 269-70; Gen. P.C. March to Wilson, Dec. 30, 1918, Wilson Papers, Sers. 5B (with troop figures for 1917-1918).

[50] Pratt's tables at *Hearings, 1920*, II, 1235-36; Frothingham, *Naval History*, III, 285.

[51] Baker, *Wilson*, VIII, 326.

[52] Palmer, *Baker*, II, 220-21, 315-316.

[53] W. R. Braisted, *The United States Navy in the Pacific, 1909-1922* (Austin and London, 1971), 282, 326, 330.

[54] D. F. Trask, *Captains and Cabinets: Anglo-American Naval Relations, 1917-1918* (Columbia, Mo., 1972), 112.

[55] Daniels at *Hearings, 1920*, II, 2822, 3076; Braisted, *Navy in Pacific*, 331-32.

[56] Guthrie to Lansing, Feb. 16, 1916, USDSM 423, roll 2; Page to Lansing, Aug. 17, 1916, *ibid.*

[57] Gillis to Secretary of State, Feb. 27, 1917, *ibid.*

[58] Lansing to Wilson (with O'Laughlin's report), Apr. 30, 1917, *ibid*; Braisted, *Navy in Pacific*, 332; *War Memoirs of Robert Lansing, Secretary of State* (Indianapolis, 1925), 279, 293.

[59] Braisted, *Navy in Pacific*, 333; Spring-Rice to Balfour, Sept. 21, 1917, Balfour Papers, 49470, on Ishii's Monroe Doctrine request; U. S. minister at Stockholm Ira N. Morris to Lansing, May 17, 1918, USDSM 423, roll 3, with press reports about Japan and Sakhalin; War Cabinet minutes for Mar. 8, 13, and 20, 1918, CAB/23/6.

[60] Pratt to Sims, May 27, 1917, and Apr. 2, 1918, Sims Papers; House to Wilson. Sept. 6, 1917, Wilson Papers; A. W. Lane and L. H. Wall, eds., *The Letters of Franklin K. Lane, Personal and Political* (Boston and New York, 1922), 237; a certain Theodore Price to Wilson, c. May 11, 1917, Wilson Papers, Sers. 2, Box 160.

[61] G. W. Guthrie to Lansing, Sept. 5, 1916, USDM 423, roll 2; R.R.M. Emmett to Sims every few days, May 19-June 25, 1917, Sims Papers.

[62] Braisted, *Navy in Pacific*, 327, 333-34.

[63] M. A. Ouden to Frank I. Polk (Counsellor of Dept. of State), Dec. 22, 1917, USDSM 423, roll 2; J. Nahoum, *The Key to National Prosperity* (New York, 1923), 132, 96, 99.

[64] Braisted, *Navy in Pacific*, 336, 329; U. S. Consul at Darien A. Williamson to Secretary of State, Apr. 12, 1918, USDSM 423, roll 3; Sims' staff's Intelligence Memorandum No. 35, © Oct. 2, 1918, USNSF, TJ file; Sims to Benson, June 10, 1918, *ibid.*, TX file.

[65] See also Braisted, *Navy in Pacific*, Book IV.

[66] Close adviser Leo S. Amery to Lloyd George, June 15, 1918, Lloyd George Papers, F/2/1/15.

[67] War Cabinet minutes for May 1, Sept. 27, Oct. 16, and Nov. 1, 1917, CAB/23/2-4; Navy General Board Report, May 19, 1917, GB425 SN730, ONRL; Cronon, ed., *Daniels Diaries*, Aug. 24 and Nov. 26, 1917; Lansing to Jusserand, Oct. 24, 1917, *Lansing Papers*, II, 55-56; Lane and Wall, eds., *Lane Letters*, 266; Cronon, ed., *Daniels Diaries*, Oct. 11, 1917; War Cabinet minutes for Sept. 27, Oct. 16, Nov. 1 and 22, 1917, and Feb. 25, 1918, CAB/23/3-5.

[68] Milner to Lloyd George, June 9, 1918, Lloyd George Papers, F/38/?/37.

[69] Daniels to Rear Admiral J. S. McKean (Bureau of Operations), June 16, 1919, Daniels Papers.

[70] Lansing to Wilson, Apr. 25, 1918, Wilson Papers, enclosing copies of two January cables from Morris.
   War Cabinet minutes for Jan. 24, Feb. 14, and Mar. 13, 1918, CAB/23/5 and 6; Ambassador Sato's remarks to Lansing, Dec. 29, 1917, Baker, *Wilson*, VII, 436.

[71] Notes on Wilson's cabinet meeting of Feb. 28, 1918, Lane and Wall, eds., *Lane Letters*, 266-67. Baker, *Wilson*, VIII, 235.

[72] Sims to Benson, Mar. 7 and Apr. 20, 1918, Sims Papers; Benson to Daniels, June 22, 1918, Daniels Papers.

[73] E. V. Gillis of Dept. of State to Dept. of Navy, copy to Sims © Apr. 14, 1918, Sims Papers.

[74] *PPWW*, V, 200-201.

[75] Redfield to Wilson, June 8 and 26, 1918, Wilson Papers; Lansing to Wilson, June 13 and 27, 1918, *ibid.*; House to Wilson, June 21, 1918, *ibid.* Redfield to Wilson, July 9, 1918, *ibid.*

[76] Balfour to Lord Reading (Br. ambassador to U. S.), July 25, 1918, FO/800/225; Reading to Balfour, July 26, 1918, FO/800/428, P.R.O.

[77] Wiseman to Lloyd George, July 13, 1918, Balfour Papers, 49642, and Balfour's appended note to Lloyd George of the 16th: this showed Washington's ignorance of British political life; moreover, a tsarist restoration would be "a misfortune for the British Empire." American Red Cross commissioner in Russia Raymond Robins to Lansing May 14, 1918, National Archives mf. 333, roll 3, *Records of the Department of State Relating to Political Relations Between the United States and Russia and the Soviet Union, 1910-1929*, hereafter cited as USDSM 333; U. S. Consul at Moscow D. C. Poole to Lansing May 15, 1918, *ibid.*; Cronon, ed., *Daniels Diaries*, Jan. 9, 1919.

[78] Sims to Benson, Aug. 3 and 10, 1918, Sims Papers; Cronon, ed., *Daniels Diaries*, Nov. 26, 1917; Benson to Sims, Aug. 17, 1918, Sims Papers.

[79] DuPuy, *Military Heritage*, 379, 389.

[80] J. Rennell Rodd, *Social and Diplomatic Memories* (London, 1925), III, 370; Baker, *Wilson*, VIII, 541-42(with note); C.R.M.F. Crutwell, *A History of the Great War: 1914-1918* (Oxford, 1934), 602-603 (with note).

[81] Rodd, *Memories*, III, 370-71; Baker, Wilson, VIII, 541-42 (with notes).

[82] Pratt at *Hearings, 1920*, (, 1236; Sims to Benson, Aug. 10, Sept 17 and Oct. 2, 1918, Sims Papers; Sir Llewellyn Woodward, *Great Britain and the War of 1914-1918* (London, 1967), 427-28.

6

THE PROSPECT OF VICTORY INCREASES ALLIED-U.S. TENSION

July-November 1918

IN AUGUST 1918, PRATT appealed to Sims to help those "of us who really wish for the betterment of the Anglo-Saxon race" save the remnants of the spirit of Anglo-American partnership. These two powers alone were emerging from the maelstrom with the maritime, financial, and moral power to attempt a resuscitation of civilized values. But the decision makers in the United States and Britain were fixing their sights upon the economic and naval race between their two nations. The animosity of Americans who had "no love for England" seemed "apt to grow" as they saw German power fade. The burgeoning of "as great [a] commercial rivalry and misunderstanding as . . . [the foes of Anglo-American partnership] were capable of" was being promoted. Pratt was evangelizing American and British leaders to meet "each other frankly and openly in the field of commercial endeavor, stating what our aims are, and attempting to pool . . . or divide business . . . on a fifty-fifty basis."[1]

Pratt and Sims feared that Britain would resist America's challenge to her naval and economic position, that after the Armistice these two nations would devote their maritime and financial resources to a contest between themselves instead of using them ot restore stability and hope for the world's future. Pratt argued that if Canada, Australia, and other parts of the Empire threw their resources behind Britain while they developed demographically and economically as the United States had done, a naval and merchant marine construction race of formidable proportions would ensue. The American taxpayer would find himself overburdened by the cost of trying to keep ahead of the British Empire in a see-saw contest. Pratt probably did not know that the Dominions had recently rejected an Admiralty proposal for a unified naval development policy for the Empire.[2]

Sims knew that Wilson and Benson were bent upon expanding America's worldwide economic interests; he believed, however, that they should do so in cooperation with Britain. Instead, the administration aimed to do so by reducing British power and acquiring a dominant American influence on the world. Sims regarded the progress of western civilization under the pre-1914 aegis of British maritime and commercial supremacy as an article of faith; so did Pratt and Theodore Roosevelt. "Leave the sea to Great Britain" and the American economy would continue to flourish, Sims urged visiting Congressmen.[3]

The President feared that the American quest for markets might undermine his political strength at the Peace Conference. In August, he instructed Federal Trade Commission Chairman Edward N. Hurley not to speak again in public of expansionist ambitions for America's foreign commerce because he wanted to avoid giving the British "even the slightest . . . excuse for what they are doing." Unfortunately, "the impression made by past utterances [of Wilsonian officials] has been that we, like the English, are planning to dominate everything and oust everybody we can oust. : . . " Doubtless Wilson was also concerned that such utterances would provide fuel for Theodore Roosevelt's pro-Allied crusade to win an anti-Wilsonian majority in the impending Congressional elections. During this campaign, Roosevelt, ignoring the argument that nationalist pride had precluded such a course, denounced the President for not having gotten divisions into combat during the first of the great German offensives. With the Republican victory of November 1918, the former President exhorted the Allies to ignore Wilson at the Peace Conference, saying he had been repudiated by the American voters. The dominion of the seas, he declared, should be left to Great Britain.[4]

Sims's difficulties with Washington mounted during the last months of the war. In July-August, the Navy Department rejected his scheme for recompensing the Admiralty for the man-hours it had lost repairing and maintaining American vessels. Behind Washington's refusal lay fresh British offences. In May, while Hurley was telling Wilson how to acquire control of most of the world's raw materials, the British were acquiring control of important sources of them in South America. In April, Balfour had informed the War Cabinet that Chile's government feared that nation would soon be overawed by American investments in its resources; Chile looked to Britain to prevent this. A British mission, headed by Sir Maurice de Bunsen, sailed for Brazil, Argentina, and Chile aboard several of His Majesty's warships. In Rio de Janeiro, the mission gained an exclusive right for Britons (among foreigners) to develop Brazil's vast iron ore deposits and an exclusive franchise to construct merchant ships in that country. De Bunsen won additional raw material concessions in Chile. Nine days after the Armistice, Daniels was to cite this mission's economic conquests as a justification for a great new naval building program. Meanwhile, the news of these British successes reached an indignant Daniels in mid-July along with Sims's Admiralty compensation proposals.[5]

Benson and Sims had long agreed that neither the French nor the Italians were willing or able to repair and maintain American naval craft

Former President Theodore Roosevelt. Underwood & Underwood photo.

in their waters. Therefore, beginning in April 1918, Sims had induced the British Admiralty to take on this work for his vessels in southern waters. The British had earlier commenced working on his craft based in their waters. They told him, however, that their manpower diverted to his ships had subtracted from the number which they would otherwise have built for themselves. They were particularly short of oil tankers. When Sims urged that the fairest arrangement would be for the Navy Department to turn over some of its oilers, Daniels disgustedly observed that "the worst of it is Sims approved[.]"[6]

No adequate explanation of why the British reduced the number of American troops to Europe in the last months of the war has been given. New evidence is the basis for this account. On August 9, 1918, an angry President reacted to a cable from Pershing quoting a message from Lloyd George to Clemenceau. "How characteristic" it was of the British that "after urging the 100 division programme" for Pershing's Army, the would not now even support an eighty-division total for 1919. The fact that on the day before the Hindenburg line, for the first time in the war, had been broken by the British Army doubtless confirmed Lloyd George's decision that the fewer American troops brought to France henceforth, the better. Yet it was some time before Wilson even partially grasped what lay behind the British decision, if he ever learned all of their motives. Although 307,000 went over in July, only 288,000 did so in August, 257,000 in September, and 186,000 in October. In the face of this, Pershing and Bliss fumed that Washington must *"force"* the British to furnish shipping to help bring over more troops. Wilson told Secretary Baker that "we must now insist that the decision be definite and final as to what they can do."[7]

Following Lloyd George's decision, however, Clemenceau and Foch at first receded only to an eighty-division program. But when Baker, in France to "force a showdown" with Foch over this issue, was told on October 4 by the Generalissimo that forty was all he wanted, the Secretary protested that there were already about forty American divisions in France. "Forty," repeated Foch, who knew where France's interest lay. Lloyd George's decision was an early manifestation of the fact that Wilson's intention of getting the Entente into his power through financial, naval, military, and moral leverage was largely doomed. To the limit of his abilities and opportunities, Sims helped to bring this about. To visiting Congressmen and in public speeches, he extolled the Anglo-American naval effort in terms which stressed the much greater British contribution to the struggle against the enemy at sea. He and fellow speakers of the English-speaking Union countered Washington's claim to ascendency over the Allies in the financial field by lauding Britain for loaning as much money to her Allies as America loaned to the Kingdom. They adumbrated the French and Italian argument, made at the Peace Conference, that when the costs to Britain, France, and Italy, were proportionately weighed against their national wealth and population, they had each expended more on waging the war than had America. To help Britain in the coming American assault on her territorial ambitions, Sims, and a group of American and British literary luminaries to which he belonged, announced the desirability of expanding America's territorial responsibilities so that she would acquire at least one protectorate in the Levant.[8]

The Americans were to be persuaded that Britain was not merely making additions to an over-gorged Empire; she was assuming new burdens on behalf of western civilization. By sharing in these responsibilities, the Americans would cease to criticize Britain's endeavor to uplift less fortunate peoples. One hoped that this would dissipate some of Washington's passion for the great navy of the future. In the summer of 1918, Lloyd George's trusted adviser, Leopold Amery, was urging a program similar to Sims's to the Prime Minister.[9]

Responsibility for some distant, needy people was to be offered to Wilson. The President was anxious to acquire oil-rich Levantine lands, but without getting them as gifts from Lloyd George, which would obligate him to London. The Turkish pashas hoped to profit from Wilson's ambitions. They needed American capital to resuscitate whatever domains the Armistice and Peace Conference left to them; Washington would try to insure that the post-war conditions imposed upon them allowed scope for profitable American investments. The Allies, on the other hand, had less money to invest and harsher territorial terms to impose. Lloyd George resolved to prevent Wilson from gaining peace-terms leverage by threatening to withhold American capital and then claiming "that it was this threat . . . that had brought Turkey to terms." By the time the German offensives were spent in July, it had long been plain that Wilson intended to assume the role of *arbiter mundi* during the Armistice and Peace Conferences. Therefore, the exhaustion of the Hindenburg-Ludendorff drives signalled Lloyd George that it was time to minimize the future role of Pershing's Army.[10]

American anger at the British over the cutback in troops for Pershing stemmed largely from an assumption that the war would last well into 1919. Even at the beginning of November, Lloyd George was concerned lest too harsh armistice terms incite the Germans to additional months of resistance. Yet, in early August, he resolved to reduce Pershing's role, even at the cost of more casualties for Britain's forces. There were, in August, some thirty combat-ready American divisions in France; eleven more were either training there or enroute from America. Bliss reported on October 14 part of the logic behind the Anglo-French attitude: "They think that they do not need as much help as they were crying for a little while ago;" they were now making an "attempt to minimize the American effort as much as possible." Indeed, Smuts urged the British War Cabinet that it would be highly advantageous to end the war quickly with limited victory that would be due mainly to British feats of battle. Otherwise, the Americans would acquire an ascendancy over the Peace Conference.[11]

Laying the groundwork for a British-dominated peace conference, Lloyd George mellowed towards his foes at the Admiralty and War Office. In late October, he announced the line to take: "the most impressive fact of this war" was the triumphant might of the "splendid" Royal Navy. "Even our Allies . . . had at last begun to realise that . . . [it] had provided the essential foundation for victory." Turning to his arch-antagonist Haig, he felt gratified that if the Germans capitulated soon, "it would be mainly due to these victories of the British Army" which the Field Marshal and "his magnificent troops" had won "within the last few weeks."[12]

On August 8, Lloyd George confirmed to Clemenceau the trend of his July 13 message to him on Pershing's Army. The Americans were conceding that their 100 division program for July 1919 would overwhelm Allied and United States shipping resources; Lloyd George pointed out that even their "80 division programme can only be accomplished if British assistance is given." Britain had been forced to make "great sacrifices" to help bring over and support Pershing's Army. He did not dwell upon loss of commercial markets by British companies to American competitors; he emphasized that ships devoted to Pershing's forces could supply coal to France and Italy. Admittedly, he was concerned about the British laborers thrown out of work by the loss of imports and exports the American troops in France had caused. Therefore, his Government could not "see their way clear to supply the additional cargo tonnage required by the United States of America even for the reduced programme of 80 divisions." Moreover, he suspected "that the scale on which the American Army [then in France] is being supplied will have to be reduced." This meant that Washington would have to give up some lucrative commerce if it wished to satisfy Pershing's ever-rising demands for weapons, munitions, aircraft, and other items. In July, Pershing unavailingly asked that Washington divert "at least 500,000 tons of deadweight shipping" to his military needs. [13]

Lloyd George probably never doubted that Clemenceau would soon spring to his side of this issue. The British merchant marine was much more helpful than the American. The British Army and Navy controlled most of France's territorial claims in the Ottoman Empire and in Africa. Besides, the British had (as previously noted) sounded out the French about bribing Wilson with protectorates in the Levant; this had alarmed the French, who wanted no American big business near their family-style operations. On the other hand, the British might find the Americans more reliable and profitable to deal with than the French as administrators of underdeveloped lands, especially if they could get Wilson's assent to a Monroe Doctrine-style arrangement for the British Empire. [14]

In August, the London War Cabinet decided to commence both a drastic reduction in naval building and an acceleration of merchant ship construction. The Admiralty intended that, in view of its new naval construction reductions, it would reduce unwanted burdens for ships afloat. Whitehall was taking its cue about a reduction of tonnage for Pershing from British Army spokesmen at special meetings of the War Cabinet. Why waste resources on incorrigibly incompetent American generals? Typical of the British attitude was the General Staff spokesman's report to the Cabinet on October 26. Coping with his caste's taboo against boasting, "General Harrington . . . admitted that our own Army was . . . the only Army fighting properly. The French Army was extremely tired and was, so to speak, leaning against the enemy, only advancing when the enemy gave way. The American Army was not in much better condition." [15]

Furthermore, in June and July, the Prime Minister had advanced other reasons for reducing support for Pershing's divisions. During the fourth and fifth enemy drives, he had noted that "American troops were now pouring into France, but we had no guarantee that they would be available" to help halt the German drives. He was certain that Clemenceau and Foch intended to deprive "us of the support of American troops" for the coming Haig offensive; they were bent on forcing "us to keep up our present total of 59 divisions regardless of the effect upon our industries and national life generally. It was intolerable that the French should put the screw upon us in that way and he was determined to refuse the French any ships for the conveyance of American troops to France."[16] Meanwhile, Haig's Army would bear extra casualties owing to its lack of help from Pershing's. The delay in Clemenceau's conversion to London's stand on shipping for Pershing may be in part attributable to such a consideration.

On October 24, the Inner British War Cabinet linked this issue with the others just discussed. They "had to bear in mind, from a *post*-war point of view, the extensions which were being made to the American mercantile marine." Hence, they must take ships from Pershing to offset economic gains being made by American competitors and force them to divert shipping to Pershing. Moreover, the war might last into 1919; a fresh, potent U-boat campaign was anticipated in the spring. But Washington was not likely to send Sims more American vessels to fend them off; "the United States' promises were apparently as untrustworthy in naval as they were in military matters," the inner War Cabinet concluded. Therefore, "the only way to press the Americans was to threaten to withhold our shipping [from Pershing]." Washington, however, was still kept in the dark about this intended leverage to be gained from the curtailment; House was to be presented with it when he came over for the Armistice bargaining. Then he was to "be told straight out that the Americans were making a mess of it" in France. The British stance would not be reversed "unless a drastic change of method were made" in Pershing's operations. These were so "inferior as to prevent them [the American generals] from achieving any considerable results" now and "they would not [otherwise] be materially better next year."[17]

Meanwhile, Clemenceau had taken up the cry against the supposed incompetencies of both Pershing and his generals, and of Diaz and his field commanders. One surmises that the French Premier intended to drown both Wilson's and Orlando's voices at the armistice and peace talks in the mire of their alleged military breakdowns; he and Lloyd George would then have the spoils of that war to themselves to haggle over. Turning his ire first on the Italians (in August), he told Lloyd George that Rome's generals continued to refuse to make an offensive against the Austrians in Italy; they had just treacherously retreated in Albania leaving the French position exposed. Clemenceau could participate in no further inter-Allied war councils where the Italians were present. Naturally he had cut off all French artillery shipments to Italy. As one must hold a session of the Supreme War Council soon in order to work out the plan of operations for the impending Allied drive from Salonika to the North, he and Lloyd George should meet à *deux*, arrange the Balkan campaign, and present the Italians with a *fait accompli*.[18]

But the British refused to exclude the Italians from the planning of the Balkan campaign, and Lloyd George alarmed Clemenceau by telling him that the Treaty of London could not be used to exclude Wilson from a voice in the disposition of the Ottoman Empire.[19] The Prime Minister sought to keep his relations with Clemenceau, Orlando, and Wilson on a footing which would enable him to play off his two main Allies and his American associate against each other.

Clemenceau then laid the groundwork for an ultimatum to Wilson demanding Pershing's dismissal. Since he did this on October 21, after all four of the Central Powers had asked for armistice terms (in fact, Bulgaria had surrendered), his claim that he sought Pershing's dismissal to enhance the likelihood of a more efficient American army for future fighting was dubious. He actually sought a club for use against Wilson and House during the armistice and peace negotiations. He wrote Foch that he, Clemenceau, would be "a criminal" if he allowed the American army to continue its appalling performance; its performance was causing his *poilus* to die in excessive numbers. Since Pershing was incapable of getting his troops to fight efficiently and refused to obey Foch, Foch must act. The Marshal, however, refused. He could not expect that the American President would now, at the eleventh hour of the war, reverse his previous policy of supporting Pershing's intransigence; to do so would be to admit American ineptitude and give away bargaining leverage at the armistice negotiations. On the other hand, Foch was willing to assist his Premier in diminishing Pershing's role in the war. He replied that rather than demand that Wilson dismiss Pershing to "diminish the weakness of the [American] High Command," it would be more effective to transfer some of Pershing's divisions to the command of French and British generals, owing to the inexperience of the American "corps and division commanders and staffs." As for Pershing's failure to advance while the British and French were driving back the Germans, "there is no denying the magnitude of the effort made by the American Army . . . in exchange for small gains on a narrow front, it is true, but over particularly difficult terrain and in the face of serious resistance."[20] This German resistance was about to weaken as demoralization and revolution overtook the Reich.

Meanwhile, the British Admiralty had provided a diplomatic explanation of part of the reduction of the flow of troops to Pershing. This was necessary to pave the way for Sir Eric Geddes's mission to Washington seeking advantages for Britain. To assuage American alarm that German surface raiders might be lurking off of American ports, London had obligingly sent ships to Montreal to embark American soldiers. There their cruisers and transports had gone and waited in vain for the expected troops to arrive. Apparently, Geddes opined, an oversight in coordinating this new arrangement with the War Department had occurred.[21]

The War Department, tardily learning of this, protested that encampment shelter for troops awaiting embarkation from the new sites were too inadequate and that ice kept the St. Lawrence closed for too much of the year to send many via this route. Actually, Geddes, while offering this account for American consumption, was complaining to the War Cabinet about construction time lost maintaining

Sims's ships, the use of British ships to transport 60 percent of Pershing's troops and 45 percent of the imports of France and Italy, and the alarming fact that, while American, Japanese, and British merchant shipbuilding now well exceeded total losses to U-boats, British losses were still 100,000 tons a month greater than British construction. Now the American merchant marine was approaching the status of half the tonnage of the British. It was time to get ships out of service to the Americans and use them for profitable trades and to acquire raw materials from overseas.[22]

Nevertheless, the Germans might launch an accelerated U-boat campaign in the spring of 1919. Sir Eric would induce Washington to send Sims a much higher proportion of its anti-submarine craft to meet this threat. Above all, he would persuade Washington of the fairness of transferring the main burden of new construction of anti-U-boat craft to America so that Britain could turn from emphasis on them to the construction of merchant ships to make up for her disproportionately high sacrifices of them in the service of supplying Pershing's Army, the French, and the Italians. Geddes intended to convince Wilson, Daniels, and Benson to divert America's 1919 construction from merchant ships and dreadnoughts. On August 30, however, Wiseman told Lloyd George of the ominous conviction in Washington that London was "openly out to make up Britain's loss of trade."[23]

Wilson had Lloyd George informed that he regarded his speech of July 31 as an endeavor to promote aims of the Paris Economic Conference. The Prime Minister evasively countered that he had reached no final decision on these goals, that he was a prisoner of the British electorate. The Australian Prime Minister, William Hughes, had recently argued with the President in the White House over whether Australia should be allowed to retain German New Guinea. Wilson presumably believed that Australian retention would advance the British Empire toward a Monroe Doctrine-style claim over the lands neighboring the Empire in Asia as well as over the East Indies. It would also provide an excuse for a parallel Japanese retention of German territory desired by the United States in the Pacific north of the equator. Furthermore, Prime Minister Hughes had recently lauded the Paris Economic Conference in New York. The President then instructed the State Department to refuse the Australian Prime Minister an entrance visa for his scheduled return. Finally Wilson agreed to let him into the country on the condition that Lloyd George would keep him silent on the Paris Economic Conference during his visit. If Hughes violated this condition, the President would publicly denounce both him and Lloyd George. Beginning in August, the Americans ignored the most routine requests from the British without even a diplomatic excuse. If any of the steel plates on order for Britain were intended for use in construction of Royal Navy ships, none could be allowed to go, Washington told London.[24]

Under these diplomatic skies, Franklin D. Roosevelt undertook his July-September mission in London, Paris, and Rome. His avowed purposes were to look into contract deficiencies in Britain and France, and to brief Sims "on the exact state of affairs at home." At one point, Sims observed that Roosevelt "was very much pleased with himself. But he was that before he came over here." Nevertheless, Sims had a staunch supporter in the Assistant Secretary. With consummate skill and tact, Roosevelt reported, Sims surmounted the many obstacles to working efficiently with the several Allies. Jellicoe ought to be made admiral-in-chief in the Mediterranean. More publicity ought to be given to Anglo-American harmony in their common endeavors.[25]

But while Geddes was persuading Roosevelt of the justice of his proposals for the reorientation of American and British maritime construction, he was cautioning the War Cabinet that Hurley's words bore out his own admonitions that the new, great American merchant marine was intended to enhance the United States' capacity "to develop trade and industry in other countries." American merchant ship production was accelerating. To Roosevelt, however, Geddes was silent about his intention to seize the lion's share of the High Seas Fleet, as well as the Reich's merchant ships in its home waters when Berlin sued for a cease-fire.[26]

Probably not fully aware of the Admiralty's rival plans, Roosevelt broached to Daniels the topic of Geddes's proposals with an innocuously informative air. The large, new mercantile shipyards at Bristol were nearing completion. "Geddes and Wemyss . . . brought up the possibility of dovetailing the British programme for new construction in with our programme, in order that we may not build too many of one type of vessel . . . for next year's operations." Roosevelt added blandly that this raised the question "of whether the British or ourselves should build many additional destroyers . . . "[27]

When Geddes arrived in Washington early in October, Pratt observed that he seemed "most interested . . . in our merchant marine." Yet Pratt could "see no reason why we cannot arrange things openly and frankly with" the British. Neither, upon his return to Washington, could Roosevelt. On October 1, he urged Daniels that "common sense requires that we should . . . avoid duplication of effort . . . and . . . be perfectly frank . . . and meet the British half-way."[28]

On August 21, Geddes told the War Cabinet that he would go to Washington. Roosevelt was too suspect in Daniels' and Wilson's eyes to be much help. Once Geddes had convinced the Washington authorities of "the magnitude" of Britain's maritime achievements in the common cause and they had agreed to do the right thing about naval and merchant ship building, he would reopen the question of Sims's oil tanker compensation proposition. Preparatory to his mission to Washington, Geddes waxed eloquent to visiting American dignitaries about Britain's paramount role and achievements at sea during this war. Upon reading his speech, however, the President wrote to Daniels: "I don't like it even a little bit." Geddes' address paralleled his complaint to Lloyd George on August 26: "up to now they [the Americans] have done very little" in the naval war against the Central Powers.[29]

Geddes failed in Washington. Although the President saw him, he gave more specific responses to Wiseman in a separate White House interview. The President's threats were blandly cast; if they succeeded he could still hope for British cooperation in a number of areas, such as blocking claims of the exclusionary French and Italians in the Balkans and the Levant. Perhaps he could yet drive a wedge between London and Tokyo. He would need British acquiescence in his League of Nations charter, unless he were successful in mustering most of the other nations against her. He had insisted that the British Phillimore Report on the League's structure and functions be withheld from the press, so that he would be free to frame the essentials of the Charter. [30] The President "admitted that the British Navy had in the past acted as a sort of Naval Police Force." The day when it could do so, however, was done. Other powers were resolved to end British naval supremacy. Wilson coldly "wondered whether the rest of the world would be willing to go on doing so [submitting to British dominion of the seas — a hint that he would seek to rally its support for offsetting the Royal Navy's existing two to one superiority over that of the United States]." The President feared a fresh global conflict, as "many nations, great and small, chafed under the feeling that their sea-borne trade and maritime development proceeded only with the permission and under the shadow of the British Navy." He had always felt that the most deeply rooted cause of the present war was this feeling in Germany. He turned to his formula for avoiding a new conflagration: "the great power of the British Navy might . . . be used in connection with the league of nations [sic] and thereby cease to be a cause of jealousy and irritation." Wilson hinted that Lloyd George was not going to be able to use Alsace-Lorraine as a bait to keep the French from joining his side over the Royal Navy; he could not fathom how Clemenceau could have misunderstood his stand on this issue: "it must go to France, he [had] meant." [31]

Not only was Britain's naval power to be submerged by his League of Nations. The President told Wiseman that peace terms must guarantee "equality of trade opportunities everywhere and [there could be] no economic boycott [of any power] except as . . . imposed by the League of Nations." As the people of other nations, "including many people in America," felt a "great jealousy" of the enormity of the British Empire, "it would create much bad feeling immediately if the German colonies were handed over to us," Wiseman reported Wilson had told him. The President had stated that "they could be held in trust" for the League of Nations.

Obviously Geddes's maritime construction scheme had never stood a chance of success with the President. The First Lord gave the War Cabinet his assessment of Wilson's post-armistice intent. During the war, America had "continued to build capital ships [more a reference to the period prior to October 1917; since then relatively few had been under construction] when the whole of her energies ought to have been thrown into building destroyers for the convoying and escorting of her own Army." Now it was apparent that the President aimed to employ "the exercise of sea power to . . . enforce anything which the League of Nations, as he sees it, wish to enforce." Moreover, "by combination with other powers jealous of our seapower," he aimed to muster "the equivalent of, or greater than, the sea power of the British Empire . . . . In other words, he is pursuing the 'Balance of Power' theory . . . and is applying it in sea power . . . to world politics." Colonel House confirmed Geddes's worst fears a few days later by telling him that the League of Nations "would control recalcitrant members . . . by the exercise of sea power."[32]

House, on September 3, urged Wilson to begin pressuring the Allies over the Armistice and peace terms. Time was running out: "as the Allies succeed [against the Central Powers], your influence will diminish . . . commit the Allies now [to your war aims] . . . you are not as strong among labor circles of either France or England as you were a few months ago." Indeed, Ray Stannard Baker had just cautioned Wilson that Britain's workers were now skeptical "of our war purposes." Bolsheviks rejuvenated their public indictments of "Moses Wilson," the "prophet of American imperialism." He aimed for profits from "the exploitation of" the "little nations" of Europe after the ousting of "German capital" from them allowed "Anglo-American capital" to enter under the guise of assisting them in their postwar "economic reconstruction."[33]

House pressed the President to impose the terms of his version of the League's charter upon the Entente. The Charter should be acceptable to Germany and "so shorten the war," the Colonel reminded him. The President realized that "the time had come to pledge the Allies to his principles, . . . [but] direct negotiations with the British and French he discarded." After three more weeks of mulling over the problem, he tried to commit them with a new speech. The German authorities liked it; eight days later they asked him for an armistice in accordance with "the program laid down in his . . . [several] pronouncements, particularly in his address of September 27, 1918." Wilson justified his delay in confronting the Allies directly by telling his Cabinet that he would do so at the Peace Conference. There, "armed with many weapons," he would be "cold and firm" with Lloyd George and Clemenceau.[34] He perhaps was waiting to see if Pershing would yet dominate the military field and the Navy complete the mine barrage. One is reminded of Daniels's later assertion that it was primarily the American-laid North Sea barrage which had brought revolution and surrender to Germany. In addition to the leverage these feats might provide him, he could hope that, when he presented the Allies with the armistice terms he and William II had agreed upon, the Allied people would force their leaders to accept them. Thus he would have gone far towards predetermining the final terms of the peace treaties.

The British War Cabinet's recent public pronouncements did little to encourage the President to adopt a more Pratt-Sims-Roosevelt approach to his relations with them. Private exchanges between War Cabinet members showed that they still anticipated implementing the measures called for by the Paris Economic Conference. Their logic was not always impeccable. On the one hand, the London authorities sometimes argued that the menace of German "dumping" had been extinguished along with the Reich's exportable items, its output of civilian consumer goods for its own people, and its stockpiles of raw materials for manufacturing. On the other hand, even the usually logical Balfour, in the summer of 1918, argued from the assumption that this danger still existed.[35] Perhaps he sought to endow this ghost with flesh in order to justify measures which could be turned against the real competition of American commerce in the months ahead.

The British War Cabinet lent substance to Wilson's suspicions. Andrew Bonar Law, Deputy Prime Minister (as well as Chancellor of the Exchequer) told the House of Commons in May 1918 (while the de Bunsen mission was gathering in raw material and merchant ship concessions in South America) that "the government still adhered to the Paris [Economic Conference] Resolutions." In July (as noted), Lloyd George publicly spoke in favor of them. In October, Bonar Law set the line to be taken by the Lloyd George coalition in the impending elections. He began loftily: the tragedies of this war demanded unselfish British economic concern for the welfare of all the Allies, great and small. This required that the nation give "special consideration to the needs of our Allies" through a British "measure of control over trade" so that their "great demand . . . for raw materials of all kinds" would be satisfied for "a long time after the war" through London's continued control of shipping resources. This signaled British control over the commerce and raw materials of their own and their Allies' overseas empires, the protectorates they might acquire from the Central Powers, and perhaps much of the remainder of the earth's surface. This dominion might help the Entente powers, but the Americans were not their "allies." Moreover, Law called for measures to increase the Kingdom's industrial output and safeguard its "home markets . . . against unfair competition."[36] This buttressing would encourage the imperial trade preference movement then afoot in London, which aimed at placing rivals outside of the Empire at a commercial disadvantage to those inside of it.

But Wilson aimed to open opportunities to export commodities such as cotton, and to invest capital everywhere, including in the retreating Central Powers. Hence he told Geddes and Wiseman at the White House in October interviews that they must not try to impose "undue humiliation" upon Germany. He would rally the French and Italians, as well as the Belgians and others, to his program against the British. The bait of continued American financial aid would be used. He would appeal to the world's masses to rally behind him. Despite House's and Baker's uneasiness, many sources assured him that his moral strength remained intact.[37]

However, one future Republican, Herbert Hoover, and two Democrats, Edward Hurley and William Benson, as soon as the Armistice was signed, would help the President to break every possible administrative partnership with Britain. Among the few pre-Armistice period pieces of his correspondence that Wilson took with him to the Peace Conference, presumably for guidance over the details of the settlement, was a study from his trusted advisor Hurley of May 1918. This asserted that

Britain's wickedness and America's virtues justified a grandiose American economic expansion and world-wide dominion.

Hurley reminded Wilson that the world's moral leadership depended on America's economic power. He explained why it was necessary for the United States to acquire (through public funds if private investors were too laggard) foreign mineral rights so that "we would soon be in control of 60 percent of the cotton of the world, 73 percent of the copper, and together with Mexico 75 percent of the oil of the world." More was expected from the exploitation of an expanded American economic empire in Latin America. "The iron mines and manganese ore of Brazil, the nitrates of Chile," and other raw materials of foreign countries would enable Wilson "to say to the rest of the world" what price all these "would be sold at, plus [the] ocean freight rates" at which they would be hauled. This would be "the same price that purchasers in our country would pay." Thus the world's markets would be made to conform to the interests of America's industries and brokers.[38]

Hurley justified all this by contrasting the past and present British and German economic ambitions and their past and present "grasping" trade practices with the "altruistic methods" pursued by the United States in "Cuba, Porto [sic] Rico, and the Philippines." Britain's past economic successes had been "backed . . . always . . . with supremacy on the sea." Even now London was encouraging "combinations of capital" to challenge Americans for control of the world's mineral resources. Americans striving to achieve Hurley's goals were aided (it will be recalled) by passage of the 1918 administration sponsored Webb-Pomerene Act, which exempted American firms from the anti-trust laws in their operations abroad to help them against the " 'rings' of England and the cartels of Germany," to use Wilson's words.

Benson believed that naval power was crucial to success in this economic struggle. When he was defeated at Paris over his naval terms for Germany, on November 4, 1918, he had part of Sims's staff draw up an analysis which he submitted to the President for guidance at the Peace Conference. Germany's defeat in this war signified that she had just become the fourth great commercial challenger to fall victim to "Great Britain and her fugitive Allies. A fifth . . . [America, is now arising and] already the signs of jealousy are visible" in London. Just as Benson and House arrived in Paris to come to grips with the Entente over this issue, Wilson received a warning from one of Hurley's colleagues on the United States' Shipping Board. The British intended not only to keep most of Germany's colonies and take "practically the whole" of her High Seas Fleet, but to "demand the German commercial fleet including . . . ships which we now hold" using the excuse that her wartime losses to submarines and mines entitled her to them. Wilson responded the same day that he was "very keenly alive to the danger upon which it [Sherman Whipple's letter] very properly dwells."[39]

As the armistice period approached, Wilson was also keenly alive to another unpleasant fact. On September 23, Hurley pointed out that during the past few months the British had carried about 60 percent of

Pershing's men across the Atlantic. American ships devoted to this service could not bring them home in less than eighteen months. If the British continued to refuse to help, Pershing's troops might become "hostages" to the Entente if serious "disagreement" over the peace conditions arose between Washington and the Allies. Daniels noted that the Administration worried that, if it pressed Britain for help in this matter, "now she will demand ships from us," presumably to be taken out of profitable trade traffic to help transport and supply Pershing's divisions. Soon McAdoo was pointing out that, unless London were made to contribute shipping to bring American troops home following the armistice, the British would have additional cargo space to increase their trade at Americans' expense.[40]

On September 26, Wilson saw a promising wedge for intervention in imposing armistice terms upon a Central Power. He had hoped to succeed in imposing terms upon Bulgaria which he would then dictate to the Allies. This precedent would enhance his chances of imposing the other armistices upon both sides by Presidential fiat. Patently, however, he was at some disadvantage in that he had done nothing to force the Bulgarians to their knees and they had addressed their request to Lloyd George. They had sent their request through neutral American diplomatic channels. When it got as far as the American minister to the Netherlands, however, he sent a copy to Washington. Wilson then acted as if it had been addressed to him. The President instructed his envoy at Sophia to induce the King to cable the White House saying that he was authorizing Wilson "to say to the Allies that the conditions of the armistice are left to me for decision and that the Bulgarian government will accept the conditions I impose." The Bulgarians, in the process of military rout and collapse, clutched at this unexpected intervention by the President who had proclaimed his goals to be peace without annexations or indemnities. Unfortunately for them, the dissolution of their army was accelerating; they could not hold out while Wilson tried to dictate terms to their enemies. Moreover, Clemenceau ordered the Allied Balkan theatre commander (Sarrail's replacement, d'Esperey) to impose the cease-fire conditions so that neither Lloyd George nor Wilson could do so. As for "the United States Minister at Sofia's note to d'Esperey demanding the mediation of President Wilson" in setting these terms, Clemenceau telegraphed d'Esperey to ignore him.[41]

The President had been frustrated, but the Constantinople government might emulate Sofia's government and the President might have more success in trying to dictate terms to the Allies and the Turks. Not only would this lure Berlin into following these examples; Wilson might gain an additional advantage in Turkey. On September 18, House reminded Wilson that hostilities had not roused the Bulgarians against allowing Americans to profit from their postwar development: this "will mean after war reconstruction and financing" of them from America.[42]

Two weeks after Wilson's failure over the Bulgarian armistice, the Sublime Porte asked his intervention in obtaining an armistice. At stake was the eventual disposition of the sprawling Ottoman Empire and its petroleum deposits — "by all odds the richest spoils of the war." But Lloyd George was resolved that the British should acquire the lion's share of investment opportunities here. Unfortunately for both Wilson's and Clemenceau's rival aspirations, advancing British divisions in the Empire had by now captured Damascus and were driving north toward Anatolia itself. Lloyd George acted. Privately fuming at both Wilson and Clemenceau for attempting to intervene, he publicly brushed aside their efforts with some civility. A British admiral dictated the cease fire terms. The Prime Minister then awaited a more auspicious moment to offer Wilson some Ottoman territory to administer. As has been discussed, he intended to dampen American jealousy of the British Empire and its fresh acquisitions by giving them charge, as Sims put it, over "peoples not capable of governing themselves in such a manner as to advance in civilization." Sims suggested that "Palestine, Syria, Armenia, etc." would do admirably for America's share of lands to uplift. The United States should also police and "guarantee the neutrality of the Dardenelles," he held.[43] On the other hand, Lloyd George was determined that Wilson should learn that "he was not in a position to dictate the terms of peace to those who had won the right on the field of battle to do so." He reminded his Cabinet of his willingness to offer Wilson some mandate such as Palestine. But the President was going to get nothing from his meddling; only when it was obvious to all that what Wilson received had come to him as a gift won by British feats of battle, would he be offered something.[44]

As matters turned out, the Prime Minister decided against offering Palestine. Amery warned him that to set the Americans with "their crude ideas" of administration over aliens "down" in Palestine would see them mismanage affairs so that the Arabs and Jews would get at each others' throats and the turmoil would spill over into nearby British protectorates. Besides, it would be unfair to natives who "genuinely preferred" British rule to force the Americans upon them. The Tanganyikans were not so enlightened as to prefer British to American administrators; they might be offered to Wilson. When House and Benson arrived in Paris at the end of October for the German armistice negotiations with the Allies, Lloyd George offered Colonel House German East Africa as an opening gambit. The suspicious Colonel, however, reported to the President that the British wanted him to "accept something so they might more freely take what they desire."[45]

As Wilson prepared for the Peace Conference, Benson urged him to accept no African mandates as such an acceptance would leave the Allies in control of most of that continent. Instead, he should press for economic gains there by getting Africa internationalized under the League of Nations. Exceptions would have to be made for South Africa and Algeria, where many Europeans had settled. In October, the Operations Chief tried to rush a dreadnought to Smyrna on Turkey's coast to strengthen Wilson's hand there. His traditional pretext for doing so, however, was dissipated when Constantinople authorities denied that American lives or property were being menaced; besides they had mined the entrance to Smyrna. As the Turks made no offer to guide the battleship or to clear a path, Benson abandoned this scheme. The Turks capitulated to Britain's Admiral Calthorpe on October 30. In response to the Allies' rebuff of his attempted intervention in the Bulgarian cease-fire terms, the President had London, Paris, and Rome told "very frankly" that, unless he were granted influence over the final peace terms for the Balkans, they were likely to get no support from the United States in "re-opening . . . the treaties of Brest-Litovsk and Bucharest," presumably for the purpose of fixing boundaries to be defended by the Allies and the United States and to establish pro-Allied governments in Finland, Poland, the Baltic States, and possibly the Ukraine.[46]

Hence, on October 6, when Berlin asked the President for armistice negotiations, House successfully urged Wilson to "delay without seeming [to do] so." By purposely responding in non-committal phrases which prolonged the fighting, the President would gain time "to get the Central Powers to accept the terms of the note which you . . . sent Bulgaria." Thus Wilson would acquire a carte blanche as the agent plenipotentiary of Germany and Austria. The consequent exchange of notes between Berlin and Washington in which Wilson did not consult the Allies in casting his cables, however, did not lead to the hoped-for result. The British and French went ahead with their own plans for imposing the armistice terms. Washington chose Bliss and Pershing to represent its army during the final stages of the armistice negotiations. But Wilson sent Benson to represent his maritime interests. The President intended to go to the Peace Conference himself "armed with . . . many weapons" to thwart "Great Britain's selfish policy." Benson rushed to Paris intent on propping up Scheer's fleet so that it would exercise "a balancing influence on the British Fleet" and thus relatively strengthen Wilson's position as against King George V's. The President instructed Pershing (on October 27) to try to keep even the U-boats out of the Allies' hands. The British, believing that Wilson and Benson aimed to preserve German naval power to help offset that of the Royal Navy (perhaps with French help), hardened their resolve to get Scheer's fleet into their own hands. French embassy circles in Washington seemed willing to support at least part of the American program to weaken British seapower.[47]

By October 26, the day Benson reached Paris, the Allies' success at defying Wilson over armistice terms persuaded him to abandon his efforts to draw out the war to gain time to get them more into his grasp. He reverted to House's position of September 3. Daniels noted the reorientation on October 22: the President now felt that "today America can have more influence in peace meetings than in future . . . . If we continue to win their [the Allies'] selfish aims will begin to be asserted."[48] In Paris, House presented Lloyd George, Clemenceau, and Orlando with America's current interpretation of the Fourteen Points. This exposition damaged any chance that Wilson and House could wean the French and Italians to their side over continued British domination of the seas. Simultaneously, a serious weakening of the President's domestic support was weakening House's threats to the

Allies. Theodore Roosevelt led a dual-purpose attack on the home front designed to thwart the President's armistice aims and prevent the reelection of a pro-Wilson majority in Congress. The Rough Rider exhorted the Senate to "declare against the adoption of the Fourteen Points . . . and [to] find out what the President means by referring to this country as the associate instead of the ally [of the Entente]." Germany must retain no naval or land power: the voters must repudiate Wilson's "chat about peace" and "dictate peace to the hammering of guns."[49]

Ominous portents of the outcome of the November 5 elections reached the White House. The Inquiry's economic experts had drawn up recommendations for the President for the postwar world. Although these exempted special economic ties between the United States and the other nations of North and South America from Wilson's injunctions against "special" and "selfish" economic blocs, Democratic Senator P. M. Simmons now protested to the President against his stance. The high-sounding Wilsonian precepts in the economic field were all too susceptible to being made into barriers to the advancement of America's own ambitions. The President castigated such protests against his call for "the removal . . . of all economic barriers . . . among the nations" as a malicious attempt "to pervert this great principle" by raising the "the bogey of free trade." Not very successfully, if the election's results were a gauge, he denounced "discriminatory trade agreements" as "a prolific breeder of war."[50]

In Paris, the Allied leaders bridled at House's announcement that they must bind themselves for peace treaty purposes to the updated provisions of the Fourteen Points as issued by Washington. On the other hand, compromise possibilities were enhanced by the British War Cabinet's outlook on the day House and Benson reached Paris. On October 25th, Lloyd George was still uncertain about whether an armistice should wait until he could persuade Clemenceau and Orlando to join him in defiance of Wilson's freedom-of-the-seas plank. But the next day he decided on an early armistice after listening to arguments that delay would strengthen Wilson's hand. As Smuts expressed it, the Germans must be given some concessions: "if we were to beat Germany to nothingness, then we must beat Europe to nothingness too. As Europe went down, so America would rise. In time the United States of America would dictate to the world in naval, military, diplomatic, and financial matters." His Majesty's ambassador at Washington, Lord Reading, was present and seconded this prognostication. "Every month the war continued increased the power of the United States . . . [where] important influences . . . were getting the idea that America should dictate the conditions. Hence by continuing the war, it might become more difficult for us to hold our own."[51] Thus, for divergent reasons, Lloyd George and Wilson now wanted to end the war quickly. House sought subtly to coerce the Allies. Still uncertain about what lay behind the drastic cut in the flow of American troops to Europe, on October 30 he urged the President to strengthen his hand by curtailing the number of American troops still being shipped to

Pershing. Diplomatic excuses would be proffered to the Entente. Then, "a little later . . . you begin to gently shut down upon money, food, and raw material," he counseled. From House's tactful prodding, the Allies would grasp the President's purpose and bend to his will over the armistice terms in order to restore American aid in defeating the enemy. Presumably Wilson felt that it was not too late to benefit from this advice on November 6, when he ordered his cabinet to let Britain and France have "nothing . . . till peace."[52]

In Paris, House threatened Lloyd George: America would not "submit to Great Britain's complete domination of the seas any more than to Germany's domination of the land." It "would build a navy and maintain an army greater than" Britain's; Lloyd George was taking "the same attitude that Germany took in the spring of 1914 regarding her army . . . . But Germany came to grief and . . . it was inevitable that Great Britain would likewise . . . . " This followed hard on his warning that "the United States went to war . . . with Germany in 1917 upon the same [maritime] question."[53]

On October 29, House decided to seek Lloyd George's help against French and Italian resistance because "the British had intimated that an agreement with Wilson might be possible on all points but freedom of the seas and reparations." The Prime Minister, however, was not sufficiently helpful over Points 1, 3, and 14. On October 31, the President insisted that "terms one, two, three, and fourteen are the essentially American terms . . . and I cannot . . . consent to end with only European arrangements of peace." In his Fourteen Points address, Wilson had demanded in these four essential points: " . . . there shall be no private international understandings of any kind . . . ; absolute freedom of navigation upon the seas . . . in peace and in war . . . except as the seas may be closed . . . by . . . [the League] . . . ; the re-moval . . . of all economic barriers and the establishment of an equality of trade conditions among all the nations . . . [joining the League] . . . ; a [league] of nations . . . [to afford] guarantees of political independence and territorial integrity to great and small states alike." Of these four essential points, the Lippman-Cobb elucidation endorsed by Wilson said 1) negotiations could be confidential, but no part of an international agreement could be valid unless it were made public; 2) if the League went to war to enforce its rules, it would allow no commerical intercourse with the "outlaw nation."; 3) "the destruction of all special agreements, each putting the trade of every other nation in the League on the same basis . . . . "; 4) for Point 14, the Allies should refer to the President's speech of September 27, 1918, which required "no further elucidation."[54]

"The five particulars of September 27, 1918," were

1. . . . no discrimination between those to whom we wish to be just and those to whom we do not wish to be just . . . .
2. No special or separate interest of any single nation or group of nations can be . . . any part of the peace settlement . . . .
3. . . . no leagues or alliances or special covenants or understandings . . . .
4. And more specifically, there can be no special, selfish, economic

combinations within the League, and no . . . form of economic boycott or exclusion except as the power of conomic penalty by exclusion from the markets of the world may be vested in the League of Nations itself as a means of discipline and control.
5. All international agreements . . . of every kind must be made known in their entirety.[55]

With respect to Points 1, 3, and 14, Wilson would be charging in 1920 that Britain was using a new, secret international understanding to exclude the United States from access to Middle Eastern oil resources. (A further discussion is presented in Chapter 7.) It was to protect such American rights that he insisted that Points 1, 2, 3, and 14 were the essential ones, and that Point 2 was the most essential of all. Britain, by her refusal to accept Point 2, signified that she meant to keep her supremacy of the seas. With this superiority, she could negate the intended effects of all four of Wilson's essential points, especially if she succeeded in eliminating Germany's naval power by the armistice terms. With freedom from Point 2, Britain could succeed in pursuing the aims of the Paris Economic Conference; she could obtain fresh "private international understandings" having similar purposes; she could intimidate "small states" into granting her special economic advantages, additional lease ports, and spheres of influences; she could declare new "protectorates," as she had over Egypt four years earlier. Hence, on October 31, the President instructed House to tell the Allies that unless Britain yielded over Point 2, he would get Congress to approve the United States' separate withdrawal from the war on his terms instead of continuing to spend "American lives for British naval control." To this threat, Lloyd George replied that he "would be sorry" to see the Americans depart, but "we will fight on" without them. Clemenceau seconded him. A month later, Paul Cambon, the French ambassador at London, told Balfour that Britain and France must be prepared to fight "a future great war . . . a death struggle with a German and an American Republic." Although Balfour judged this "from the point of view of immediate diplomacy . . . [to be] little short of insanity," it indicated the orientation of France's attitude toward Wilson as the guns fell silent.[56]

On November 4, however, Wilson sullenly accepted Lloyd George's compromise offer. Although the Prime Minister would not accept Point 2 with respect to the German Armistice terms, at the Peace Conference he would be "willing to discuss the Freedom of the Seas in the light of the new conditions that have arisen in the course of the present war." The President's acceptance telegraph implied that he suspected that the Prime Minister meant that he was willing merely to seek to outlaw the torpedoing of British merchant ships by submarines. Wilson qualified his acceptance with a warning that if Britain did not yield over Point 2 at the Peace Conference, she could be certain that America would "build up the strongest Navy that our resources permit . . . ."[57] And at the Peace Conference, he was to decline to assent to the British proposal to outlaw submarine attacks on merchant ships. (Further discussion is in Chapter 7.)

Perhaps Wilson yielded temporarily over Point 2 on November 4, owing in part to the fears attributed to him by the Earl of Derby (Ambassador to France) on December 20, 1918. "He is afraid of the English Navy now that the German Navy has disappeared." Benson, in Paris, gave the President a copy of his staff study of November 4 (the date the armistice terms were set) about this change in the relative naval strength of Britain and America on December 18. On December 2, the Navy General Board expressed a similar alarm about the weakened power of the American navy owing to the loss of "the balancing effect" of the German navy on Britain's. An Anglo-American conflict would constrict rather than expand American commerce. Derby reported that Wilson was rushing over to London from Paris to dampen down British anger at "the American Naval programme . . . because he feels that . . . in case of a row . . . American seaport towns would be entirely at the mercy of the British Fleet." The President was also coming to enlist Britain's aid in thwarting "the demands for territorial aggrandizement of France . . . and Italy."[58]

On October 29, Wilson had telegraphed House, counting on Britain's dislike of most of the territorial claims of the exclusionary French and Italians for Lloyd George's help over Points 4-13. He had also counted on Clemenceau and Orlando to help him against the British over Point 2: "England cannot dispense with our friendship in the future and the other Allies cannot without our assistance get their rights as against England." But when Colonel House presented the Lippman-Cobb explanations of Points 4-13 to the Allies, Clemenceau and Orlando realized that in Britain's seapower lay their main hope of eluding Wilson's grasp. Reluctantly, they yielded to Lloyd George's lead on all Fourteen Points. On November 2, House telegraphed the President that Clemenceau and Orlando would accept whatever "the English will agree to concerning Article 2 . . . ."[59]

Among the Wilson-endorsed elaborations of Points 4-13 that frightened the French and Italians were the following. Under Point 5, colonial "exploitation should be conducted on the principle of the 'open door,' and under the strictest regulations as to labor conditions, profits, and taxes . . . . subject to international inquiry . . . and a colonial code binding on [all] colonial powers." Point 8 said that France should not be allowed to have the Saar. Point 9 gave Italy "less, of course, than the territory allotted by the Treaty of London . . . ." Clemenceau and Orlando shuddered at Point 10: *"German Austria* . . . should of right be permitted to join Germany . . . ." The Italians were thoroughly alarmed at the prospect of a postwar Germany, in her old partnership with the Hungarians, succeeding as the more efficient heirs of Habsburg power in the Balkans. Clemenceau was equally aroused at the prospect of a Reich larger than that of 1914. Moreover, Point 10 dealt a blow to his hope of erecting a greater Poland as a bastion against German and Russian power: "Eastern Galicia is in large measure Ukranian . . . and does not of right belong in Poland." Owing to the seeming success of Wilson's threats over Point 2 and Lloyd George's help over most of the other Points, House telegraphed

Wilson that the Allies' acceptance of all his principles except those on freedom of the seas and reparations represented "a great diplomatic victory . . . in the face of a hostile and influential junta in the United States and the thoroughly unsympathetic . . . Entente Governments." The Allies, however, thought they had evaded a commitment to the specifics of how these principles would be interpreted and put into practice at the Peace Conference. House's "victory" message implied this: "I doubt whether . . . the Allied governments . . . realize how far they are now committed to the American peace programme." Indeed, when Orlando renewed his objections to Point 9 the day before (November 3), Lloyd George suggested reminding Wilson that Point 9 had "no bearing" on the German armistice terms. House replied that it would be best not to point out this obvious truth to Wilson, "so Italian objections to the Fourteen Points had to await the Peace Conference."[60]

In fact, Wilson had avoided committing himself to much that was very specific in Points 4-13 when he telegraphed his approval of the Lippmann-Cobb explanations of his Fourteen Points: "the details of application mentioned should be regarded as merely illustrative suggestions and reserved for [the] peace conference."[61]

Meanwhile, the President found that other planks in his program for shoring up postwar German power were being cracked by the mounting domestic opposition against his generous armistice terms endeavors. Behind the scenes, Wilson was trying to leave the Kaiser on his throne. Irrational public hatred of Germany, however, had driven her language from school curricula and her composers' works from American concert halls. With the imminent Congressional elections on his mind, a Democratic Senator asked for a public Presidential denial of an attempt to save the German monarchy. Wilson's rejoinder, "had you rather have the Kaiser or the Bolsheviks" reigning in Germany, failed to arrest the Senator's stare from pointing out the disastrous effect this would have upon his Party's chances. By October 23, the President had hardened his position toward Berlin, but only somewhat. Democrat Party stalwarts protested. Wilson retorted that he would brazen out the people's wrath by taking refuge in a cyclone cellar. Then, "after 48 hours, the people will quit being hysterical and become reasonable." His Cabinet, however, insisted that the voters would not relent before election day. A few hours later, Wilson dispatched a harsher message: the German people must rid themselves of their monarch and generals; otherwise he would impose "not peace negotiations, but surrender" upon them.[62]

When he went to Paris, Benson called over three of Sims's staff planners to help him forge the naval armistice terms. Benson had carefully selected the four captains of Sims's planning staff. In summer 1917, he had reminded Daniels that Britain was "conducting her maritime operations in such a way as to diminish the possibility of postwar commercial competition from friend and foe alike." Concerned that any officers he sent Sims would become "obsessed with all things British to the detriment of clear judgment," he had stipulated that these officers be "fully imbued with our national and naval policy and ideas."[63]

At the height of the great German offensives of 1918, Benson had cabled asking this staff how soon the nation could resume capital ship construction. The captains (as they explained at armistice time) had based their May 1918 reply on the likelihood that "a peace in Europe [would] be established through [compromise] agreement or through the partial victory of Germany." In that light, they had replied that "the most likely combination of Powers against which the United States must [build in order to] be prepared to operate . . . would be Germany, Austria, and Japan." Lenin, it might be noted, had surrendered the enfeebled remnants of the Russian Navy in March at Brest Litovsk. The staff's May advice, however, had left the door ajar to the possibility that the war's end would restore Britain to the position of America's foremost potential enemy against which she must build: "war is the ultimate form of economic competition" and "the three aggressive powers" in this field were Great Britain, Germany, and Japan. Dreadnought construction could be resumed as soon as the ongoing war ceased to be "the controlling factor." The twenty-one super dreadnoughts they urged, in addition to completion of the 1916 program, would give the United States Navy a comfortable superiority of firepower over either a German-Austrian-Japanese combination or over the Royal Navy (or even over the Royal and Japanese navies).[64]

The Reich's request for an armistice galvanized these officers into promoting Great Britain into the position of prime potential enemy. The study of October 24 held that the German fleet must be left in German hands or Britain could "do with our new merchant marine as she saw fit." She could also "stop the importation of food . . . necessary to all the countries of Europe" and thus coerce them to adopt anti-American policies. Although Sims refused to allow this memorandum to leave his headquarters, once Benson got three of these officers over to Paris, they repeated their anti-British arguments for his use in advising Colonel House.[65]

Wilson had already adopted a similar stance over the armistice terms. He summoned Pratt (as noted earlier) to tell him to cable Benson that the word "interned" (rather than "surrendered" or "transferred") was to be applied to the armistice condition of Germany's warships. For, as he chose to tell the Anglophile Pratt, or Pratt chose to edit him in 1939 (without mentioning the fact that the President's instruction would have had a mainly anti-British result), "he wished not a weakened Germany, but one strong enough to halt Bolshevism in its westward sweep through Europe."[66] This reasoning was specious. The German authorities needed an army, not a navy, to halt Bolshevism's sweep through Poland, Hungary, and the streets of Berlin and the Ruhr. Besides, Lenin had no navy. Moreover, at virtually the moment Wilson was instructing Pratt, he had Daniels (on October 28) introducing a request to Congress for funds for a new three-year building program of ten super-dreadnoughts and six enormous battlecruisers which the General Board had recently advanced as part of its new, larger program to place more firepower on American decks than the British had on theirs. Two days later, Benson cabled that the Allies had resolved to cripple the German Navy. Pratt then argued to Daniels that this humiliation was likely to force the Germans "back into the hands of the Military or into those of the Bolsheviks."[67] In this indirectly anti-Bolshevik sense, Wilson may genuinely have sought to preserve German naval power to avoid "a weakened Germany," but he certainly intended her navy to have a restraining effect on Britain.

At armistice time, as William Reynolds Braisted has put it, the main objective of "the most powerful voices in American naval councils . . . was at least a navy second-to-none . . . to meet a possible combined threat from Britain and Japan." Of the two powers, "Britain seemed the more immediately ominous . . . ." Not surprisingly, Lloyd George and his Continental allies refused to countenance Wilson's plan for "the internment of [Germany's] submarines and the return of the bulk enemy surface fleet to its home bases."[68] As Benson's Paris staff explained the armistice terms, the three Allies reached agreement "by which Great Britain and France dictated the German armistice terms and Great Britain and Italy dictated the Austrian armistice terms" after holding "councils on this subject from which we have been excluded."

In the last month of the war, the President declared that he might have to combat "such intolerant [American] hatred of Germans" by becoming "their advocate for justice" over peace terms. Such "justice" as Wilson sought in this instance would have the effect of keeping the Royal Navy distracted by German seapower. On November 3, he instructed Daniels to cable Benson that the President's "judgment is clear that it ought to be distinctly understood that all armed vessels taken from the enemy should be held in trust and that it is possible to go too far in demanding excessive security" against a German renewal of the war. The President's deteriorated domestic and diplomatic position, however, doubtless animated his weakening qualification: he had Benson authorized "to use your judgment" in advising Colonel House as to what was possible of achievement.[69]

The armistice terms stipulated that the most powerful units of Scheer's High Seas Fleet were to be "interned in neutral ports, or failing them, Allied ports . . . ." The Germans had to surrender all submarines into their enemies' custody. Neither Benson nor Sims (nor Pershing) participated in the formal capitulation — Wemyss and Foch alone signed the Armistice on behalf of the Allies and the United States.[70] Sims watched the cortege of German dreadnoughts, battlecruisers, cruisers, and destroyers steam into captivity under the Grand Fleet's guns at Scapa Flow.

Notes on Chapter 6

[1] Pratt to Sims, Aug. 15, 1918, Sims Papers; Pratt to Benson and Sims, Nov. 12, 1918, *ibid.*

[2] *Ibid.*; W. R. Braisted, *The United States Navy in the Pacific,1909-1922* (Austin and London, 1971), 410-11.

[3] Congressmen James F. Byrnes and C. C. Carlin and Senator Carter Glass at *Hearings, 1920*, I, 329-40, II, 2083.

[4] Wilson to Hurley, Aug. 29, 1918, R. S. Baker, *Woodrow Wilson: Life and Letters* (Garden City, 1927-39), VIII, 365-66; *New York Times*, Oct. 29, 1918; S. W. Livermore, *Politics is Adjourned: Woodrow Wilson and the War Congress, 1916-1918* (Middletown, Conn., 1966), 206.

[5] Balfour to War Cabinet, Apr. 16, 1918, Balfour Papers, 49699; E. David Cronon, ed., *The Cabinet Diaries of Josephus Daniels, 1913-1921* (Lincoln, 1963), Nov. 20 and July 19, 1918; for details of the effects of the de Bunsen mission, see Mary Klachko, "Anglo-American Naval Competition, 1918-1922," Ph. D. dissertation, Columbia University, 1962, 25ff.

[6] Sims to Benson, Apr. 2, June 1, and Aug. 15, 1918, Sims Papers; Benson to Sims, July 24, 1918, *ibid.*, Cronon, ed., *Daniels Diaries*, Aug. 21, 1918.

[7] The "Rough Draft of a letter from the Prime Minister to M. Clemenceau," © Aug. 8, 1918, (Lloyd George Papers, F/23/3/7) is identical to the excerpts quoted by Pershing to Baker, Aug. 9, 1918, in Frederick Palmer, *Newton D. Baker* (New York, 1931), II, 338, except that it gives a fuller explanation; Baker, *Wilson*, VIII, 328; Gen. P. C. March to Wilson, © Nov. 30, 1918, Wilson Papers, Sers. 2, Box 188.

[8] Palmer, *Baker*, II, 348; *Hearings, 1920*, I, 328-37; Joseph P. O'Grady, *The Immigrants' Influence on Wilson's Peace Policies* (Lexington, 1963), 93, 107; G. L. McEntee, *Italy's Part in Winning the World War* (Princeton, 1934), 110; Cronon, ed., *Daniels Diaries*, Feb. 25, 1919; Sims to Mrs. Sims, Oct. 22 and Nov. 22, 1918, Sims Papers.

[9] Amery to Lloyd George, June 8 and 15, Aug. 16, and Oct. 19, 1918, Lloyd George Papers, F/2/1/24, 25, 29, and 31, and July 19, F/23/3/82; "Report [s] of the Imperial War Committee on Territorial Desiderata for the Terms of Peace," 1917-1918, *passim*, CAB/21/77, P.R.O.

[10] Amery urged that as the Americans had just occupied "Hayti and Santo Domingo without a word said to anyone," their consent to such a doctrine for the security of the British Empire should be sought. In exchange, London could adopt a benevolent attitude if Washington wanted to try overawing Mexico again or try to exploit the Belgian Congo without assuming political responsibility for the natives. Amery to Lloyd George, June 8 and Aug. 16, 1918, F/2/1/24 and 29.

[11] Palmer, *Baker*, II, 366; Special War Cabinet minutes for Oct. 26, 1918, CAB/23/14.

[12] Special War Cabinet minutes for Oct. 21 and 26, 1918, CAB/23/14.

[13] See note 7, above; Lloyd George to Clemenceau, July 13, 1918, Lloyd George Papers, F/50/3/8; Palmer, *Baker*, II, 262-63.

[14] See note 10, above.

[15] Special War Cabinet minutes for Oct. 24 and 26, 1918, CAB/23/14.

[16] Minutes of "Conversations" between Lloyd George and certain close advisers, most often Milner, Amery, and Hankey, marked "X minutes," for June 24 and 26, 1918, CAB/23/17, P.R.O. See also Daniel R. Beaver, *Newton D. Baker and the American War Effort, 1917-1919* (Lincoln, 1966), 171.

[17] Special War Cabinet minutes for Oct. 24, 1918, CAB/23/14.

[18] Br. ambassador at Paris Lord Derby to Balfour, Aug. 17, 1918, Lloyd George Papers, F/52/2/29.

[19] Derby to Lloyd George, Sept. 13 and Oct. 7, 1918, *ibid.*, F/52/2/31 and 27.

[20] Palmer, *Baker*, II, 367-68, 370.

[21] Geddes to Lloyd George, Aug. 29, 1918, Lloyd George Papers, F/18/2/12; "Admiralty Study of Merchant Ship Uses," Aug. 8, 1918, *ibid.*, F/35/2/75 and 77.

[22] *Ibid.*; Geddes to War Cabinet, Aug. 1, 1918, ADM/116/1909, P.R.O.; Balfour (as chairman of Admiralty-Cabinet committee) to War Cabinet, Aug. 16, 1918, ADM/116/1808; Admiralty to War Cabinet, Aug. 24, 1918, ADM/116/1809; Geddes to Gen. Sir E. H. Allenby, Aug. 5, 1918, ADM/116/1808; Memorandum (of matters to be discussed by Geddes in Washington), Sept. 19, 1918, ADM/116/1809; Special War Cabinet minutes for Sept. 4, 1918, CAB/23/14; Admiralty to War Cabinet, Sept. 19, 1918, ADM/116/1809, saying that it had reduced naval building for more merchant ship building, but was uneasy about it.

[23] Wiseman to Ambassador Reading (in London), Aug. 20 and 30, 1918, FO/800/225, P.R.O.

[24] Wiseman to Reading, Aug. 20, 27, 28, and 30, Sept. 5, 12, and 15, *ibid.*

[25] Frank Freidel, *Franklin D. Roosevelt* (Boston, 1952), I, 343; Sims to Mrs. Sims, July 28, 1918, Sims Papers; FDR to Daniels, July 28 and Oct. 1, 1918, Daniels Papers.

[26] Special War Cabinet minutes for Sept. 17, 1918, CAB/23/14.

[27] Sims to Benson with copy of this FDR letter to Daniels, Sept. 6, 1918, Sims Papers.

[28] Pratt to Sims, Oct. 15, 1918, *ibid.*

[29] War Cabinet minutes for Aug. 21, 1918, CAB/23/7; Geddes to Lloyd George, Aug. 26, 1918, Lloyd George Papers, F/18/2/11; Wilson to Daniels, Oct. 2, 1918, Wilson Papers.

[30] Baker, *Wilson*, VIII, 344.

[31] Geddes' copy of Wiseman's "Notes of an Interview with the President at the White House," Oct. 16, 1918, ADM/116/1806, P. R. O.

[32] Geddes' "Memorandum to the War Cabinet: United States Naval Policy," Nov. 7, 1918, W. P. 43, P.R.O.

[33] Charles Seymour, ed., *The Intimate Papers of Colonel House* (Boston and New York, 1926-28), IV, 65-66; House to Wilson, Sept. 3, 1918, Wilson Papers; Baker, *Wilson*, VIII, 346; unsigned dispatch to Lansing, Oct. 8, 1918, with copy of Karl Radek's article in *Izvestia*, same date, National Archives mf. 333, roll 3, *Records of the Department of State Relating to Political Relations Between the United States and Russia and the Soviet Union, 1910-29* (hereafter USDSM 333).

[34] Seymour, ed., *House Papers*, IV, 66-71; *PPWW*, V, 253-61; Cronon, ed., *Daniels Diaries*, Oct. 17 and Nov. 6, 1918.

[35] Report of Br. Reconstruction Committee, "Post War Commercial Policy . . . ," Apr. 11, 1917, CAB/24/10, P.R.O.; Balfour to Bonar Law, dated by archivist "Summer 1918," Balfour Papers, 49693.

[36] Bonar Law to Sir Edward Carson, Oct. 25, 1918, Papers of Andrew Bonar Law, Beaverbrook Library, London, 84/7/95.

[37] Baker, *Wilson*, VIII, 341-42; such assurances of mass support given by a variety of American leaders are to be seen in the August-November 1918 correspondence in the Wilson Papers, Sers. 2.

[38] Hurley to Wilson, May 27, 1918, Wilson Papers, Sers. 5A.

[39] Benson Paris staff memorandum, "United States Naval Interests in Armistice Terms," Nov. 4, 1918, sent to Wilson Dec. 17, 1918, Wilson Papers, Sers. 5B; Whipple to Wilson, Wilson to Whipple, both on Oct. 29, 1918, Wilson Papers.

[40] Hurley to Wilson, Sept. 23, 1918, Wilson Papers; Cronon, ed., *Daniels Diaries*, Sept. 25, 1918; McAdoo to Wilson, Oct. 26, 1918, Baker, *Wilson*, VIII, 516-17.

[41] Baker, *Wilson*, VIII, 425, 428-29; Seymour, ed., *House Papers*, IV, 60; Derby to

Lloyd George, Sept. 30, 1918, Lloyd George Papers, F/51/2/33.

[42] House to Wilson, Sept. 18, 1918, Wilson Papers.

[43] Clemenceau to Lloyd George, Oct. 21, 1918, Lloyd George Papers, F/52/2/37; Lloyd George to Clemenceau, Oct. 25, 1918, *ibid.*, F/52/2/39; Baker, *Wilson*, VIII, 479, 509; Sims to Mrs. Sims, Nov. 23, 1918, Sims Papers.

[44] Special War Cabinet minutes for Oct. 3, 1918, CAB/23/14.

[45] Amery to Lloyd George, June 8 and 15, July 21 (strongly endorsed by Hankey), 1918, Lloyd George Papers, F/2/1/24, 25, and 32.

[46] Benson to Wilson, Dec. 17, 1918 (with Nov. 4 study), Wilson Papers, Sers. 5B; unsigned message to Daniels on conditions in Smyrna, Oct. 10, 1918, Daniels Papers, Box 41.

[47] Seymour, ed., *House Papers*, IV, 75-76; Cronon, ed., *Daniels Diaries*, Oct. 17, 1918; Baker, *Wilson*, VIII, 521; Special War Cabinet minutes for Oct. 26, 1918, CAB/23/14.

[48] Cronon, ed., *Daniels Diaries*, Oct. 22, 1918.

[49] Baker, *Wilson*, VIII, 510-11.

[50] Lawrence E. Gelfand, *The Inquiry: American Preparations for Peace* (New Haven, 1963), 295, 299.

[51] Special War Cabinet minutes for Oct. 25 and 26, 1918, CAB/23/14.

[52] Baker, *Wilson*, VIII, 529; ibid., 531; Cronon, ed., *Daniels Diaries*, Nov. 6, 1918.

[53] Seymour, ed., *House Papers*, IV, 160, 178-85.

[54] Harry R. Rudin, *Armistice 1918* (New Haven, 1944), 272, 274, 412-21.

[55] *Ibid.*, 403.

[56] *Ibid.*, 274; Seymour, ed., *House Papers*, IV, 164; Balfour to Lloyd George, Nov. 29, 1918, Lloyd George Papers, F/52/2/54.

[57] Rudin, *Armistice*, 280, 282.

[58] Derby to Lloyd George, Dec. 20, 1918, Lloyd George Papers, F/52/2/54; Benson's Paris staff memo., Nov. 4, 1918, to Wilson Dec. 17, 1918, Wilson Papers, Sers. 5B.

[59] Baker, *Wilson*, VIII, 529; Rudin, *Armistice*, 278; Clemenceau demanded that Lloyd George pledge "at once" his opposition to any attempt at "the incorporation of German-Austria into Germany." — Special War Cabinet minutes for Oct. 26, 1918, CAB/23/14; George Creel to Wilson, Sept. 23, 1918, Wilson Papers, reporting Sonnino's vehement objection to such an *Anschluss*.

[60] Rudin, *Armistice*, 412-21, 283, 280.

[61] *Ibid.*, 267.

[62] Cronon, ed., *Daniels Diaries*, Oct. 8, 16, 21, and 23, 1918; Baker, *Wilson*, VIII, 371.

[63] W. R. Schilling, "Admirals and Foreign Policy, 1913-1919," Ph. D. diss., Yale Univ., 1954, 134; Benson to Daniels, dated only "Nov. 1917," USNSF, TX file, Box 567.

[64] Schilling, *"Admirals and Foreign Policy,"* 124; Benson's Paris staff Memo. No. 67, Nov. 21, 1918, USNSF, TX file; Sims' staff Memo. No. 21, May 11, 1918, *ibid.*

[65] Unsent Sims' staff memo., Oct. 24, 1918, *ibid;* Benson's Paris staff Memo. Nos. 65 and 67, Nov. 4 and 21, 1918, *ibid.*

[66] Pratt's unpublished autobiography, Chap. XIV, p. 28, Library of Congress.

[67] H. and M. Sprout, *Toward a New Order of Seapower: American Naval Policy and the World Scene, 1918-1922* (Princeton, 1940), 50-55; Baker, *Wilson*, VIII, 502; Schilling, "Admirals and Foreign Policy," 185-86.

[68] *Navy in Pacific*, 410; David F. Trask, *Captains and Cabinets . . .* (Columbia, Mo., 1972), 334.

[69] Cronon, ed., *Daniels Diaries*, Nov. 3, 1918.

[70] H. W. V. Temperley, ed., *A History of the Peace Conference of Paris* (London, 1920-24), I, 466, 470.

7

THE PEACE CONFERENCE

December 1918 - June 1919

Prosperity of United States depends on complete adoption of ... 14 Points .... it is necessary to insist on United States shipbuilding programme to insure biggest fleet. By no other means can Great Britain be forced to accept our terms at the Peace Conference.

> Benson to Daniels, January 1919.

[President Wilson] is threatening us with an immense fleet, he is allowing his country to pursue a policy very hostile to us in trade.

> First Lord of the Admiralty Long to Lloyd George, March 1919.

Great Britain would be very glad to have some sort of an alliance with us ... [and jointly police the world's seas with us. This would] be a most wise thing [for us] to do.

> Pratt to Benson and Sims, November 1918.

America should concede naval supremacy to England ... [as] the British Navy is the most potent instrumentality making for world peace.

> Theodore Roosevelt speech, December 1918.

It will indeed be a disastrous consequence of the Peace Conference if the moral leadership of the nations passes from us to the United States.

> Lord Robert Cecil to Lloyd George, May 1919.

A FEW DAYS AFTER the Armistice terms struggle, Sims learned of the Navy Department's massive new building request to Congress. He sourly answered the Secretary's congratulations that he would, except for Benson, shortly become the nation's only full admiral: "It is to be regretted that I could not have had this rank in carrying out my duties during the war," and "that I . . . must give it up as soon as I am detached from this position."[1]

In December 1918, Sims's prestige raised a vexing problem for the Administration. By statute, Benson would retire from active duty in mid-1919; Sims was his logical successor. The new admiral, however, confided to his wife that considering their aims, he would not be happy working at close quarters with the Secretary and the President. He saved them from some embarrassment by asking that he be allowed to resume his position as President of the War College.[2] Sims requested a Presidential audience. His tone damned his chances. He sought to persuade Wilson of "the real attitude and feeling" of good will of the London Government, lying fallow for want of American cultivation. Wilson replied that his busy schedule prevented a talk with Sims. Lloyd George was informed that Wilsonian officials were inciting a "widespread" publicity campaign "at all levels of government" to denigrate Britain's war efforts. Official Washington was taking the line that the war had been won largely by the United States' efforts; now Britain was seeking "selfish gain" from a predominately American victory.[3]

Under anti-British pressures from Wilson, Daniels, and Benson, acting Chief of Naval Operations Pratt (in mid-November) countered with a compromise proposal by which Lloyd George could "yield gracefully" to Washington's demand for naval "equality" by joining Wilson in placing both navies at the disposal of the League of Nations and reducing the Royal Navy's tonnage. The British could then "unite with us in policing the seas" in "some sort of alliance with us." But in early December, as the President neared Brest, he castigated the Sims-Pratt-Theodore Roosevelt concept of a new world order of justice enforced by an Anglo-American naval partnership: this was "militaristic propaganda." In a shipboard interview with Dr. Isaiah Bowman of the Inquiry, he fumed that had not Germany's U-boats precipitated his entrance into the war against her, he "would have been ready to have it out then and there with Great Britain . . . ."[4]

By January 1919, Sims was prepared to let the American people know "the whole truth" about "the nature of our operations" during the war. He awaited the reconvention and reorganization of Congress later in the year; then "if our Republican friends insist and if I am called before a Congressional Committee . . . I shall tell the truth." On the other hand, Benson was then cabling Daniels to do what he could about offending sections of the American press: they "should be instructed to . . . stop their sentimental attitude towards the Allies." They were "ruining our interests and peace proposals"; they were undermining the President's moral leverage over the Entente; the "prosperity of the United States depends upon complete adoption of . . . [the] 14 Points. Without appearing antagonistic it is necessary to insure [the] biggest fleet [for the United States]. By no other means can Great Britain be forced to accept our terms at [the] Peace Conference."[5]

Wilson echoed the essence of Benson's message in one of his own to Daniels on January 27. The Secretary must tell the leaders of the balky Congress that he had instructed him to say "with very deliberate conviction that it is necessary for the accomplishment of our objects here that the three year building program should be adopted . . . ." Precisely in what "our objects here" consisted, the President left for a suspicious Congress to infer. Geddes assured Lloyd George that one was "to reduce comparatively the preponderance in seapower of the British Empire." To this end, Wilson and Benson were resolved that the German warships, now mostly in British hands, must be pried loose. Wilson's pre-Armistice assumption that "England fears France and Italy and small nations will side with me to get their rights" against the preponderance of the Royal Navy had been dashed. He now saw the French in his foe's camp: "the French and British leaders fear that I might lead the small nations against them." He would fetter the British navy by getting it under the control of his League of Nations. He would complete the 1916 construction program and launch a new one — unless, so Paul Cravath (legal adviser from the State Department to the American Peace Commission) told the British, Lloyd George agreed to sell him a satisfactory number of "first class ships" from among those which Britain "might acquire from Germany, or those she might decide to immobilise." Furthermore, if London declared that its "naval standard applied only to Europe [which had no powerful navy] and not to America," then the President's "naval programme would be cut down at once." It would also be reduced if Britain gave the United States some of her share of Germany's dreadnoughts, if the Allies divided them among themselves.[6]

Daniels publicly declared that the new building program was essential because the United States was the "leader of the democratic impulse." The American people must "accept the burden" of "world police" duty. This required a navy "as powerful as that of any other nation" so that America could "play her proper part" in the defense of "the freedom of the seas" and the maintenance of the new world order which was to be upheld by the League's "world police." This force was to "be very largely naval"; the United States' share of it must be "upon a scale commensurate with its wealth." The Secretary urged the House of Representatives Naval Affairs Committee to bear in mind the success of the British de Bunsen mission's "attempt to monopolize in Brazil" when considering the size of naval appropriations.[7]

Clemenceau sent Lloyd George his *Paris Temps* account of Secretary Daniels's February 1 speech. The sanction which the Monroe Doctrine gave to the United States to be the Latin Americans' guardian against the other great powers was to be enlarged to embrace the entire globe: the navy must be expanded "for the maintenance . . . of the rights of all the little nations of the world." If the powers could not agree to naval strength reductions at Paris, Daniels had recently told

Congress, America would need a navy "bigger than any other in the world." As Japan, with the third largest Navy, had but six dreadnoughts to America's seventeen, the British and French premiers could readily divine from whom "all the little nations of the world" were to get protection from America's new guns afloat. By sending this, Clemenceau was emphasizing to Lloyd George that attaining divergent British and French aims at the Peace Conference required that they support each other against Wilson. Indeed, as the President had prepared to sail for France, the State Department had compiled a summary of chief offender Britain's recent transgressions against the United States. She was in collusion with Japan to promote her economic interests in China and Siberia; she planned to keep American investors from sharing in the exploitation of the oil deposits in her zone of influence in Persia; she was acquiring new investments in Latin America's resources, and she was striving "to wrest from America this [Latin America's] trade." Her officially-sponsored de Bunsen mission had "emphasized the aggressiveness of British policy." Balfour should be told that the economic domain of Latin America was of primary importance to "the United States and that Britain would have to base her actions accordingly."[8]

Additional post-Armistice evidence that the British were putting into effect Paris Economic Conference methods (as anticipated by Wilson) came from the American envoy to Denmark. The British were using their control of Baltic cables and censorship of mail to try to monopolize American entrepreneurs out of the competition for the markets of Scandinavia. A British naval flotilla in the Baltic was providing an advantageous background for the blandishments of their commercial attachés. The President quickly approved the doubling of American commercial attachés throughout Europe, but he could do little about the cables. His frustration over British cable practices helps explain his 1920 order for United States naval guns to fire on a British-owned company's men and equipment (Western Electric's) if they tried to lay a cable off the Florida coast to connect the United States with Latin America (despite a license granted them to do so by the unfortunate Baker).[9]

In April 1919, Benson gave Wilson another instance of the link between the coercive power of the Royal Navy and Britain's grasp on the world's cable network; he cited the recent (December-January) Anglo-French defiance of Washington's interest in Liberia. Backed by British seapower, London and Paris were moving to gain financial domination of that country. The State Department warned that this would lead to political control. The British intended to gain control of the cable-wireless links between Monrovia and other parts of Africa. They would, Washington suspected, transmit British and French commercial messages first, American messages when convenient. The British merchant marine (protected by the Royal Navy) was being brought into play to brace Clemenceau against Wilsonian economic coercion. The British, Wilson was told, were "endeavoring to increase the obligations of France . . . [to themselves] by providing France with 500,000 tons of shipping." They were telling the French (in December

1918) not to worry "if the Americans won't do business with [you], the British will."[10]

To counteract British naval and mercantile power, the administration, in December-January, sent the chairman of the General Board, Admiral Charles J. Badger, as well as Admiral Mayo and other flag officers, before Congress to justify its request for eighteen more capital ships. They were aided in their task by the belief among "informed" Americans that naval power was needed to guarantee access to the world's oil resources and their belief "that the untapped petroleum resources of the world lay in British hands." Although the President neglected to keep Congress informed of his struggle against the British, French, and Italians in Paris over access to the oil resources of the Middle East and his use of naval units to open the door to opportunity in the Mediterranean, the Department generated some building support. It was aided by alarm at the pending sale of American holdings of oil concessions in Mexico to a British-controlled company, which Herbert Hoover's deputy, Mark Lawrence, decried as "a national disaster." In January, when Daniels attended a dinner for the Vice-President, the table "talked of oil and how Great Britain was controlling [it] all over the world." In April, Daniels bewailed the expansion of British oil holdings in anti-American Mexico at the Standard Oil Company's expense. Great Britain was "reaching out everywhere to obtain oil in order to strengthen its maritime commerce," he lamented. The Secretary looked to the League's Covenant to insure that "all mandatory countries . . . were kept open on equal terms to all allied countries. Otherwise GB [sic] will control oil in Mesipotamia [sic] and other countries where it is the mandatory power while enjoying equal or better advantages with U.S. in US [sic] and countries where U.S. has power."[11]

America's industrial propserity was dependent upon a plentiful supply of oil. The General Board had, in September 1918, set forth arguments for the Administration's imminent approval of a three-year program to Congress for eighteen capital ships in 1919 that would give the nation a navy at least equal to any other in the world by 1925. Badger told a Congressional hearing in December that the Navy "must keep the trade routes of the world open to our shipping," especially as the nation was "building a great merchant marine" to get "our fair share of the carrying trade of the world." There were, however, misgivings in Congress about the need for government subsidies to keep this great merchant marine in operation. Badger's next assertion depended for its success on the mixed feelings in Congress about commitments to the League of Nations; the United States must be able "to contribute a very large share of the international police force to render . . . [the League] effective . . . ." He moved into safer waters with his statement that a superior navy was required "to give due weight to diplomatic remonstrances in peace," but he alarmed many solons with his declaration that it was needed "to enforce its [the nation's] policies in war." For the foreseeable future, he could only mean for a war against Britain, legislators were quick to point out. Mayo's admission that he aimed at winning a naval race with Britain hurt the administration's quest for a majority vote. The Board's intent, however, was to prepare America for a "spectacular future as the world's dominant mercantile power, a destiny . . . not expected to be fulfilled without a navy powerful enough to command the distant seas."[12]

On November 11, Benson's recently-formed Washington planning staff drew up its desiderata for an anticipated League navy. One stipulated that "the total naval force of the League at all times in tonnage and personnel shall be at least equal to twice that of any other state" (meaning Great Britain). Benson protested to Daniels against the inclusion of the six battlecruisers in the eighteen warships of the requested 1919 program (even though Britain had four under construction); he correctly pointed out that Jutland had demonstrated their unreliability.[13] However, Japan had four (or eight, if certain modified cruisers were counted), and the Anglophiles in Congress might prove more likely to accept her than Britain as their building stimulus. The insurmountable argument against this hope turned out to be Congressional alertness to the existing superiority of the America's navy over Japan's.

Benson and his Paris staff correctly judged that the Mikado's government was not going to risk its inferior navy against America's war-strengthened fleet, unless Tokyo was certain that Britain's fleet would join it against the United States'.[14]

In December 1918, the General Board unsuccessfully urged the President to make Japan an offer of eastern Siberia in exchange for concessions over the Pacific islands. House and Lansing had toyed with similar notions, but Wilson hoped to prop open the door in Siberia through a cooperative native government. Newton Baker, nevertheless, importuned the President on November 17, 1918, that the defeat of Germany left no valid excuse for the continuation of American military intervention at Murmansk and Archangel. The argument that the Americans could not leave Siberia while the Japanese remained or that they were needed "as guardians and police for any civil relief effort we are able to direct toward Siberia" was equally indefensible. The longer the troops stayed, "the more Japanese there are and the more difficult it will be to induce Japan to withdraw her forces . . . ." As for the Doughboys' alleged mission as protectors of potential relief missions, Baker told the President: "I frankly do not believe this, nor do I believe we have a right to use military force to compel the reception of our relief agencies." Wilson leisurely replied six weeks later via Bliss: as "the whole Russian question would . . . be one of the very first for consideration by the Peace Conference, he [Wilson] thought it better to let the status quo remain unchanged for the present."[15] It remained so for many months while Wilson hoped for an anti-Communist victory and continued his struggle with the European Allies over maritime, economic, and territorial issues.

In March, Benson pleaded in vain with the French, Italian, and Japanese naval delegates at Paris for their support against Britain: all nations, great and small "will be drawn towards association with Great

Britain as a matter of pure interest . . . even though right may be on the side of weakness," and "equality of opportunity in trade . . . will remain a dream" unless Britain were constrained to reduce the size of her navy (presumably while America built hers up).[16]

Wilson fully shared Benson's view. He pressed for the new 1919 naval program which would give America "incomparably the greatest navy in the world" (as he had described his goal in 1916). He did not, as many Congressmen and journalists at the time and some historians have since thought, keep it before Congress until May 1919 merely for the bargaining leverage it would give him over freedom of the seas (which he had abandoned by December), arms limitations (which he did not want without a navy at least equal to Britain's), and to pressure Britain into supporting the League (it was his naval construction endeavors that were alienating her from the League). Certainly he would have welcomed any Peace Conference concessions that could be wrested by rattling the guns of warships not yet built if Congressional resistance and British counter-pressure over them had not largely removed this negotiating advantage from his hand. His promise to Congress in January 1919 that he would refrain from letting contracts for the new program "until Congress is consulted" should an international agreement to reduce armaments be made did not signify that he merely wanted the program sanctioned so that he could negotiate such a treaty. He had included the same "proviso" in his request for the 1916 program "to calm Congressional opposition." For this purpose, "ever since 1913, Daniels had prefaced his demands for more ships with the hope that an international agreement would soon render competitive naval building unnecessary." The only such agreement that would have animated Wilson voluntarily to drop the 1916 or the 1919 program would have been one by which Britain relinquished her mastery of the sea. Throughout the war and the Armistice and Peace Conference negotiations, she provided the President with ample evidence that she had no intention of doing so. Moreover, as Warner Schilling has concluded, "Wilson did not consider America's pursuit of economic power to be selfish, since he believed it was America's destiny to give the world moral leadership. It is likely that he saw the American pursuit of naval power in the same perspective."[17] As an American editor reported the case for the naval expansionists at Paris, "once having abandoned our aloofness in world politics, we cannot . . . permit any nation to hold stronger weapons than we hold."[18]

Why the President abandoned his struggle for "freedom of the seas" without even bringing up this point at the Peace Conference has not been adequately explained. It will be recalled that House had pressed Clemenceau to support Wilson's freedom of the seas stance, lest France and Britain be at war against each other one day and Britain be free to repeat her oppression of neutral rights to trade with her enemies as she had done in 1914-1918. The League of Nations would be powerless to stop the Royal Navy from doing so unless most of the other naval powers took the United States' stand, House had entreated. During the Peace Conference Benson warned Wilson that Britain had emerged from the war with such a superiority of naval power that she could dictate to other members what course of action the League would pursue. Yet in a September 1919 speech, the President explained that, although he had set out for Paris "most insisting on . . . freedom of the seas," he had soon grasped the supposed fact that by raising this issue, he had merely played a "practical joke on myself." He now understood that "under the League . . . there are no neutrals . . . . All nations . . . being comrades in arms, and partners in a common sense, we all have equal rights to use the seas."[19] But that was apparent to him in October-November 1918, as his approval of the Lippmann-Cobb explanations of Points 2 and 14 showed.

The evidence suggests that soon after the Armistice, the President realized that the British would join no league whose covenant paralyzed their Navy in war with Wilsonian rules that enhanced their enemies' chances of defeating them. In December 1918, House informed him that the British were saying that "your League of Nations" would be acceptable to them, except that they were "very much disturbed concerning your freedom of the seas . . . stand."[20] Without the help of idealistic British supporters of the League concept, the President could get no League worthy of the name. Clemenceau's denigration of the League in late December (which won him a very large vote of confidence in the Chamber of Deputies) and the profound Japanese apprehensions of the League's purposes meant that no important power except the United States would support it. With the Germans and Russians outcasts, Wilson had to induce the British as well as the suspicious French, Italians, and Japanese to join his band of "comrades in arms." Then, perhaps, he could impose upon them the economic and territorial conditions of his Covenant favorable to the United States and to a durable peace.

Abandoning the freedom of-the-seas plank would reduce Anglo-American tensions to a more tolerable level. It would, so the President must have hoped, enable him to advance his other goals. It was then that Daniels appealed for Sims to help him assuage British anger at his recent pronouncements.[21]

Daniels rushed the General Board's December 2 warnings to Wilson virtually as the President started up the gangplank for Europe on December 4. Its admirals wanted "freedom of the seas" dropped. If a conflict with Britain erupted in the near future, not enough American dreadnoughts would have been built. Submarines, mines, and aircraft were needed to strike down her dreadnoughts and merchant ships in such a war. But the President must not prevent their use by inducing the Peace Conference to adopt his rules on wartime rights at sea. The Board noted that Germany had come close to victory through unrestricted use of her U-boats; the United States, too, would face the formidable prospect of trying to strangle, with a "smaller naval establishment, a superior enemy seapower." Therefore, America must "have the right of the use of submarine and aerial craft . . . to carry on war successfully against a stronger surface antagonist" who possessed "a stronger surface Navy and a large over-sea trade." This was also essential because the United States was "a nation with many ports all of which could not be protected by the presence of the fleet." The President must recede from Point 2 and modify Point 4 (on world disarmament) of his Fourteen Points. The American Navy must expand "under the conditions now obtaining and likely to obtain for some time . . . ." This greater American firepower was essential owing to the "intense commercial competition that will inevitably take place" now that the war was over.[22]

It will be recalled that in 1917 Wilson had opined to the British that dreadnoughts would probably not be decisive in a future war. He did not, however, say that they would not be a help in war or in underlining peacetime remonstrances on behalf of American rights. As world opinion still regarded battleships as the most impressive evidence of naval power, he wanted both dreadnoughts and submarines. When the British urged the Peace Conference to outlaw the use of submarines against merchant ships, Wilson sidestepped them. When Colonel House reminded him on May 22, 1919, that the issue had not been settled, the President contentedly wrote back, "not for the Conference I think."[23] Submarines would be useful against both Britain and Japan. In June 1920, the President implied that he found it advantageous to leave the British with the impression that America was free to use British and German naval practices to which he had formerly objected. He told his cabinet that he "[had?] favored freedom of the seas but wished the American flag to float there and was strong for merchant shipping." He continued on this general topic. "Speaking of British shipping and oil the President said 'Daniels and I know . . . the British and their selfishness. We were up against that in Paris[.]'" Paul Cravath told the British in November 1918 that Wilson would drop freedom of the seas for a favorable change in the American to British dreadnought ratio. As for neutral rights, in December, Lloyd George gathered that Wilson had accepted his face-saving suggestion that discussion of the issue be postponed until the League was functioning.[24] The League, however, could not be fully satisfactory to the President unless the Royal Navy was incapable of defying American remonstrances to it on behalf of equality of opportunity for Americans.

The friction foreseen by Benson quickly materialized. Consequently, Anglo-American cooperation in fashioning a just and durable peace was hobbled. British cooperation or indifference helped Wilson advance some of his aims. But the evidence suggests that the President adopted or changed to some positions in a way harmful to the world's future at least partly from a desire to spite the British. Wilson gave belated support to some of the French and Italian demands the British were resisting partially to try to win their support against Lloyd George after his own initial Peace Conference attempts to get them into his grasp had failed. Late in 1918, Washington sought to induce the Allies to accept more loans, which would have placed them further in Wilson's debt. It would also have strengthened the American economy by unloading excess commodities upon them at prices higher than they paid elsewhere upon their refusal. Hoover asserted that the Entente's refusal to make these purchases probably spelled "the total demobilization of American industry."[25]

The President sailed towards the Paris Peace Conference resolved that his League of Nations Covenant would bar the British from achieving the goals of the Paris Economic Conference. Illustratively, he declared that he would insist that Germany's colonies "be declared the common property of the League of Nations and administered by small nations." Then "the resources of each colony should be available to all members of the League." However, the urgings of such Americans as Senator John Sharp Williams on behalf of a League dominated by British and American seapower were raising apprehensions among non-English speaking people. None were more aroused than the Japanese. Their vociferous stance drove the President into further dependence upon British approval of his League.

In January-March, 1919, the Japanese were urging the Chinese to unite with them in outsing the Americans from East Asia. The Monroe Doctrine had "become a doctrine of imperialism"; America's economic tentacles, having embraced first Latin America, and then China, were now groping for Siberia, where they sought to squeeze Japan out of her rightful markets, Tokyo's agents asserted. The President's naval construction goals, as well as his other ambitions which his League Covenant was designed to promote, aimed at the humiliation and ruin of Japan.[26] The influential Prince Konoye's charges were typical of the Japanese press: "the economic imperialism with which . . . [Britain and the United States] threaten the world is no less a menace than [German] military imperialism." The kind of League "favored by America and Great Britain . . . will [give] them the lion's share of the advantages while others, deprived of the arms to resist economic aggression, will be obliged to submit to . . . these two powers. If Great Britain closes her colonies to foreign countries [through imperial preference], how can Japan maintain her existence with her limited territory [and] slender resources . . . ? Japan will be obliged to assume the same position as Germany before the war and destroy the status quo . . . . The discriminatory treatment accorded the Yellow race in America and Britain must be removed." Such charges, however, apparently served to harden Wilson against the Sino-Japanese proposal on racial equality in the League Covenant. When he helped to suppress it, the Clemenceau-inspired French press charged him with racism.[27]

To be freer to work for his economic goals, Wilson, following the Armistice, withdrew America's participation in the work of the various inter-Allied organizations, despite London's protests that in these were embodied benign nuclei for the organs of the embryonic League of Nations. They were, however, tainted with British leadership. Simultaneously, Benson ordered the nine dreadnoughts under Sims's command home, so that Mayo's fleet could commence battle exercises off Cuba as soon as possible. Daniels overruled several of his admirals' opinions that it would be "suicide" to cram some of Pershing's soldiers onto warships to bring them back to America.[28]

The British divined what lay behind America's independence of

Allied organizations. Hoover was "to be *the* food controller of the world," Lloyd George was advised. From this vantage point, Hoover could furnish Wilson with power to "influence the political reorganisation of Central Europe." Hurley was adopting a similar stance about shipping coordination. On the other hand, he was telling Wilson that Lord Reading, then in Paris, was employing "his usual cunning" to alienate the French and Italians from the President's leadership. Reading was assuring the Latins that the Americans were refusing to cooperate with the Allies so that Wilson and his agents could retain for themselves "all the credit . . . for the aid given to the enemy countries and to the liberated peoples." Hurley thought that Reading was telling the French and Italians that selfish American commercial motives lay behind this largess, that the Americans "want to hold all the advantages we have and gather in new ones."[29]

On January 31, the Inquiry reminded the President that propinquity entitled the United States to make privileged economic arrangements in North and South America and that the peace settlement ought to sanction the Open Door in Europe, Asia, and Africa. France, Italy, and Japan, the Inquiry warned, had a long history of exclusionary practices in their imperial territories. Perhaps the reports that the American Peace Commission had a plan afoot to gain control of the trade of East Central Europe for American firms figured in Reading's bill of particulars. In any case, Benson was helping Wilson, Hurley, and Hoover to achieve their goals. He had naval vessels and supply ships rendering essential support to Hoover and other administration agents.[30]

Despite such efforts, Wilson's ambitions for a merchant marine equal to Britain's were being dashed by the bankruptcy closing American shipyards. The President's hopes for an expanding export trade were temporarily becalmed in the doldrums brought on by cheaper prices asked for British goods throughout the world. To survive, many American firms were contracting with more economical British shipping companies.[31] Most aggravating to Washington was the fate of 850,000 tons of ships at issue in the Anglo-American dispute over Wilson's "wantonly provocative steps" (in London's eyes) to prevent American shareholders in the International Mercantile Company from accepting English purchase offers. Daniels told Wilson that this was an attempt "backed by the British Admiralty" to acquire "the greatest fleet and the largest ships in the world." By March 1919, Wilson receded from his November 1918 stand from which he had "emphatically" instructed the Shipping Board to prevent British purchase of ships. When McClay stated that these ships would be forcibly seized if American resistance continued, the President yielded to the invisible but ever-present weight of the Grand Fleet's firepower.[32] Moreover, pressure from the American business community and Congress struck from Wilson's hand the wartime powers he had hoped to retain over the allocation of raw materials.

Vital to Wilson's purposes was the necessity of making certain that his anti-British efforts at Paris were not going to be hobbled by

American Peace Conference Commissioners of dubious intentions. This largely explains the mystery of why the President preferred to run the risk of the further erosion of his domestic political support rather than appease the Senate with the nomination of at least one luminary of each political party to the five-man commission he headed. Vice President Thomas R. Marshall "rather talked against the League." Secretary of the Interior Lane, at Theodore Roosevelt's unexpected death in January 1919, found himself "terribly broken up." John Sharp Williams, leader of the Senate's Democrats, called upon his post-Armistice audiences to "thank your God for the British fleet" and lauded "Teddy Roosevelt" for exhorting his compatriots to leave the sea's trident to Britain and join her in a naval partnership in which "there will be no jealousy between our navies." The most obvious choice among Republican Senators for Wilson's five-man Paris commission was the incoming majority leader and Chairman of the Foreign Affairs Committee, Roosevelt's cohort, Henry Cabot Lodge.[33] Hence, the President sailed with a team commanding a negligible political following and under his own control.

As the Americans and British sparred for position at the Peace Conference, Daniels carried out a more rapid demobilization of the American navy than Benson had anticipated. The uninformed admiral, in distant Paris, still envisioned Mayo's assembled fleet flexing newly swollen muscles in the Caribbean with adequate personnel. Daniels was going to try to induce the several powers to accept amicably American naval parity with Britain; Sims could help him to do so. The Secretary was in closer touch with American domestic politics than was Benson in Paris. He was inherently a pacifist, and he had a new motive for refusing the role Benson wanted him to play. Notions of himself as President had arisen. But the isolationist-pacifist-populist-progressive circles which talked of running him had conditions: Wilson would not seek a third term and the Republicans would "put up [a] military man."[34]

Sims refused to try to help Daniels calm the British. The Secretary sent him copies of his own speeches; he asked him to explain in London that the hostility which they had aroused was unjustified. After a five weeks' delay, Sims rejoined that British alarm was not due to any distorted construction put upon his words.[35]

By the time Daniels reached Paris, the Congressional and public clamor against the League Covenant was reaching irresistable proportions. This probably surprised Wilson. Was he not pursuing (albeit behind closed doors) a policy in consonance with such "typical" wartime senatorial statements as the ones which held that the war was providing America "with an opportunity to build up its foreign commerce such as we have never had before" and would the war's end not see "in our control and not in the control of Great Britain . . . the largest number of merchant ships?" But the President now saw that he would have to undo some concessions to his domestic foes over the Monroe Doctrine. Lloyd George seized upon Wilson's weakened domestic position to use the Monroe Doctrine in his opening salvo of "the sea battle of Paris." Daniels later explained the cause of the "red-hot debate" between Benson and Wemyss: "Wilson went to Paris resolved that the . . . ambition . . . [manifest in] the dreadnoughts of Britain . . . that one nation should rule the waves should no longer prevail. Every warlike nation aspired to be mistress of the seas . . . . Control of the seas and imperialism have always been twins." The President had to have a superior navy to thwart British greed.[36]

But, in early March, Wilson had given Daniels an indication that he might recede from the new three-year program. Three weeks later, the Admiralty's new First Lord, Walter Long, gathered that Daniels was in retreat and that Benson therefore had gotten him far from Paris.[37] The First Lord urged Lloyd George to instruct Cecil, who had been selected to thrash the naval issue out with House, to stand fast. Wilson's call for a greater American navy was "very dangerous both for us and for the U.S.A." The President was trying "to get the credit for all that we have done in achieving victory," in spite of "the fact that we were fighting and spending every farthing we had in support of the war," while America "was making money hand over fist." Moreover, "although the best citizens of the United States are friendly to us, . . . a vigorous campaign is . . . on foot to promote hostility to England." The President "is threatening us with an immense fleet . . . while allowing his country to pursue a policy very hostile to us in trade." The British people must prepare themselves for the strain of outbuilding America.[38]

Cecil told House that British assent to incorporation of the Monroe Doctrine in the League Covenant was the price Lloyd George would pay for the President's abandonment of new naval construction. Wilson and House were anxious to preclude any extended Peace Conference discussion of it. Clemenceau and Orlando still looked to Lloyd George to help them achieve their eastern territorial claims and a share of German warships. They might fan anti-American resentment in Latin America. Ambassador Thomas Nelson Page had alerted the American Peace Commission to the fact that Italy and Brazil were drawing "very close"; Rome had dispatched an anti-American ambassador to Rio de Janeiro; Italy was experiencing "a recrudescence of" the talk about the "Latin race and its mission"; Orlando had made "a very gushing statement" about "Franco-Italian relations."[39] On the other hand, the British placed a higher priority on halting American naval building than they did upon thwarting Japanese demands for a Monroe Doctrine for East Asia. Wilson and House saw that, once a row over the Monroe Doctrine got underway, both Japan and Britain might demand that their own claims to Monroe Doctrines be included in the Covenant.[40] This would tend to confine American economic expansion to the Western Hemisphere.

House tried pained surprise that the British could see a connection between the Monroe Doctrine and the naval issue. Privately, Cecil pleaded with Lloyd George that Britain's demands on the Americans be divested of the aura of an ultimatum with which the Admiralty seemed intent on surrounding them. Cecil won his point. He and House assured each other that they deplored the incendiary attitudes of Wemyss,

Benson, and their staffs. House said that statements by Royal Navy officers that they hoped for war "now . . . so that they could finish them [the Americans] once and for all" before Wilson's new dreadnoughts got launched ought to be stopped. The Colonel assured Lord Robert (with diplomatic license) that "there was no idea in the President's mind of building a fleet in competition with that of Great Britain." But, as contracts for all of 1916 American construction program had to be let "under the authority of Congress he was himself doubtful whether the President could interfere with it." Cecil asked that Wilson "postpone the commencement of those ships which had not been actually begun until after the Treaty of Peace had been signed, so that we might have time to discuss and consider the matter together. He [House] said he thought that might be possible, and would see what could be done in that direction," Cecil reported. Moreover, House had now received "the President's approval" for meeting Cecil's request that the United States "abandon or modify our new [1919] naval programme."[41] This latter was not much of a concession, as the 1919 building request appeared quite unlikely to win Congressional approval. Congress was even skeptical of funding completion of the 1916 program. The same day that House gave this assurance, April 10, he and Wilson rushed their Monroe Doctrine request before the League Covenant Commission. They were just in time. The French were on the verge of launching an anti-Wilson publicity campaign over his alleged oppression of Latin American nations. Clemenceau unsuccessfully sought to shackle the United States with a League Covenant prohibition that "would limit the right of the United States to insist upon its own interpretation of that Doctrine in the future as in the past." The British, however, helped Wilson suppress an "ungracious" attempt by the French to get Wilson's Monroe Doctrine proposal rejected. On this same day, April 11, the Commission accepted Wilson's proposal. In May, the President formally withdrew his support for the new three-year building program.[42]

In refusing Daniels' request for help in assuaging British feelings over the proposed American construction program, Sims told him of a British analysis of Washington's ambitions. The new dreadnoughts could only signal a challenge to Britain, particularly as a parallel economic gauntlet had been thrown down in "recent statements made by Mr. Hurley, Mr. Schwab, and Mr. Dolan" with respect to ambitions for the American merchant marine. American naval utterances were "universally" being taken as "a threat . . . [about] what America intends to do if the peace conference does not accomplish certain results." Sims inferred that the other Allies had taken shelter under Britain's naval umbrella. The Entente "nations" had "the distinct impression that they have been threatened."[43]

But in November 1918, the American people, in electing a Republican majority to the incoming Congress, had strengthened Theodore Roosevelt's hand. In December, he and other Republicans (as well as some Democrats) declared against the Wilsonian intent "to challenge Great Britain's naval supremacy. Privately, Roosevelt went even further and sent word indirectly to Lloyd George that the new Congress would absolutely decline to authorize the 1918 [request for the 1919] program."[44]

When the new Republican Congress met in the spring, an anti-construction majority quickly appeared. It was sustained by the voters' demand for tax relief, by pro-British sentiment (sometimes disguised), by idealists' apprehension that "a greater naval program might well lead us along the road to imperialism — a course trending inexorably toward a head-on collision with Great Britain," and by legislators' resentment at the war-spawned growth of executive power. Many were irritated at the President's failure to consult with or even inform the Senate of what was happening in Paris. Republicans were also motivated by partisan opposition to the Democrat in the White House.[45]

Benson reacted to the concessions made to the Allies by pressing the President to take up a course which would enable the United States eventually to turn her Paris defeats into victory. Wilson adopted this course to a degree significant to the history of the following decades. How instrumental the Admiral was in determining his decision to do so is difficult to assess. This question, however, is of modest importance compared to the fact that the President acted in large measure as Benson recommended. Through Benson's solution to the frustration they felt in April and May of 1919, American leadership continued their struggle against Britain.

As the naval contest on the Seine had approached its climax, Benson, as previously noted, had appealed to the naval delegates of all the great powers: unless "Great Britain should reduce her Fleet . . . equality of opportunity in world trade . . . will remain a dream." Three days prior to the Wilson-House capitulation to the Lloyd George-Cecil demand, Benson held that "Lloyd George is very earnest . . . in saying that he would not give a snap of his fingers for the League of Nations if we keep on building." The Admiral also drew Daniels' attention to the latest British "duplicity" in seeking to expand their control of world communications by laying a new cable within the United States itself.[46]

On April 28, Benson exhorted the President to hold fast against the British: "it is evident that commercial interest is underlying every factor under consideration by the various nations, except ourselves. This is particularly true of Great Britain." On May 5, he laid further groundwork for persuading Wilson to adopt his solution to the deterioration of America's naval, economic, and moral grip over the Peace Conference: "it must be quite evident to you that in practically all questions that have come up Great Britain has been able to maintain her position through the dominant influence . . . of her tremendous naval superiority." Evil resulted. "During the six months of conferences" in which Benson had participated, he had "tried in every possible way to interpret your views and to anticipate your ideals and objects." The Admiral had, however, been defeated "from the very beginning . . . . [by] the fact . . . that American interests, the American viewpoint, American aims, and American ideals were entirely foreign to those of the other powers and that in practically all important cases the . . . other powers have sided with Great Britain." Now, owing to American retreats before Britain and her allies, "the League of Nations, instead of being what we are striving for . . . will be a stronger British Empire." To reverse this, it was necessary to increase the size of the American navy and to decrease or "at least prevent an increase in the naval strength of Great Britain, France, and Japan."[47]

Wilson replied the next day. He was better informed than Benson about the tensions between Britain and these two "allies" as well as about the resistance of taxpayers everywhere to a naval construction race. "I . . . take very much the view of the matter that you do. While it was impossible to get the words that you and I desired into the treaty, I do not . . . despair of bringing about the same result, chiefly because I do not believe that the taxpayers of these countries will consent to bear the burden of a larger naval establishment."[48] He thus avoided coming to grips with Benson's objections to allowing the status quo in naval strength to continue. Owing to the mood of Congress, there was little Wilson could do about this.

On the same day, Benson outlined for Daniels what the President must do to salvage something from the wreck of America's interests at the Peace Conference. Wilson "should create a situation that will compel him to break with the Allies." Then he should go home. The American naval force in the Mediterranean should remain for what influence it could exercise on the settlements yet to be made there. Considering the disadvantages under which the American delegation had labored, the President had got about all he could out of the Allies by participation in the Peace Conference. On his return to America, the President should say that "all the Allies agreed in the beginning to make peace on the basis of the Fourteen Points," but they had subsequently subverted them. Now "the strongest card he could possibly play" was that of American virtue withdrawn from the den of iniquity which the Europeans had made of the Peace Conference. "Eventually, by putting proper economic pressure on the European nations, we can secure the League of Nations on terms that will at least put us in a much stronger position."[49]

Benson's notion spread. Three weeks after he urged this, Cecil took alarm. "Some of the American delegation are already saying that . . . they are ready to say that they have struggled for milder terms and that it was the English who made it impossible for that struggle to be successful." He pleaded to Lloyd George that the terms to the Germans must be softened. "For the last two generations at any rate the greatest national asset we have had in foreign affairs has been the belief in our justice." The inequities of the peace terms gave the Americans too strong a leverage for the future; British idealists were also disturbed. "It will indeed be a disastrous consequence of the Conference if the moral leadership of the nations passes from us to the United States."[50]

The Prime Minister launched a crusade to make the terms for the

Germans more "just." Had the President joined Lloyd George's endeavor of May 7-June 28, he might have held the allegiance of some of his disciples who now turned against him. Sir Harold Nicolson protested: "I cannot understand Wilson. Here is a chance of improving the thing and he won't take it. Lloyd George, however, is fighting like a little terrier all by himself." On May 28, Philip Snowden publicly broke with the President. Among the American Peace Conference advisers who also did so were Samuel Eliot Morison and William C. Bullitt. Bullitt (already dissatisfied over Wilson's lack of interest in his solution for ending the intervention in Russia) charged that the President had "consented now to deliver the suffering peoples of the world to new oppressions . . . a new century of war." Wilson grudgingly yielded a little to Lloyd George's revisionist demands. He agreed to a plebiscite in Upper Silesia and a modest reduction in the conditions of the Rhineland's occupation, but he gave no real ground over the German indemnity terms. He stood by Clemenceau over the Poles' expansionist ambitions, too. He fought the Prime Minister with assertions that of course the terms were "hard but the Germans earned that." Lloyd George denounced the Clemenceau-Wilson protegé, Paderewski, over the Poles' oppression of "other races than their own." To an indignant Wilson he retorted that he was "simply standing by his Fourteen Points and fighting them through." The President, nevertheless, insisted on placing the now violently resisting Ukranians (and their oil deposits) under Polish rule.[51]

When Lloyd George began his revisionist effort, Wilson told Ray Stannard Baker (who was to be his chosen biographer and historian of the Peace Conference with sole access to his papers for years to come) that the Prime Minister was in "a perfect funk" because he had earlier resisted Lloyd George's efforts to get generous terms for the Germans, and he now feared that his greedy ambitions would be revealed to the world. Wilson "disgustedly" added that Lloyd George's present effort made him "very sick." Later, from his sickbed, Wilson assured this acolyte that his version of the history of the Peace Conference "will be of the highest value." Lloyd George presumably sensed the futility of renewing his March 27 argument that the transfer of the Germans in the "Polish Corridor" and Danzig to Polish dominion was likely to incite a second world war.[52]

The President could not publicly break with the Allies until he got the Senate's pro-British and pacifist votes for membership in the League. He could not yield to Lloyd George's revisionist demands without losing ground from which to charge Britain in the future with a betrayal of the Fourteen Points and the cause of a just peace. By retaining this moral advantage, he might subsequently be able to get a revision of the League Covenant (as Benson urged) that gave more specific safeguards to American Open Door rights (and more specific punishment of Allied transgressions against them). He might also, after American and Allied public opinion softened, get the Germans easier peace terms that included a revival of their naval power. At the moment, to yield to Lloyd George's revisionist demands would lose

Wilson senatorial support that might prove necessary for American membership in the League.

Some evidence suggests that one reason the President wanted Danzig transferred to Polish control (via the League) was that the grateful Poles would help with American trade expansion in East-Central Europe. German press reports in January 1919 asserted that the Americans were implementing a plan to deprive Germany's ports "of their part in the trade connection between Central and Eastern Europe" so that they could establish new routes "assuring American control over the whole of Eastern Europe." In May, Wilson frankly told the Council of Four that German merchants and investors must not be allowed to gain the principal markets of Central Europe and the Balkans. He may have resisted Lloyd George's efforts for more lenient peace terms in part because the chief beneficiaries were likely to be the Germans and the British instead of the Americans. The Smuts-Keynes argument was that as Britain and Germany had been each others' best customers before the war, generous terms to Germany were necessary to Britain's prosperity. Bliss had gathered in January that although the French wanted "to bring complete and lasting ruin on Germany," the British might be intending merely to restrain "German industrialism and commercialism . . . until they themselves are well in the lead in the race."[53]

Reports reaching Wilson's Paris Peace Commission strengthened his motives for a peace settlement that restricted German and British competition with Americans. In April, acting Chief of Naval Operations Josiah S. McKean cabled that Argentina had renewed "the German concession for High Power Radio Stations . . . . This affords Germany excellent opportunity to . . . facilitate German commercial activities in Western Hemisphere to detriment of . . . American trade with South America." In that same month, the British delegation to the Peace Conference's Supreme Economic Council waxed indignant that "a great congestion of goods imported from Allied countries [meaning chiefly Britain]" into the occupied Rhineland was being refused admittance into unoccuppied Germany. Doubtless the Berlin authorities were refusing them in order to pressure the British over the blockade and peace terms. The American delegation protested that "responsibility for all measures dealing with the economic life of the Rhineland . . . rests with the Supreme Economic Council and not with the military authorities [of Britain and France]." They worked at getting a Peace Treaty provision that would prevent the British and Germans from making discriminatory arrangements with each other at the expense of American businessmen. In May, the President (with Benson present) urged that the Council of Four accept Benson's recommendation that Austria be allowed to manufacture naval armaments, even though Germany might prove to be the principal purchaser of these wares. His stated purpose was "to wean her away from her old ally" by encouraging industries in her truncated territory because "Germany had been the chief archenemy of peace." A week later, he protested against the three European Allies' intention of making the new states "arising out of the former Austro-Hungarian Empire ... share in the Reparations debt" by pointing to "a danger that these states, being placed in a position of co-debtors with Germany, might turn in that direction for their economic development ... "[54]

Unfortunately for Wilson's purposes at Paris, the American people had little knowledge of his endeavors there. They shared his resolve of May-June to keep Germany economically handicapped; their vehemence may have encouraged his resistance to Lloyd George's revisionist campaign. During the early weeks of the Peace Conference, administration spokesmen had called for fairness to Germany. American businessmen assumed in April that their President was seeking peace terms harmful to them. One business journal declaimed that the Administration was seeking "to open our home markets to the Huns" while Britain and France were embargoing American imports to promote home industries. The Wilsonian "Free-Trade slogan to give the Germans equal rights with our home workingmen on our home markets is an insult to every Doughboy who crossed the seas ...." Moreover, the Germans' relief from taxation for large armed forces would help them gain the world's trade lead.[55] A harsh peace would slow German economic expansion.

As Lloyd George's generous impulses toward the Germans did not extend to giving them reciprocal rights in Britain's home markets, he and Wilson agreed in the Peace Treaty that "the Allied and Associated Powers ... impose on Germany ... non-reciprocal conditions in ... commercial exchanges." Germany could not bribe any of the victors; she could not grant "special preferences ... to an Allied or Associated country" for five years. Lloyd George did not intend giving either the Germans or the Americans an equal opportunity with Britons to garner markets in Russia. The President protested on June 17, that since Britain was not at war with Russia, she must cease blockading her. The Prime Minister replied that not to blockade her would leave the commerce of Russia to "German exploitation." At the same Council of Four sessions, Wilson protested the British seizure of American ships bound for German ports "with foodstuffs for Poland and Czechoslovakia." Although Lloyd George tried to suggest that their seizure had somehow been intended to coerce the Germans into signing the Peace Treaty, he ordered them released.[56]

Not only Germany, but France and Italy were rivals with the United States for economic penetration of the Balkans. At Armistice time (as previously noted), the President had warned the Allies against trying to exclude him from the peace settlement for the area. He announced to the Council of Four that although America had never been at war with Bulgaria, he was going to sign the Peace Treaty with her "through the operation of the League of Nations Covenant which ... would be included in the Treaty ... [and make] the United States ... in some degree a guarantor of the results of the Treaty ...." Among other advantages, this Treaty, coupled with the League Covenant, would give Washington a voice in the regulation of traffic on the Danube, the main commercial artery of the Balkans and Austria,

Seated together in Paris are the Big Four during the Peace Conference, 1919.
Left to right: Vittorio Orlando of Italy, David Lloyd George of Great Britain,
Georges Clemenceau of France, and Woodrow Wilson of the United States.
World Wide photo.

and an important connection with Czechoslovakia. Wilson was determined to keep Fiume, the principal Adriatic port for the Balkans, out
of Italian hands, as it was, he told the Council, not only "important to
Jugo-Slavia . . . . but . . . an   international   port   serving   Roumania,
Hungary, and Czecho-Slovakia." He intended, he added, "to build up
new States [out of the former Habsburg Empire] linked for the future
with the new order . . . . [and] one of the essentials of the new order
was that control of the Great Powers should be withdrawn from the
Balkans." In May, he instructed Benson to keep himself "fully
informed of what the Italians, French, and British were doing in and
about Fiume" and to send "a vessel of as much power as possible" to
that port. Neither the Italians nor the French were going to gain
advantages from which they could discriminate against American goods
and capital in the Balkans (the British presence was supposed to
discourage the Latins). In September, American marines were landed in
Dalmatia to forestall Italian ambitions there. In October, the President
told Daniels not to answer any Congressional queries about what
American naval units were doing in the Adriatic or the Mediterranean.
He himself would respond, if he thought it in the national interest to do

so.[57] No doubt Senator Lodge's commiseration with Italian-American voters about Wilson's public denunciation of Orlando's Adriatic aspirations prompted this covertness.

The rivalry among Wilson, Lloyd George, and Clemenceau for advantageous ground in the Turkish Empire did not preclude the collaboration of the President and the French Premier (with part-time assistance from the British Prime Minister) in trying to shut Italy out of the rewards promised her in Anatolia by Britain and France. The President declared that all mandates should be administered for the good of the natives. He insisted that their good included their unhindered access to American products and capital investments. He did not expect difficulty in mustering Congressional support for mandates over Armenia or Constantinople and the Straits (of the Bosporus and the Dardanelles). Control of Constantinople and the Straits would give Washington control over access to Russia's most heavily used ports, over access to the Black Sea ports of Turkish Armenia and Transcaucasia, and over access to the mouth of the Danube. American naval units were anchored at Constantinople and patrolled the Black Sea beginning in early 1919. An American food relief mission was dispatched to the long-suffering Armenians (among whom American missionaries had long offered solace). An American military mission operated in Transcaucasia (with headquarters in Tiflis) and sent anxious reports to the American Peace Commission in Paris about the local Menshevik government's inclination to nationalize the globally-important manganese mines of Georgia. The British, by virtue of their relatively large occupation force in Transcaucasia, were the overseers of the region. The region consisted of Georgia, Azerbaijan (with rich oil deposits) and Russian Armenia. These three provinces had declared their independence of Russia following the overthrow of the Romonovs, and formed the Transcaucasian Republic. By the Treaty of Brest-Litovsk (of March 1918), Lenin had abandoned all claim to the area. The advance of Turkish troops into the area had, in mid-1918, forced the dissolution of the Transcaucasian Republic. Upon the arrival of British troops, the Allies resolved to unite Russian and Turkish Armenia. Some American advisers on the question of Turkish mandates recommended (in early 1919) that the President include in the Armenian mandate all three provinces (as well as another Turkish province), which they tentatively styled the "Armeno-Caucasian Federation of Azerbaijan, Georgia, Armenia," and Cilicia (the last in eastern Anatolia), owing to their complimentary mineral and agricultural resources.[58]

Although Wilson did not commit himself to the inclusion of territory beyond the two Armenias in his mandate request, control of them and Constantinople would give Americans advantages in acquiring concessions to the vital manganese of Georgia and the oil of Azerbaijan, provided local sentiment in favor of nationalization could be overcome and Lenin remained helpless to reannex these provinces. The British possessed the world's other chief source of manganese in India and were anxious to withdraw from the Transcaucasian region, owing to their occupational expenses. Wilson, however, was determined that they should remain until Congress sanctioned an American mandate for Armenia because both the Italians and the French were expressing interest in a mandate over all or part of Transcaucasia. The Italians' proposal that they send two divisions there precipitated a Presidential cable to Secretary of War Baker on February 8. Wilson asked if sentiment in America would permit the sending of American troops to Armenia, pending a settlement of mandate question. The President explained to Baker that he sought to relieve the British of some of their burdens by substituting American troops for theirs in "portions of the Turkish Empire, such as Constantinople and Armenia and Mesopotamia pending the . . . designation of mandatories for such regions." He assumed that "the occupation of Constantinople and Armenia would not strike the [American] people as unreasonable." Although they might be cool to an American occupation "of the Syrian [Turkish Syria included Lebanon and northern Palestine] and Arabian countries," he was sure that American troops "would be more welcome and serviceable in those places than any other troops would be." Although the British had no intention of giving up the known oil deposits of Mesopotamia or the potential oil pipelines of Palestine, the President stated that it was "only fair that we should consider . . . sharing the burden of occupations of which nobody but the whole group of nations [under his open-door League Covenant and mandates rules] is to get the benefit." Baker replied, however, that the public was too "insistant [*sic*] upon the return of our troops" to venture sending any to any region south "of Turkey proper and Armenia." It would be better not to dispatch any even to Armenia or Constantinople before Wilson presented the case for doing so to the people; it was politically impossible to send any to Syria or Mesopotamia unless he returned to America and persuaded the people of the need to do so. This was underlined by the fact that "public opinion at home has been restless about our troops in Russia . . . ."[59]

The French were displeased at the British and American intention to award Constantinople to the Americans; they pointed to their own cultural ties with that city. Wilson was displeased that British, French, and Italian trade missions had begun pouring into the city soon after the Armistice. On May 14, Balfour proposed to the Council of Four that "some international body for finance" be established for Turkey. Wilson took this to be an effort to advance the Allies' interests in Turkey; he was "altogether opposed to that." He also opposed the Allies' proposal that their "prior claims in regard to concessions" in Turkey be honored; he "pointed out that this was contrary to the principle provided in the League of Nation's Covenant for equal opportunity to all nations in mandated territory." But, he assured the worried Allies, "this did not mean that the United States of America would rush in everywhere . . . ."[60]

Lansing thought that the Italians were unsuccessful at Paris partly because they "urged their claims frankly . . . while others, seeking to hide their nationalistic purposes, demanded that their claims should be recognized on the ground . . . of the future peace of the world and the welfare of the inhabitants of the territories . . . they coveted." The Italians' real frankness failed, while "apparent frankness, seasoned by assertions of unctuous platitudes, succeeded. . . . To admit openly that one was impelled by selfish motives was an offense to those who proclaimed their own altruism . . . . It was not playing the game according to the rules." In any case, the Italians offended Wilson. When Lloyd George suggested on April 21 giving Italy "a sphere of influence" somewhere, the President objected that that would be "paying the Italians for something they had no right to." If he could not get Armenia and Syria for the United States, he wanted Britain to keep them. The natives were less likely to revolt, and, so he told Lloyd George, he did not expect Britain to "interfere unduly" in her mandates. He no doubt meant this to stimulate open-door style behavior from the British authorities. A week later the Italians landed on the southwestern coast of Anatolia. From there, they extended their occupation to include all of the southwestern quarter of Asia Minor (which had been promised them by Britain and France). On May 2, Benson ordered Rear Admiral Mark L. Bristol to steam with his naval units from Constantinople to Smyrna to discourage the Italians from attempting to take that city. Benson added that he was trying to rush a dreadnought to join Bristol's command at Smyrna. He ordered that no destroyer in the Mediterranean return home and ordered back three that had reached Gibraltar.[61]

The Italian landings dampened French interest in Latin solidarity against the Anglo-Saxon powers. On May 14, the Venizelos government, with French and British help and Wilson's consent, landed Greek troops at Smyrna. It was understood that the Greeks would safeguard French, British, and American interests. Meanwhile, on May 5, the Italians angered Wilson by bluntly stating that they wanted to send troops to Transcaucasia "as there was oil there." The President vetoed their proposal. In late June, the President informed the Italian government that if Italy remained "in Asia Minor, the other Powers will be forced to infer that it desires to be left to its own resources."[62] This threat to cut off coal and food to Italy failed to propel her troops home.

In March, the American advisers on Turkish mandates proposed that a joint Allied-American team of pollsters tour parts of the Turkish Empire to ascertain the natives' preferences about who should become their mandatory power. They listed three cities in French-coveted Syria-Lebanon and two in British-coveted Mesopotamia. The President successfully urged that the Council of Four approve the pollsters' mission and that they be allowed to extend their enquiries "beyond the confines of Syria." The British did not want the French to get Syria, but neither did they want to offer a gross offence to the French by participating fully in Wilson's endeavor to deprive them of it. A few weeks later, Clemenceau declared that no Frenchmen would participate in the poll-taking mission until the "British troops in Syria were replaced with French troops." Lloyd George refused to replace the troops, but he tactfully said that no Briton would participate in the polling in the absence of the French. Wilson then volunteered that the Americans would go polling alone. Lloyd George declared he "was quite willing to abide by the decision of the inhabitants as interpreted by the [American] commission." Wilson rejoined that the Syrians could not have independence because "they required guidance and some intimate superintendance . . . ."[63]

The Americans reported that the Syrians would prefer an American mandate, in part as they anticipated that it would be the most short-lived. Failing this, they infinitely preferred a British protectorate to a French one. The majority of the Palestinians, which included the Arabs west of the Jordan River, declared that their principal goal was to prevent the fulfillment of the Balfour Declaration which they anticipated would bring a large Jewish immigration. Wilson backtracked. As the mission reported that Jewish immigration could be upheld only by force of arms, and that the strong influence of American Jewish voters on any Washington administration would bring almost irresistible pressure to bear to permit large-scale migration into Palestine, Lloyd George could have it. Ray Stannard Baker blamed the Allied-American struggle over the Ottoman Empire largely on the *Allies'* quest for "oil rights, railways, and pipelines," including control of the proposed line from Mesopotamian oil fields to the Syrian port of Tripoli. The Allies' resisted Wilson's effort to get control of Syria and Palestine (and the French even worked to prevent an American mandate over Constantinople) because it was obvious that at stake were the "untouched deposits of oil, copper, silver" and other riches of the Turkish Empire itself, plus "the opening to . . . exploitation . . . of Persia. The control of the eastern Mediterranean also turned upon the possession of the coastal cities of Asia Minor, Syria, and Palestine."[64]

Despite the objections of the Syrians, the American commissioners ended up recommending that they be placed under French administration owing to the overriding "need of preserving friendly relations between France and Great Britain." They recommended "a British mandate for Mesopotamia, based on British fitness and the general desires of the peoples involved." They also approved "Great Britain's general supervision of Arabia, with the proviso that she be held strictly responsible for the maintenance of the 'open door' for all members of the League of Nations."[65] Owing to their rivalries, however, the Allies and the Americans required a year following Wilson's departure from Paris to cast their Peace Treaty for Turkey.

In June, the Germans removed one source of concern to Wilson and Benson; they scuttled most of their warships at Scapa Flow. The President left Paris for home on June 28, never to return. House, with whom Wilson's relations were growing increasingly cool, and other Americans stayed on for the months of Peace Conference work to be done on the Adriatic and Levantine settlements. This proved as helpful to the Wilson-Baker version of the President's martyrdom at the hand of the Peace Conference delegates as did the President's absences from Paris during some of the earlier weeks of the Conference. Baker claimed that America's assent to unfair terms for the Germans had been gained by Allied deceptions which had taken in an unwitting House and a Lansing who "had no glimmer of the President's vision of peace, or the part America should play in it." Of the two men, House had done more damage, owing to his alleged lack of Wilson's "own clear, vivid, swift leaping logical processes." House had fallen into the pit dug for him by the unregenerate Lloyd George and his continental accomplices when the President's strong hand was not there to sustain him. When "Wilson, the leader and prophet, . . . had gone away, they set up a golden calf . . . the men there [in Paris] had their eyes on some immediate selfish purpose which obliterated everything else."[66]

Back in the United States during the summer of 1919, the President bent his failing energies to his unavailing campaign to build fires of voters' indignation under the Senate. Wilson refused to make the concessions needed to convert that body's simple majority in favor of League membership into the necessary two-thirds vote. His intransigence is in part explained by his inferred belief that behind the senatorial demands for alterations in the League's Covenant there might be lurking a scheme for large American corporations to share the world's markets with large European corporations by having them act in collusion with each other. The pro-Wilson *New Republic* had charged in its November 30, 1918, issue that Roosevelt, Lodge, and their Congressional cohorts sought to do so by dividing up markets behind "strategic frontiers and economic discriminations." A few days later Daniels appealed to a Congressional committee to support a "government monopoly of wireless" stations abroad rather than allow "a foreign owned or controlled corporation" obtain the "concessions in South American Republics" it was seeking. "Special interests," however, were lobbying against him. In May 1919, Daniels worked to prevent the General Electric Company from making arrangements to form a wireless company in collusion with the British-owned Marconi Company by which General Electric "would give that English Company [patents and] too much power in world communication."[67] Lodge, or even the President's more naive foes in the Senate, might, through their revisions of the League Covenant, make his own task of making subsequent changes more difficult to force onto the Allies. Besides, once Lloyd George got hold of their proposals, he would probably seek to renew his own efforts at revising the German terms to which Wilson had bound the League Covenant. Lodge's proposed reservation on Article X would weaken a future League justification for a navy at least equal to George V's. It would even force "Great Britain to assume most of the burden of enforcing collective security" that Wilson sought for America. As Benson had reminded him, "the smooth and leisurely phrases of diplomacy derive their pungency from a vision of the force in readiness that lies behind them . . . if England cannot get by . . . diplomatic notes the decisions she desires . . . she . . . uncovers the idea of military superiority."[68]

On the eve of his departure from Paris, the President successfully insisted that the minutes of the Council of Four's meetings be kept secret. A few weeks later, he denied to the Senate Foreign Relations Committee (headed by Lodge) that he had had any knowledge of the Treaty of London or related Allied pacts before he arrived at the Peace Conference. To have permitted the Peace Conference records of his endeavors in Paris to be published or to have admitted that Balfour had provided him with copies of the Treaty of London and the Sykes-Picot Agreements in May 1917 would have marred his image as a noble crusader to the wicked Allies. Publication would have enabled his Congressional foes to charge he had given tacit approval to the secret treaties by his wartime silence about them. If he had replied that he had merely been awaiting the day he got the Allies into his hands to force them to abandon their treaty programs, Lloyd George, Clemenceau, and Orlando would probably have published minutes showing his Council of Four efforts to seize Russia's share of the London Treaty's spoils and deprive the Allies of their share. They might have also decided to alter the League of Nations Covenant to remove the provisions advantageous to the Americans. Moreover, admission and publication would have demonstrated strong motives for his wartime withholding of naval and military aid to the Allies and lent support to charges that he had deliberately done so. Instead of admitting this, he wanted to magnify America's achievements and minimize the Allies' efforts in winning the war and their consequent right to economic and territorial rewards.

By his secrecy about his endeavors at the Peace Conference and his denial of prior knowledge of the Allies' territorial agreements, Wilson suppressed evidence of his own materialistic acquisitiveness. This helped his effort to hold moral advantages over the Allies and their American collaborators. In April 1920, he told his Cabinet that the British "financial experts at Paris had [had] no heart and were trying to grab everything in sight." Many British and French "devils" there had "taken him up the high mountain" to tempt him. He could not now trust them to abide by the good terms he had forced them to put in the Peace Treaty. His secrecy and denial enabled a partisan of his campaign to force Senate acceptance of his League Covenant to compare (in October 1919) those resisting Wilson with the Israelites who were worshipping the golden calf when Moses first extolled the Ten Commandments to them.[69]

Meanwhile, what Seth Tillman has termed "the breakdown of Anglo-American cooperation in the final stages of the peace conference" was painfully visible. The American and British delegates filled the conference rooms with "mutual recriminations." They stubbornly continued their disagreement over the Adriatic question, allowing the political life of Italy to be further poisoned until conditions were ripe for Mussolini's seizure of power in 1922. The Americans continued to support the "dubious Polish claims to Eastern Galicia while Great Britain [unsuccessfully] resisted them." Anglo-American broils over the Levantine settlement also indicated that Washington and London were largely intent on thwarting each other. Washington continued the struggle against the British over merchant ships. The British seized ships

The Prince of Wales and Admiral Sims in procession to receive honorary degrees from Cambridge University, 1921. Photo courtesy of William S. Sims II and Tom Aitken, London.

flying the American flag; Benson's Shipping Board, defying British protests, refused to honor an agreement to relinquish certain seized German ships.[70]

Whether a Wilson decision to join instead of resisting Lloyd George's efforts for softening the German's peace terms would have sufficiently reduced the causes of the rise of Adolph Hitler, and the outbreak of the second World War is impossible to say with certainty. It does seem clear that his struggle to maintain his position against the British interferred with his effort to eliminate the seeds of a new general war.

Embittered by the administration's conduct at the Peace Conference, Sims got a public forum from which to air his indictment of the Navy Department's role in the war. Early in 1920, the Republican majority on the Senate Naval Affairs Committee gave him his opportunity. Daniels and Benson rejoined with arguments to exonerate the policies that they had pursued. Some officers felt that if Sim's charges were accepted, respect for the Navy would suffer. They testified in defense of the Navy's wartime performance. Other senior officers testified in support of Sims's claims. The conflicting testimony, and especially Daniels' long-winded perambulations and evasions tended to confuse and bore the public. Although the Republican majority on the committee voted that Sims's charges had been sustained by the evidence, these hearings probably contributed little to the size of the 1920 Republican landslide.

Although these hearings did not help the pro-British cause much, only three dreadnoughts of the 1916 program were ever completed (the first not until 1921).[71] Lloyd George, however, was sufficiently relieved at Wilson's partial retreat over naval construction and his loss of influence over Congress that the Prime Minister retired a number of older battleships without building new ones. He was encouraged to do so by the harried British taxpayer. Thus, by the time the Washington Arms Conference agreed in 1922 to naval parity in capital ships between Britain and the United States, the gap between their sizes had been markedly narrowed.

In 1922, at the statutory age of sixty-four, Sims retired from active duty. His sorrow at Theodore Roosevelt's early death was the deeper as he had longed to see him elected President in 1920 so that he could reverse the course of Anglo-American relations. Roosevelt, like Sims, believed that the affinity of America's and Britain's moral and material interests overrode their rivalry; George V's Navy and Empire should be maintained to sustain an Anglo-American partnership against would-be "evildoers." Roosevelt had sought to throw America's weight behind such British power as had survived the war in order to forge a *Pax Britannica-Americana.* This would promote the standards, values, and stability of the lost *Pax Britannica* in the face of a potentially resurgent Germany and Russia and an expansionist Japan. Whether the implementation of Roosevelt's program would have resulted in a less tragic history of the ensuing decades than the one Versailles fashioned is a question to which no certain answer can be given. It would have been difficult for Roosevelt to divide the world's markets with the British without going as far as Wilson did in giving American big companies and banks advantages in their quest for foreign markets.

In the event, the long shadow of the Paris Economic Conference and the Treaty of London fell across Anglo-American relations in 1920. In May, Washington charged that London was violating the Peace Conference agreement on "equal opportunity in the acquisition of concessions" in its "administration of Palestine and Mesopotamia" by giving "advantages to British oil interests that were not accorded to American companies" and by preparing for exclusive British control "of the oil resources of this region." Secretary of State Colby (with whom Wilson had replaced the dismissed Lansing) subsequently accused the British of arranging to give "France preferential treatment" in "the disposition of petroleum" extracted from the region. He also charged that Britain had just induced the League of Nations to confirm her as the mandatory power over it by "making a friendly arrangement with

Italy" about Mesopotamia. In addition, London's administrators were discriminating against American businessmen in what had been German East Africa.[72]

Foreign Secretary Curzon curtly dismissed these assertions. He added that as the American government had not joined the League of Nations, it would not be allowed to participate in couching the economic rules to be applied to its protectorates and mandates, which were about to be drawn up. Moreover, he charged that upon Wilson's seizure of Haiti in 1913, the American government had voided the oil concession granted to Britons by the Haitian Legislature and President. "More recently," Curzon asserted, Washington had pressured the Costa Rican government into rescinding the "oil concession to a British subject granted by the previous Government." He closed with the charge that it was the United States, and not Britain, who was trying to seize control of the world's oil resources. [73]

According to Ray Stannard Baker, in whom the President frequently confided during the Peace Conference, Wilson had felt at Paris that he dared not attempt to coerce the Allies into "more controversial economic agreements. Already the Republican party . . . with its . . . protectionism, was in control of the Senate!" The difficulties of how to get greater guarantees of "equal treatment" for American businessmen the President felt he had to leave "to the League to solve in the future." In 1920, however, Curzon went far toward dashing this hope. Even Baker placed some of the blame for the continuation of international economic rivalry and tension on Wilson. The American policy at Paris, Baker wrote, was "to go back to the old economic rivalries with each nation playing a lone hand." The President had foreshadowed this policy when he wrote on October 22, 1918, Baker noted, that his peace terms would "leave every nation free to determine its own economic policy except . . . that its policy must be the same for all nations." Baker objected that America's policy of the " 'open door' and 'equality of trade conditions' " encouraged "a free scramble for the good things of the earth. This is a policy . . . for the great and strong, like America, but where does it leave the smaller, crowded nations? And will it bring peace?" Baker doubted it.[74] The "have nots" justified his doubts in the 1930s.

Baker concluded that the Americans offered only one positive, "broadly international economic proposal" at Paris — over cables. But here, the British outmaneuvered the Americans. The recovery of Europe was handicapped because "the Americans wanted international cooperation where it would help them, and the British wanted it where it would help them; and each either opposed or was apathetic toward the other . . . ." In 1920, as in 1919, the Allies resisted the American demand for "a removal of all economic barriers so that our unharmed and mighty private business interests could rush into every market."[75]

The Harding Administration proved to be almost as anti-British as Wilson's. Finally, in February 1922, Britain consented to dreadnought parity with America. Not surprisingly, Benson denounced the pact for letting Britain temporarily retain a higher capital ship tonnage than

America (to compensate for the more recent vintage of the average American dreadnought) and Wemyss bitterly criticized it for permitting American "equality." Sims was dismayed both by the treaty's implications for the world's future and by Wemyss's denigration of the value of seeking Anglo-American friendship. In an article rebutting Wemyss, Sims urged that the Washington treaty had not really finished British dominion of the sea — if the London authorities acted wisely. Only the construction and total tonnage of British and American battleships and battlecruisers had been limited. The true capital ship of the future was the aircraft carrier. It and the submarine would be the decisive craft of the future. The parsimonious American Congress, however, was going to authorize few carriers or submarines in the foreseeable future. The British Parliament, by sanctioning many, could ensure that Britain retained the trident of the sea.[76]

As for Pratt, the passage of time gave him an ambivalent attitude toward his wartime pro-British ardor. In the late 1930s he wrote his unfinished autobiography in retirement, after serving as Chief of Operations under President Franklin Roosevelt. In it, he held that America's pre-1917 endeavors to make "the neutral view [of freedom of the seas] prevail over that of the belligerent [*sic*] . . . was in effect a selfish point of view." Instead of the neutral supplying the belligerent, "it is better . . . [for] world stability that he give up such profits since the world pays for them in the prolongation of the war."[77] Pratt's revised view was no doubt tempered by the substitution of Hitler for William II and Lenin and Stalin for Nicholas II — substitutions which might not have occurred had the first world war ended in 1916 with a negotiated peace. The logic of Pratt's view implies that without American supplies to sustain their hope of victory, the Allies would not have drawn up their Paris Economic Conference objectives and the Germans would not have felt it necessary to escalate their war aims in late 1916. Thus, the two sides might have been able to accept the compromises required for an early end to the war. Such a peace might have preserved much of the old order of 1914.

Notes on Chapter 7

[1] Sims to Daniels, Dec. 7, 1918, Sims Papers.

[2] Sims to Mrs. Sims, Jan. 10, 1919, *ibid.*

[3] Sims to Wilson, Dec. 26, 1918, Wilson Papers, Sers. 5B; Wilson to Sims, Dec. 27, 1918, *ibid.*; A. Bennett-Smith (from New York) to Lloyd George, Dec. 18, 1918, Balfour Papers, 49692.

[4] Pratt to Benson and Sims, Dec. 12, 1918, Sims Papers; quoted from the records of Charles Swem, Princeton University Library, in Arthur Walworth, *Woodrow Wilson* (New York, London, and Toronto, 1958), II, 217.

[5] Sims to Mrs. Sims, Jan. 10, 1919, Sims Papers; Geddes to Lloyd George, n. d., with "Extract from a letter dated January 17...," Lloyd George Papers, F/18/3/3, and stating that he was withholding the name of the American with access to this Benson cable (FDR? Pratt?).

[6] Wilson to Daniels (via Benson), Jan. 27, 1919, Wilson Papers, Sers. 5B; Charles Seymour, ed., *The Intimate Papers of Colonel House* (Boston and New York, 1926-28). IV, 213-14; R. S. Baker, *Woodrow Wilson, Life and Letters* (Garden City, 1927-39), VIII, 585, Drummond to Balfour, Nov. 27 and 28, 1918, FO/800/329, P.R.O., and C. F. Dormer (administrative assistant to Lord Grey, who was special envoy designate to the United States) to Drummond, Nov. 28, 1918, *ibid.*

[7] Daniels to Wilson, Jan. 4, 1919, Wilson Papers, Sers. 5B; E. David Cronon, ed., *The Cabinet Diaries of Josephus Daniels, 1913-1921* (Lincoln, 1963), Nov. 20, 1918.

[8] Clemenceau to Lloyd George, Feb. 2, 1919, Lloyd George Papers, F/57/1/8; reports of Divisions of Far Eastern, Near Eastern, and Latin American Affairs to Ass't. Secretary W. Phillips, Nov. 29, 1918, roll 2, USDSM 581.

[9] U. S. minister at Copenhagen (Osbourne) to American Peace Commission at Paris (hereafter Amission), Nov. 25, 1918, Jan. 10 and Feb. 4, 1919, Wilson Papers, Sers. 5B; Vance C. McCormick (Presidential adviser) and Redfield jointly to Wilson, Dec. 14, 1918, *ibid.*; Wilson to Tumulty, Dec. 15, 1918, *ibid.*; Cronon, ed., *Daniels Diaries*, Aug. 4, Nov. 20 and 23, Dec. 7 and 25, 1920.

[10] Benson to Wilson, Apr. 17, 1919, Daniels Papers; Acting Secretary of State Polk to Amission, c. Dec. 14, 1918, Wilson Papers, Sers. 5B, Box 6; Sharp to Amission, Jan. 15 and 18, 1919, Wilson Papers, Sers. 5B; Hurley to Wilson, Dec. 23, 1918, *ibid.*, with report he had requested from Thomas F. Logan.

[11] G. T. Davis, *A Navy Second to None* (New York, 1940), 260; Hoover to Wilson, Feb. 1, 1919, Wilson Papers, Sers. 5B; Cronon, ed., *Daniels Diaries*, Jan. 21 and Apr. 8, 1919.

[12] H. and M. Sprout, *Toward a New Order of Seapower: American Naval Policy and the World Scene, 1918-1922* (Princeton, 1940), 51-53, 104-07; W. R. Schilling, "Admirals and Foreign Policy, 1913-1919," Ph. D. diss., Yale University, 1953, 231-32.

[13] Memorandum by Rear Admiral R. E. Coontz *et al.* to Benson Nov. 11, 1918, USNSF, VL file: League of Nations: W. R. Braisted, *The United States Navy in the Pacific, 1909-1922* (Austin and London, 1971), 451.

[14] Schilling, "Admirals and Foreign Policy," 211-213.

[15] Daniels to Wilson, Dec. 3, 1918, Wilson Papers, Sers. 5B, with Gen. Bd. report 438 SN879, 2 Dec. 1918; Braisted, *Navy in Pacific*, 331; Baker to Wilson, Nov. 27, 1918, *Baker Papers*, Box 8; Bliss to Baker, Jan. 11, 1919, *ibid.*, Box 9.

[16] Benson to Daniels, Mar. 28, 1919, Daniels Papers, with memorandum he was about to read to naval representatives of the major Allies.

[17] Schilling, "Admirals and Foreign Policy," 235-36; *ibid.*, 237.

[18] Frank R. Kent in *Baltimore Sun*, Nov. 18, 1918.

[19] Benson to Wilson, Dec. 17, 1918, Wilson Papers, Sers. 5B, with his Paris staff memo. No. 65, Nov. 4, 1918; *PPWW*, VI, 294.

[20] Seymour, ed., *House Papers*, IV, 129, 134; House to Wilson, Dec. 25, 1918, Wilson Papers, Sers. 5B.

[21] Daniels to Sims, Jan. 2, 1919, Daniels Papers.

[22] See notes 16 and 20, above.

[23] Quoted in Schilling, "Admirals and Foreign Policy," 159-60.

[24] Cronon, ed., *Daniels Diaries*, June 1, 1920; see note 6, above; Schilling, "Admirals and Foreign Policy," 147, 153-54, 211-213.

[25] Hoover to Sharp (thence to Wilson), Dec. 31, 1918, Wilson Papers, Sers. 5B; Wilson to Sce. N. Baker, Jan. 9, 1919, *ibid.*; a certain Mr. Snyder of the American Food Administration to Hoover, Jan. 7, 1919, *ibid.*; a Mr. Glass of Dept. of Treasury to Hoover's assistant, a Mr. Davis, Jan. 9, 1919, *ibid.*

[26] R. S. Baker, *Woodrow Wilson and the World Settlement* (Garden City, 1922), I, 10; U. S. embassy Tokyo to Amission, Jan. 8, 1919, Wilson Papers, Sers. 5B; U. S. consul at Tsintau to Sec. of State, Mar. 14 and 24, 1919, USDSM 423, roll 3; acting Sec. of State Phillips to Amission, Mar. 26, 1919, with message from Tokyo embassy, Mar. 25, *ibid.*; U. S. legation at Peking to Sec. of State, Mar. 26, 1919, *ibid.*

[27] U. S. embassy Tokyo to Amission, Jan. 8, 1919, Lansing MSS, vol. 41; Cecil to Lloyd George, Apr. 15, 1919, Lloyd George Papers, F/16/6/29.

[28] Benson to Mayo, Dec. 12, 1918, Wilson Papers, Sers. 5B; Cronon, ed., *Daniels Diaries*, Dec. 28, 1918.

[29] Reading to Wiseman, Nov. 26, 1918, FO/800/225, P.R.O.; Hurley to Wilson, Dec. 23, 1918, Wilson Papers, Sers. 5B, endorsing study he had requested of Thomas F. Logan.

[30] Inquiry to Wilson, Jan. 21, 1919, Wilson Papers, Sers. 5B; U. S. minister to Stockholm (Morris) to Amission, Jan. 21, 1919, Wilson Papers, Sers. 5B; Benson to Daniels, Jan. 23, 1919, Daniels Papers.

[31] New York shipyard owner Franklin Remington to Wilson, Jan. 10, 1919, Wilson Papers, Sers. 5B; Ellis Dressel to Wilson, Jan. 13, 1919, *ibid.*; acting Sec. of State Polk to Amission, Jan. 17 and Feb. 5, 1919, *ibid.*; William Sutherland (of Ministry of Shipping) to Lloyd George, Jan. 1, 1919, Lloyd George Papers, F/93/2/10.

[32] Wilson to Bainbridge Colby (of U. S. Shipping Board), Nov. 18, 1918, Wilson Papers, Sers. 2; Colby to Wilson, Nov. 30, 1918, *ibid.*; McClay to Lloyd George, Dec. 27, 1918, Lloyd George Papers, F/35/2/95; Daniels to Wilson, Nov. 18, 1918, Daniels Papers; Cronon, ed., *Daniels Diaries*, Mar. 1, 1919.

[33] Cronon, ed., *Daniels Diaries*, Feb. 20 and 22, 1919; A. W. Lane and L. H. Wall, eds., *The Letters of Franklin K. Lane, Personal and Political* (Boston and New York, 1922), 306, 372; account of William's speech in *Baltimore Manufacturer's Record*, Nov. 21, 1918, Wilson Papers, Sers. 2; Williams to Wilson, Dec. 11, 1918, *ibid.*, Sers. 5B with a copy of another of his unwelcome speeches; *New York World's* Dec. 11, 1918, account of Roosevelt speech in which he urged that America "concede naval superiority to Britain and be satisfied with second place," *ibid.*

[34] Daniels to Sims, Jan. 8, 1919, Daniels Papers; Sims to Mrs. Sims, Jan. 10, 1919, Sims Papers; Cronon, ed., *Daniels Diaries*, Dec. 18, 1918, Jan. 10 and 13, Feb. 9 and July 5, 1919.

[35] Daniels to Sims, Jan. 2, 1919, Daniels Papers; Sims to Daniels, Feb. 5, 1919, *ibid.*

[36] Davis, *Navy Second to None*, 258-59, including notes; Josephus Daniels, *The Wilson Era* (Chapel Hill, 1946), II, 367-70.

[37] Wilson to Daniels, Mar. 1, 1919, Daniels Papers; Daniels to Wilson, Mar. 4, 1919, *ibid.*; Cronon, ed., *Daniels Diaries*, Apr. 7, 1919; Wemyss to Lloyd George, Mar. 29,

1919, and Long to Lloyd George, Apr. 8, 1919, Lloyd George Papers, F/192/1/4 and F/33/2/31.

[38] Long to Lloyd George, Mar. 7, 1919, Lloyd George Papers, F/33/2/22.

[39] Br. minister to Vatican, Count John de Salis, to Drummond, Dec. 1, 1919, FO/800/329, P.R.O.; Rodd to Curzon, Feb. 26 and Mar. 2, 1919, FO/425/383, *ibid.*, Sir George Grahame (from France) to Curzon, Mar. 27, 1919, *ibid.*; according to Rodd, Franco-Italian "solidarity" sprang "mainly" from "misgiving as to . . . how far their own interests are jeopardized by . . . Wilson . . . ."

[40] FDR to Wilson, Apr. 5, 1919, with cable from Gillis in Peking warning that Japanese anti-American excitement required that he "immediately establish a powerful fleet in Far Eastern waters." Daniels Papers.

[41] David Hunter Miller, *The Drafting of the Covenant* (New York and London, 1928), I, 420-21; Cecil to Lloyd George, Apr. 4 and 10, 1919, Lloyd George Papers, F/6/6/25 and 33; Seymour, ed., *House Papers*, IV, 420-21.

[42] Baker, *World Settlement*, I, chap. XVIII; David Hunter Miller in *What Really Happened at the Peace Conference, 1918-1919*, E. M. House and C. Seymour, eds. (New York, 1921), 286, 291-93; Davis, *Navy Second to None*, chap. XII.

[43] Sims to Daniels, Feb. 5, 1919, Daniels Papers.

[44] Schilling, "Admirals and Foreign Policy," 258.

[45] Sprout, *New Order of Seapower*, 102-105.

[46] Benson to Daniels, Mar. 28, 1919, with "Special memorandum" he was about to read to naval delegates of the Allies, *ibid*; Memo. for President from Sec. of Navy, Apr. 7, 1919, Daniels Papers; Benson to Daniels, May 6, 1919, *ibid.*

[47] Benson to Wilson, Apr. 28 and May 5, 1919, Daniels Papers.

[48] Wilson to Benson, May. 6, 1919, Wilson Papers, Sers. 5B.

[49] Benson to Daniels, May 6, 1919, Daniels Papers.

[50] Cecil to Lloyd George, May 27, 1919, Lloyd George Papers, F/6/6/47.

[51] Seth P. Tillman, *Anglo-American Relations at the Peace Conference of 1919* (Princeton, 1961), 346-48, 352-54, 356-62.

[52] Bailey, *Lost Peace*, 293; Paul Mantoux, *Proceedings of the Paris Peace Conference: Proceedings of the Council of Four (March 24-April 18)* (Geneva, 1964), 28-29.

[53] American minister at Stockholm (Ira N. Morris) to Amission, Jan. 21, 1919, Wilson Papers, Sers. 5B; Baker, *World Settlement* II, 357-59. Bliss to N. D. Baker, Jan. 4, 1919, Baker Papers, Box 4.

[54] McKean to Benson, Apr. 2, 1919, USNSF, VP-1 file: Diplomatic Plans and Policies, including Peace Plans, 1919-1920; Supreme Economic Council minutes, Apr. 2 and 14, 1919, 180.0501/11 and 12, roll 128, NAMf 820: Record Group 256, General Records of the American Commission to Negotiate Peace (cited hereafter as GRACNPM 820); minutes of Council of Four, May 15 and 22, 1919, 180.03401/15 and 24/½, roll 110, *ibid.*

[55] Clippings from *Manufacturer's Record*, Apr. 3, 1919, *American Economist*, Apr. 11, 1919, and unidentified periodical, © Apr. 8, 1919, Lansing MSS, vol. 42.

[56] Council of Four minutes, June 14 and 17, 1919, 180.030401/66 and 74, roll 112, GRACNPM 820.

[57] Council of Four minutes, May 23, 1919, 180.03401/28, roll 110, *ibid.*; Benson to Rear-Adm. Phillip Andrews (commander of U. S. naval forces in eastern Mediterranean), May 2, 1919, USNSF, UB file; Cronon, ed., *Daniels Diaries*, Sept. 28 and Oct. 7, 1919.

[58] Balfour to Lloyd George, Nov. 29, 1918, Lloyd George Papers, F/3/3/45; The Inquiry to Wilson, Jan. 31, 1919, Wilson Papers, Sers. 5B; W. C. Bullitt to Lansing, Feb. 6, 1919, with recommendation of Dr. W. L. Westermann on Transcaucasia, Lansing MSS, vol. 41.

[59] Appendix B, Feb. 5, 1919, to "Agenda for meeting of the Supreme War Council . . . Feb. 7, 1919," USNSF, QW file: Supreme War Council, Meetings of; minutes of 2nd meeting of 13th session of Supreme War Council, Feb. 8, 1919, *ibid.;* Wilson to Baker, Feb. 8, 1919, Baker Papers, Box 10; Baker to Wilson, Feb. 11, 1919, *ibid.*

[60] Winston Spencer Churchill to Lloyd George, Feb. 14, 1919, Lloyd George Papers, F/18/3/25 on his acrid exchange of views about Constantinople with Clemenceau; Mr. Ravndall of Am. Section of International Commission on Mandates in Turkey to Amission, Aug. 25, 1919, 181.91/215, roll 183, GRACNPM 820; Am. Commissioner at Constantinople Heck to Amission, © Jan. 8, 1919, Wilson Papers, Sers. 5B; Council of Four minutes, May 14, 1919, 180.03401/13½, roll 109, GRACNPM 820.

[61] Robert Lansing, *The Big Four and Others of the Peace Conference* (Boston and New York, 1921), 123-24; Council of Four minutes, Apr. 21, 1919, 180.03401/108, roll 113, GRACNPM 820; Benson to Andrews, May 2, 1919, USNSF, UB file.

[62] Council of Four minutes, May 5, 1919, 180.03401/144, roll 113, GRACNPM 820.

[63] Report by American committee on mandates in Turkey, "Suggestions for the Proposed Commission," © Mar. 1, 1919, 181.91/25, roll 183, GRACNPM 820; "Excerpts from the Minutes of the Meeting[s] of the Council of Four held on Mar. 20 and May 21, 1919, 181.91/49 and 132, *ibid.;* Council of Four minutes, May 22, 1919, 180.03401/22½, roll 110, *ibid.*

[64] Baker, *World Settlement,* II, 200-201, 370; "Report of the American Section of the International Commission on Mandates in Turkey . . . July 10, 1919, 181.9102/3, roll 183, GRACNPM 820.

[65] "Report[s] of the American Section of the International Commission on Mandates in Turkey," c. Aug. 20 and Aug. 28, 1919, 181.9102/7 and 9, roll 183, GRACNPM 820.

[66] Baker, *World Settlement,* I, 303, 306, 308.

[67] Cronon, ed., *Daniels Diaries,* Dec. 12, 1918, May 22 and 23, 1919.

[68] Daniel M. Smith, *The Great Departure: The United States and World War I* (New York, London, and Sydney, 1965), 196; Benson to Wilson, Apr. 9, 1919 (with Paris staff study of Apr. 7), Baker, *World Settlement,* I, 384-85.

[69] Cronon, ed., *Daniels Diaries,* Apr. 27 and 20, 1902, Oct. 22, 1919.

[70] Tillman, *Anglo-American Relations,* 365-66; Cronon, ed., *Daniels Diaries,* Oct. 21, 1919.

[71] Sprout, *New Order of Seapower,* 351.

[72] Colby to Am. embassy, London, May 10 and July 26, 1920, USNSF, VO file; Mandates: Economic Policy of British Government RE Mandate Regions in the Near East.

[73] U. S. ambassador at London John W. Davis to Colby, Aug. 11, 1920, *ibid.,* with note from Curzon, Aug. 9, *ibid.*

[74] Baker, *World Settlement,* II, 318, 326, 327.

[75] *Ibid.,* 467, 333.

[76] Schilling, "Admirals and Foreign Policy," 312; "The Status of the Navy," *Current History,* XVI (May, 1922), 187-93.

[77] Pratt's unpublished autobiography, chap. XV, 24-25, Library of Congress.

SELECTED BIBLIOGRAPHY

Private Papers

Baker, Newton D. Library of Congress, Washington, D.C.
Balfour, Arthur James. British Library, London.
Bonar Law, Andrew. Beaverbrook Library, London.
Daniels, Josephus. Library of Congress.
Hamilton, Frederick T. National Maritime Museum, Greenwich, England.
Henderson, W. H. National Maritime Museum.
Jellicoe, John R. British Library.
Jones, Hilary P. Library of Congress
Lansing, Robert. Library of Congress.
Lloyd George, David. Beaverbrook Library, London.
Pratt, William V. Library of Congress.
Richmond, H.W. National Maritime Museum.
Sims, William S. Library of Congress.
Wilson, Woodrow. Library of Congress.

The Private Papers of William S. Benson have not, for several years, been available to any researcher except his biographer, Dr. Mary L. Klachko.

Official Records

British Admiralty documents, ADM/116 series, Public Record Office, London. Some of Sir Eric Geddes's correspondence is included in this collection.

General Records of the American Commission to Negotiate Peace, 1918-1931. National Archives. Microfilm 820. Record Group 256 (USDS).

British Foreign Office Papers, FO/438 and 800 series, Public Record Office, London. The former sub-group relates to topics concerning the war and its aftermath; the latter relates to foreign affairs in general. Some papers of Balfour and other diplomatic figures are located in one or both of these files. Minutes of regular, daily meetings of the British War Cabinet in the CAB/23/1-8 series; minutes of the specially summoned meetings of certain War Cabinet Members in the CAB/23/13-14 series; records of "conversations" between Lloyd George and certain close advisers, termed "X-minutes, in the CAB/23/17 series, Public Record Office, London.

Reports, Studies, and miscellaneous papers submitted to the British War Cabinet by its various members, committees, and Secretary in the CAB/21,22, 24, 25, 26, and 27 series, Public Record Office, London.

Naval Records and Library Collection. National Archives. Record Group 45 (USNSF).

Reports and War Plans of the U. S. Navy General Board. Office of Naval Records and Library, Washington Navy Yard, Washington, D. C.

Records of the Department of State Relating to Political Relations Between the United States and Great Britain, Japan, and Russia and the Soviet Union, 1910-29. National Archives microfilms 581, 423, and 333 (USDM).

Published Documentary Sources and Memoirs

Mantoux, Paul, *Proceedings of the Council of Four (March 24-April 18).* Genève: Libraire Droz, 1964.

U. S. Department of State, *Papers Relating to the Foreign Relations of the United States.*

——————————, *Papers Relating to the Foreign Relations of the United States, the Lansing Papers, 1914-1920* (2 vols., Washington: United States Government Printing Office, 1939-1940).

U. S. Senate, Subcommittee on Naval Affairs. *Naval Investigation Hearings,* 66th Cong., 2d Sess., 1920.

U. S. Senate, Committee on Naval Affairs. *Report of the Naval Investigation: Views of the Minority of the Subcommittee on Naval Affairs* (Washington: United States Government Printing Office, 1921).

Published Papers, Diaries, and Memoirs.

The Cabinet Diaries of Josephus Daniels: 1913-1921, edited by E. David Cronon. Lincoln: University of Nebraska Press, 1963.

Daniels, Josephus. *The Wilson Era.* 2 vols. Chapel Hill: University of North Carolina Press, 1946.

The Private Papers of Douglas Haig, edited by Robert Blake. London: Eyre and Spottiswoode, 1952.

Hankey, Maurice Pascal Alers. *The Supreme Command.* 2 vols. London: George Allen and Unwin, Ltd., 1961.

The Intimate Papers of Colonel House, edited by Charles Seymour. 4 vols., Boston and New York: Houghton Mifflin Company, 1926-1928.

The Letters of Franklin K. Lane, Personal and Political, edited by Anne Wintermute Lane and Louise Hendrick Wall. Boston and New York: Houghton Mifflin Company, 1922.

Lansing, Robert. *War Memoirs of Robert Lansing, Secretary of State.* Indianapolis: Bobbs-Merril Company, 1925.

——————— . *The Peace Negotiations: A Personal Narrative.* Boston and New York: Houghton Mifflin Company, 1921.

Lloyd George, David. *War Memoirs of David Lloyd George.* 6 vols. Boston: Little, Brown and Company, 1933-1937.

——————— . *The Truth about the Peace Treaties.* 2 vols. London: Victor Gollancz, Ltd., 1938.

——————— . *Memoirs of the Peace Conference.* 2 vols. New Haven: Yale University Press, 1939.

Pershing, John J. *My Experiences in the World War.* 2 vols. New York: Frederick A. Stokes Company, 1931.

Robertson, William R. *Soldiers and Statesmen.* 2 vols. London: Cassell and Company, 1926.

Rodd, James Rennell. *Social and Diplomatic Memories,* Vol. III: *1902-1919.* London: Edward Arnold and Company, 1925.

Sims, William Sowden in collaboration with Burton J. Hendrick. *The Victory at Sea.* Garden City, New York: Doubleday, Page and Company, 1920.

The Public Papers of Woodrow Wilson, edited by Ray Stannard Baker and William E. Dodd. 6 vols. New York and London: Harper and Brothers, Publishers, 1925-1927.

BOOKS

Adler, Selig. *The Isolationist Impulse: Its Twentieth Century Reaction.* New York: Collier Books, 1961.

Bailey, Thomas A. *Woodrow Wilson and the Lost Peace.* New York: McMillan Company, 1944.

Baker, Ray Stannard. *Woodrow Wilson: Life and Letters.* 8 vols. New York: Doubleday, Doran and Company, 1927-1939.

——————, *Woodrow Wilson and the World Settlement.* 3 vols. Garden City, New York: Doubleday, Page and Company, 1922.

Beaver, Daniel R. *Newton D. Baker and the American War Effort, 1917-1919.* Lincoln, University of Nebraska Press, 1966.

Braemen, John, *et al.*, eds. *Twentieth Century American Foreign Policy.* Columbus: Ohio University Press, 1971.

Braisted, William Reynolds. *The United States Navy in the Pacific, 1909-1922.* Austin and London: University of Texas Press, 1971.

Broesamle, John J. *William Gibbs McAdoo: A Passion for Change, 1863-1921.* Port Washington, N. Y.: Kennikat Press, 1973.

Buchan, John. *A History of the Great War.* Boston: Hougton Mifflin Co., 1922. Vol. III.

Buehrig, Edward H. *Woodrow Wilson and the Balance of Power.* Bloomington: Indiana University Press, 1955.

Cronon, E. David. Editor. *Twentieth Century America: Selected Readings.* 2 vols. Homewood, Illinois: The Dorsey Press, 1965.

Coffman, Edward M. *The War to End All Wars: the American Military Experience in World War I.* New York: Oxford University Press, 1968.

Crutwell, Charles R. M. F. *A History of the Great War, 1914-1918.* Oxford: Clarendon Press, 1934.

Davis, George T. *A Navy Second to None: The Development of Modern American Naval Policy.* New York: Harcourt, Brace and Company, 1940.

Diamond, William. *The Economic Thought of Woodrow Wilson.* Baltimore: the Johns Hopkins Press, 1943.

Fischer. Fritz. *Griff Nach der Weltmacht.* 3rd ed., improved. Dusseldorf: Droste Verlag, 1964.

W. B. Fowler, *British-American Relations, 1917-1918: The Role of Sir William Wiseman.* Princeton: Princeton University Press, 1969.

Freidel, Frank. *Franklin D. Roosevelt.* vol. I, *The Apprenticeship.* Boston: Little Brown and Co., 1952.

Frothingham, Thomas G. *The Naval History of the Great War*, Vol. III: *The United States in the War*, 1917-1918. Cambridge: Harvard University Press, 1927.

Gelfand, Lawrence E. *The Inquiry: American Preparations for Peace, 1917-1919.* New Haven: Yale University Press, 1963.

Guinn, Paul. *British Strategy and Politics, 1914-1918.* Oxford: Clarendon Press, 1965.

Helmreich, Paul C. *From Paris to Sevres: The Partition of the Ottoman Empire at the Peace Conference of 1919-1920.* Columbus: Ohio State University Press, 1974.

Hendrick, Burton J. *The Life and Letters of Walter Hines Page.* 3 vols. Garden City, New York: Doubleday, Page and Company, 1922-1925.

Hogan, Michael, J. *Informal Entente: The Private Structure of Cooperation in Anglo-American Diplomacy, 1918-1928.* Columbia, University of Missouri Press, 1977.

Hoover, Herbert. *The Ordeal of Woodrow Wilson.* New York, Toronto, and London: McGraw Hill Book Company, Inc., 1958.

House, Edward Mandell, and Seymour, Charles, eds. *What Really Happened at the Peace Conference.* New York: Charles Scribner's Sons, 1921.

Israel, Jerry. *Progressivism and the Open Door: America and China, 1905-1921.* University of Pittsburgh Press, 1971.

Kaufman, Burton K. *Efficiency and Expansion: Foreign Trade Organization in the Wilson Administration, 1913-1921.* Westport, Conn. Greenwood Press, 1974.

Koebel, W. H. *South America: An Industrial and Commercial Field.* London: T. Fisher Unwin, Ltd. 1918.

Kennan, George F. *Soviet-American Relations, 1917-1920.* Princeton University Press, 1956-
 Vol. I: *Russia Leaves the War.* Princeton, 1956
 Vol. II: *The Decision to Intervene.* Princeton, 1958.

Kittredge, Tracy B. *Naval Lessons of the Great War.* Garden City; Doubleday, Page and Company, 1921.

Knox, Dudley. *A History of the United States Navy.* New York: G.P. Putnam's Sons, 1936.

Levin, Gordon, Jr. *Woodrow Wilson and World Politics.* New York: Oxford University Press, 1968.

Link, Arthur S. *et al. Wilson's Diplomacy: An International Symposium.* (The American Forum Series.) Cambridge, Mass.: Schenkman Publishing Co. 1973.

_____ *Woodrow Wilson and the Progressive Era*, 1910-1917. New York: Harper and Row, Publishers (Torchback), 1954.

Livermore, Seward W. *Politics is Adjourned: Woodrow Wilson and The War Congress, 1916-1918.* Middletown, Conn.: Wesleyan University Press, 1966.

Mamatey, Victor S. *The United States and East Central Europe.* Princeton University Press, 1957.

Marder, Arthur J. *From the Dreadnought to Scapa Flow: The Royal Navy in the Fisher Era, 1904-1919.* Vols. III-V. London: Oxford University Press, 1966-1970.

Marshall, S. L. A. *The American Heritage History of World War I.* New York: American Heritage Publishing Company, 1964.

McEntee, Girard Lindsley. *Italy's Part in Winning the World War.* Princeton University Press, 1934.

Mayer, Arno J. *Politics and Diplomacy of Peacemaking: Containment and Counterrevolution at Versailles, 1918-1919.* New York: Alfred Knopf, Inc. 1967.

Miller, David Hunter. *The Drafting of the Covenant.* 2 vols. New York and London: G. P. Putnam's Sons, 1928.

Morison, Elting E. *Admiral Sims and the Modern American Navy.* Boston: Houghton Mifflin Company, 1942.

Morrison, Joseph L. *Josephus Daniels, the Small -d Democrat.* Chapel Hill: University of North Carolina Press, 1966.

Nahoun, Jules. *The Key to National Prosperity: A Presentation of Foreign Trade in its Connection with the Development of National Prosperity.* New York: E. P. Dutton and Company, 1923.

Notter, Marley. *The Origins of the Foreign Policy of Woodrow Wilson.* Baltimore: Johns Hopkins Press, 1937.

O'Grady, Joseph P. *The Immigrants' Influence on Wilson's Peace Policies.* Lexington: University of Kentucky Press, 1968.

Palmer, Frederick, *Newton D. Baker.* 2 vols. New York: Dodd, Mead and Company, 1931.

Peterson, Horace C. *Propoganda for War: the Campaign Against American Neutrality, 1914-1917.* Norman: University of Oklahoma Press, 1939; reprinted 1968.

Pingaud, Albert. *Histoire diplomatique de la France pendant la Grande Guerre.* 3 vols. Paris: Alsatia Press, 1939-1940.

Pratt, Julius W. *A History of United States' Foreign Policy.* 2d ed. New York: Prentice Hall, Inc., 1961.

Roskill, Stephen. *Naval Policy Between the Wars,* Vol. I: *The Period of Anglo-American Antagonism, 1919-1929.* London: Collins Press, 1968.

Rothwell, V. H. *British War Aims and Peace Diplomacy, 1914-1918.* Oxford: Clarendon Press, 1971.

Rudin, Harry R. *Armistice 1918.* New Haven: Yale University Press, 1944.

Safford, Jeffery J., *Wilsonian Maritime Diplomacy, 1913-1921.* New Brunswick, N. J., Rutgers Press, 1977.

Salter, J. A. *Allied Shipping Control: An Experiment in International Administration.* Oxford: Clarenden Press, 1921.

Seth, Ronald S. *Caporetto: the Scapegoat Battle.* London: Macdonald Company, 1965.

Shannon, David A. Editor: *Between the Wars: America, 1919-1941.* Boston: Houghton Mifflin Company.

Smith, Daniel M. *American Intervention, 1917: Sentiment, Self-Interest, or Ideals?* Boston: Houghton Mifflin Company, 1966.

_____ *The Great Departure: The United States and World War I, 1914-1920.* New York, London, and Sydney: John Wiley and Sons, Inc., 1965.

Sprout, Harold and Margaret. *The Rise of American Naval Power.* Princeton University Press, 1939.

_____, *Toward a New Order of Sea Power: American Naval Policy and the World Scene, 1918-1922.* Princeton University Press, 1940.

Taylor, A. J. P. *The Struggle for the Mastery in Europe.* Oxford: Clarendon Press, 1954.

Temperley, H. A. W., ed. *A History of the Peace Conference of Paris.* 4 vols. London: Henry Frowde and Hodder and Stoughton, 1920-1924.

Tillman, Seth P. *Anglo-American Relations at the Peace Conference of 1919.* Princeton University Press, 1961.

Trask, David F. *The United States in the Supreme War Council; American War Aims and Inter-Allied Strategy, 1917-1919.* Middletown, Conn.: Wesleyan University Press, 1961.

_____ *Captains and Cabinets: Anglo-American Naval Relations, 1917-1918.* Columbia: University of Missouri Press, 1972.

Tulchin, Joseph S. *The Aftermath of War: World War I and U. S. Policy Toward Latin America.* New York: New York University Press, 1971.

Wheeler, Gerald E. *Admiral William Veazie Pratt, U. S. Navy: A Sailor's Life.* Washington: Naval Historical Division, Department of the Navy, 1974.

Willert, Arthur. *The Road to Safety: a Study in Anglo-American Relations.* New York: Frederick Z. Praeger, Inc., 1953.

Williams, William Appleman, ed. *From Colony to Empire: Essays in the History of American Foreign Relations.* New York: John Wiley and

Sons. 1972.

Wish, Harvey. *Contemporary America.* 3rd ed. New York: Harper and Row, Publishers, 1961.

Woodward, Llewellyn. *Great Britain and the War of 1914-1918.* London: Methuen and Company, 1967.

Živojinovíc, Dragan R. *America, Italy and the Birth of Yugoslavia, 1917-1919.* New York: Columbia University Press, 1973.

Articles

Allard, Dean C. "Admiral William S. Sims and United States Naval Policy in World War I." *American Neptune* 35 (Apr. 1975), 97-110.

Baldridge, Harry A. "Sims — the Iconoclast," *Proceedings of the United States Naval Institute*, LXIII (February, 1947), 1-6.

Davis, Donald E., and Trani, Eugene F. "The American YMCA and the Russian Revolution." *Slavic Review*, 33 (Sept. 1974), 469-91.

Elké, Frank W. "Japanese-German Peace Negotiations During World War I." *American Historical Review*, LXXI (October, 1965), 62-76.

Halpern, Paul G. "The Anglo-French-Italian Naval Convention of 1915," *The Historical Journal* (Cambridge, England), Vol. XIII, No. 1 (1970).

Hartig, Thomas H. "Robert Lansing and East Asian-American Relations: A Study in Motivation. " *Michigan Academician*, 7 (Fall 1974), 191-99.

Herwig, Helger H. and Trask, David F. "The Failure of Imperial Germany's Undersea Offensive Against World Shipping, February 1917-October 1918," *The Historian*, XXXIII (August, 1971).

Hogan, Michael J. "The United States and the Problem of International Economic Control: American Attitudes Toward European Economic Reconstruction." *Pacific Historical Review*, XLIV (Feb. 1975).

Kaufman, Burton J. "United States Trade and Latin America: The Wilson Years," *The Journal of American History*, LVIII (Sept. 1971), 342-63.

Kernek, Stirling J. "Distractions of Peace During War: The Lloyd George Government's Reaction to Woodrow Wilson, December, 1916-November, 1918." *Transactions of the American Philosophical Society*, 65 (Apr. 1975), 1-117.

Safford, Jeffrey J. *"Edward Hurley and American Shipping Policy: An Elaboration on Wilsonian Diplomacy, 1918-1919,"* The Historian, XXXV (August, 1973), 568-86.

Sims, William S. "The Status of the Navy," *Current History*, XVI (May, 1922), 186-94.

Wells, Samuel F. Jr. "New Perspectives on Wilsonian Diplomacy: The Secular Evangelism of American Political Economy" review essay. *Perspectives in American History* VI (1972).

Woodward, David R. "The Origins and Intent of David Lloyd George's January 5 War Aims Speech." *The Historian* XXIV (Nov. 1971), 22-39.

Živejinović, Dragan. "Robert Lansing's Comments on the Pontifical Peace Note of August 1, 1917," *Journal of American History*, LVI (December, 1969), 556-571.

Ph.D. Dissertations

Cuddy, Joseph Edward. "Irish-American and National Isolationism, 1914-1920," State University of New York at Buffalo, 1965.

Klachko, Mary L. "Anglo-American Naval Competition, 1918-1922." Columbia University, 1962.

Schilling, Warner R. "Admirals and Foreign Policy, 1913-1919." Yale University, 1953.

INDEX